189

D0355285

Oriental Philosophy

A Westerner's Guide to Eastern Thought

STUART C. HACKETT

The University of Wisconsin Press

Published 1979

The University of Wisconsin Press
114 North Murray Street
Madison, Wisconsin 53715

The University of Wisconsin Press, Ltd.
1 Gower Street, London WC1E 6HA, England

First printing

Printed in the United States of America

For LC CIP information see the colophon

ISBN 0-299-07790-X (cloth)   0-299-07794-2 (paper)

Contents

v

Preface

This book will attempt to explain, in language intelligible to the Western reader and with as few technical complications as possible, the main philosophical positions associated with the religious traditions of Confucianism, Taoism, Buddhism, Hinduism, and Jainism. It is a real introduction to oriental thought directed to the level of the upperclass college student and therefore explicitly intended as a basic text for courses in this area. It is, however, not an exhaustive treatment of the subject, and its ideal function would be to provide an expository and critical framework to be supplemented both by class lectures and by supplementary readings in primary source materials, such as those listed in the bibliography.

As it stands, the book has numerous qualities that contribute to its usefulness: it contains not only expositions of the perspectives discussed, but also evaluative critical sections which attempt to assess these views along lines carefully explained in the introduction. A further distinctive feature is the marginal outline, which provides a basis both for understanding the text and for developing organized insight into the views discussed. There is also a glossary which briefly and clearly defines the principal special terms that are used, as well as a general bibliography which will guide the reader into accessible literature on the subject in the English language. A final unusual quality of the book is that each section ends with explicit recommended readings in primary and secondary sources.

It is impossible for me to acknowledge my total indebtedness in writing this book. But I wish to thank both the Alumni Association of Wheaton College (Illinois) and the Institute for Advanced Christian

Studies for providing funds that made it possible for me to spend a year in India, along with my family, so that I could do intensive research on this project. I also want to express profound appreciation for many mentors of long standing, especially Edwin A. Burtt of Cornell University (who first introduced me to philosophy) and Raymond F. Piper of Syracuse University (who steered me through a doctoral dissertation on the philosophy of Aurobindo Ghose). Thanks are due also to Arthur F. Holmes, chairman of the Wheaton College philosophy department, for inspiring me by his example of devotion to scholarship and for providing me with every possible encouragement in my own studies in oriental philosophy as well as with extensive secretarial assistance in producing my manuscript. Further thanks are particularly due to Robert E. Frykenberg of the history and Indian studies departments at the University of Wisconsin (Madison), who, out of selfless friendship, read my entire original manuscript, believed in its worth, and successfully undertook to help me locate a suitable publisher. Of course, I owe a great debt of gratitude to Irving E. Rockwood, general editor of the University of Wisconsin Press, and to Keith E. Yandell of the philosophy department at the University of Wisconsin (Madison) for virtually endless hours spent in going over my manuscript and providing me with many useful revisionary suggestions. Finally, and above all, I want to express my deepest appreciation to my wife Joan, without whose constant support and encouragement I would have lacked both the inspiration and the determination required to carry through this project.

STUART C. HACKETT

Wheaton, Illinois
May 1978

Oriental Philosophy

Introduction

Preparing for the Journey

What follows is the record of an existential journey, the
account of one individual's struggle with the perspectives and problems of oriental philosophy. For this
reason, the understanding developed here is as much a
refraction of light through the prism of my own mind as
it is a descriptive analysis of the viewpoints considered.
Still, although I fully acknowledge a subjectively relative slant, I think I also speak as a typical child of the
Western world; I therefore hope to call forth a sym-
pathetic vibration from deep within the soul of every
other man whose interpretive categories, though essentially human, have been struck from the mould of the
same tradition. Again, my exposition reflects the mind-
set that has matured through a quarter of a century
spent in teaching both Western and Eastern philosophy
in the college classroom. And what emerges from this
background is a concern not with the historical and
cultural setting of oriental viewpoints, not even with the
religious beliefs and ritual practices that characteristically provide a context for these viewpoints, but rather
with the systematic, comparative, and critical analysis
of oriental perspectives as alternative philosophical
positions. Hence, I am interested in an organized conceptual understanding, even in the case of those classical
philosophers whose rambling style and preoccupation
with fertile aphoristic insight do not lend themselves

1. Characteris-
tics of the
present study

a. Both
descriptive of
oriental
philosophy and
reflective of
the author's
personal
viewpoint.

b. Limited to
concerns
developed in
the philosophy
classroom, and
therefore
concerned
primarily with
the
comparative
and critical
analysis of
oriental
perspectives.

1. Hence, a
concern with
systematic
explanation

3

readily to this approach. Furthermore, I want to reconstruct the grounds of the various beliefs that are a part of the positions I discuss, and that means a concern with supporting arguments and counter-arguments, even in analyzing perspectives for which such apologetic concerns are secondary, if not virtually irrelevant.

I have not attempted to add to the swelling tide of competently written, technical, scholarly books on oriental philosophy; I respect these lengthy volumes— brimming with a linguistic torrent of Sanskrit, Tibetan, Chinese, and Japanese terms, or transliterations thereof —and I hope it will be obvious to the initiated that I have made extended use of these learned treatises. But I want instead to spread a feast of insight for the common man who is at the same time deeply thoughtful and profoundly concerned with the cumulative, total human understanding of the meaning of existence, as that understanding is enshrined in the classical traditions of oriental thought. I have sincerely tried to incarnate here my best philosophical efforts; but I do not wish to obscure the viewpoints I analyze by calling continuous attention to the fact of that attempt. As a result, I have

tried to keep transliterated oriental words to an absolute minimum, and I have also tried to explain the oriental concepts analyzed not in the frequently baffling and esoteric style of the Eastern thinkers themselves, but in language that aims at the clarity and precision which, in my opinion, should characterize philosophical exposition at its best. No doubt some of the "feel" and emotive atmosphere of oriental thought will be lost in this way, but it is my conviction that the substantive content can be preserved entire, and that the gain in clarity will more than compensate for the loss in emotive impact.

My concern with supporting arguments and counter-arguments associated with the different views means that I am also interested in the critical evaluation of these views. But every such critical effort inevitably presupposes certain logically ultimate and underived criteria or standards of evaluation which, whether explicitly or not, play a decisive role in the estimate that a man makes of the positions he investigates. I have made two decisions about the treatment of these criteria: the first, in keeping with my desire to address the common man, is the decision not to discuss the problem of evaluative criteria in the sophisticated, technical vocabulary of professional philosophers. Those who require understanding in such terms will easily be able to discern how to apply them to my discussion; and those not familiar with these refinements of vocabulary and linguistic wizardry would only be confused by such a technical discussion. My second decision is to explain, as clearly and succinctly as possible, the evaluative criteria I intend to use, and to give some indication of the reasonableness of using them.

In general, there are two noticeably different attitudes toward evaluative critical principles. One of these, which I would characterize as *voluntaristic* (because it holds that an ultimate commitment of will is the decisive basis for the status of such principles as standards), maintains that these fundamental criteria are logically dependent upon the over-all system that a man accepts, whether knowingly or not. From this point of view, evaluative principles are likely to vary from one system of thought to another, and there is no neutral ground of independent logic or reason by which one can decide between opposing sets of criteria. In the end, of course, this approach means that a thinker can criticize another system only on grounds that imply his own, and that therefore all decisions between systems are ultimately arbitrary—not merely in the sense that they often *are* arbitrary, but also in the sense that it is inevitable that they *must* be. The main defense for this voluntaristic attitude consists in pointing out that however neutral evaluative criteria may superficially claim to be, exploratory analysis characteristically reveals that these criteria are in fact the reflection of some prior systematic commitment of the thinker who employs them. So the critical dice turn

a. Such standards inevitably implied in any attempt at critical assessment.
b. But
1. the problem of identifying those criteria will not be discussed in technical terms here;
2. yet the standards used will be explained and some account of their reasonableness provided.
c. There are basically two different positions about ultimate critical principles.
1. *Voluntarism.*
a. For this view such ultimate criteria inevitably reflect a man's prior commitment to a particular system of thought and are in that sense logically arbitrary.
b. But it is claimed that a descriptive analysis of these principles and systems makes this contention quite reasonable.

out to be loaded after all, and we may as well frankly admit that fact, however awkward and embarrassing it may be to do so.

The second attitude toward critical principles, an attitude which I would characterize as *rationalistic* (because it holds that there are ultimate principles of criticism which do not depend for their status on voluntary commitment to a particular over-all system, but rather reflect the nature of objective reason itself), maintains that the final grounds of all truth-claims, so far as those claims are reasonable, cut across alternative systematic perspectives and therefore need not reflect the special distinctives of any one such perspective. Such basic categories or interpretive standards would then be regarded as logically necessary presuppositions of all possible thought and being. In a way, these categories would be metaphysical, in the general sense of pertaining to the understanding of reality, since nothing could exist or be clearly thought without conforming to them; but they would not be reflective derivatives of one system of philosophy over against others. In fact, the reasonableness of *any* system of philosophy would then depend on the degree to which *it* reflected, and conformed to, those very principles. It is, of course, open to those who hold this view to maintain that a man's best efforts to identify and express these ultimate principles are characteristically no more than approximations to the principles themselves, and that these approximations are therefore tentative formulations in need of constant revision.

The main defense for this rationalistic attitude consists in pointing out that unless there is some such set of objective standards or categories (objective in the sense that these principles do not depend on the special presuppositions of a particular viewpoint), not only would any choice between philosophical systems be purely arbitrary, but any truth-claim for any proposition would be just as arbitrary, since all such claims presuppose the ultimacy of certain evaluative criteria, which would in

2. Rationalism. a. For this view there are ultimate principles of objective reason which cut across alternative perspectives,

and therefore provide a common framework of interpretive principles and standards through which the worth of different views can be assessed on grounds that do not reflect the special features of any of those views,

although the attempt to identify and express these principles may be viewed as no more than approximative.

b. In defense it is claimed that

(1) Unless there are such principles, all truth-claims would be wholly arbitrary,

that case themselves be arbitrary by hypothesis. And of course the result would be a kind of self-eliminating scepticism or denial of the possibility of objective knowledge, since even the claim that all truth-claims are arbitrary would then itself be equally arbitrary. As a matter of fact, when a voluntarist argues that presuppositions about evaluative criteria inevitably reflect the systematic viewpoint of the person propounding them, he is himself making a truth-claim that cuts across all such viewpoints and that therefore purports to transcend dependence on any one of them. Thus a thinker's aim at objectivity may still be tainted with subjectivity, but to recognize that very fact is already to move toward counteracting that taint.

Now I respect the voluntaristic attitude, and I recognize in myself and my life all manner of influences bent on deflecting me from the track of truth. But I believe in that track, and I think I would be less than an authentic man if I did not continually aim to find it and conform to it. I will therefore assume that the rationalistic attitude is essentially sound, and that there are ultimate criteria of truth which reflective thought can approximate and which are not logically dependent on commitment to some one particular systematic viewpoint over against others.

If then there are such basic principles, the fact that ideally they should be necessary presuppositions of all possible thought and being gives us a clue to their specific character. Since they make intelligible thought possible, we need only ask ourselves what it is to think intelligibly. And does not thinking intelligibly mean thinking in terms that stand for concepts which have a determinate (though not necessarily consciously defined) meaning which sets the reference of a concept apart from whatever does not belong to it, and especially from whatever is so opposed to that concept that it would be unintelligible to affirm both that concept and its opposite of the same subject at the same time and in the same sense? The assumption underlying this

and that would lead to a scepticism about the possibility of any knowledge at all;

(2). voluntarists themselves seem to appeal to just such objective principles in their attempt to support the contention that there are none.

d. Although not without some qualifications, the author assumes the basic soundness of the rationalistic attitude.

e. Whatever else these criteria may be, they function as the first principles of all intelligible thought.

1. It becomes clear that one such necessary principle is the law of rational coherence or contradiction.

a. Meaning of this principle explained.

question may be called the principle of *rational coherence,* or the principle of *contradiction,* and may be stated as a proposition of the following sort: all the concepts that intelligibly apply to the same subject of thought must be logically consistent with each other in meaning and with the concept of that subject in its meaning as well. And it follows that all the propositions that can be meaningfully thought to be true at the same time must likewise be consistent and therefore free from either explicit or implicit contradiction. Now such a principle of rational coherence embodies precisely the sort of objective and ultimate standard that is required if philosophical truth-claims are to aim at being something more than arbitrary projections of subjectivity. Of course, the truth of this principle cannot be proven, since it is itself a part of the basis of every reasonable proof without exception. But it can be justified as reasonable, since nothing whatever can be intelligibly thought except by approximating conformity to that principle itself. As an evaluative standard for philosophical systems, the principle of rational coherence means that just to the extent that such systems contain contradictory elements, the truth-claim of the systems will be unjustified in a formal logical sense.

b. This principle cannot be proven, but it can be viewed as reasonable, since it is a condition of the clarity and intelligibility of any act of thought.

A second basic criterion emerges if we remember that the whole point of a philosophical view is to give a satisfactory explanation, in systematic form, of the general characteristics of the whole range of human experience, and to do so in such a way as to provide man with an understanding that both clarifies his place in the scheme of things and suggests guidelines for meaningful living. Providing such a satisfactory explanation means giving an account of the nature of reality which, if it were true, would account for the general character of things being as they are, rather than otherwise. In this sense, a philosophical view aims at discovering and analyzing the cause or ground of things, and this aim is not realized fully in any identification of causes which themselves require futher explanation of the same kind.

2. A second criterion emerges in the recognition that a philosophy is supposed to provide an explanation of things that satisfies the claims of experience as fully as possible.
a. And this involves the search for causes or grounds which seem to

No, it can reasonably be held that a philosophical system aims at tracing the character of things up to causes or explanatory principles which, though they explain all else, are themselves self-explanatory in the sense that they require no further causal grounding or argumentative basis. If anyone should ask why it should be necessary to provide such ultimate causal explanations, his very question could in turn be interpreted as illustrating this very necessity, since he is asking for precisely such a causal explanation himself. What this fact shows is that causal explanation is itself an ultimate interpretive category or principle, and that no one can reasonably dispense with it, unless he claims to do so in a purely arbitrary fashion. Whenever anyone asks for the justification of a factual truth-claim, he is asking for a causal explanation; but no further justification of that principle itself can be reasonably required, since it would itself be a part of the basis of any such justification. Now we may call this ultimate principle, thus clarified, the principle of *experiential relevance* or *explanatory capacity*. As a test for the adequacy and reasonableness of a philosophical system, this principle would require that such a system provide a satisfactory, ultimate explanation of all the main features of the experienced world; and the truth-claim of such a system, from a factual point of view, would in that sense be proportionate to the comprehensive adequacy of its causal explanation of things.

account for the state of things as they are, without those causes requiring any further account of the same sort;

b. understood in this way, the principle of causality is an ultimate and indispensable interpretive principle,

and because of its function we may call it the principle of experiential relevance or explanatory capacity.

If then we put the two criteria of rational coherence and experiential relevance together, we confront a standard of evaluation which, rather than depending on the special characteristics of a philosophical viewpoint, reflects instead the very nature and meaningfulness of any sort of intelligible thought about reality. This standard, furthermore, does not require of a philosophical position that the detailed factual character of reality be logically deducible from the principles of that position, but it does require that the factual character of reality be reasonably explainable in terms of those principles. It

3. These two criteria together provide an evaluative standard which a. is not dependent on any special viewpoint; b. does not entail the deducibility of facts from logical principles.

follows that the most reasonable philosophical commitment for a rational man will be a commitment to that system which, in his sincere opinion, exemplifies that evaluative standard more fully than any known alternative. And if, as will surely be the case in oriental philosophy, we meet with viewpoints that attempt to bypass, limit, or go beyond this standard of objective philosophical reasonableness, we may be more than surprised to find that these critics attempt to justify going beyond that standard of reasonableness by appealing to the standard itself—by pointing out, for example, that the application of the standard leads to contradictions and fails to give a satisfactory explanation of certain identifiable aspects of human experience. We shall deal as generously as possible with these critics when we come to them, but in the meantime we may point out the remarkable strangeness of attempting to dispense with a standard of reasonableness on grounds that involve an appeal to that standard itself.

4. Even oriental views which purport to go beyond these criteria inevitably use the criteria themselves in the process of doing so.

On the other hand, it would be unrealistic to expect that, however carefully and critically we scrutinize positions with their arguments and counter-arguments, we would develop anything like a universally effective basis of persuasion. For one thing, our best efforts to achieve the truth are likely to be no more than a tentative and shifting approximation to that truth, partly because the experience on which we base knowledge-claims is rarely, if ever, complete, and partly because the most careful self-scrutiny is bound to overlook an indefinite number of culturally and subjectively variable conditioning influences which tend to limit our aim at objectivity in a variety of unpredictable ways. For another thing, when we look at these same limits from the standpoint of a person to whom an argument is presented, it seems clear that the persuasive effect of any such argument is person-relative; that is, the same argument stated in the same way commonly has noticeably different effects on different hearers, and even on the same hearer under different circumstances. And again the reasons for this

f. But the results to be expected from the use of these criteria are no more than approximative,

1. because
a. our experience is always limited,
b. there are many factors which tend to restrict our best efforts at objectivity,

c. and the persuasive effect of arguments is person-relative.

variability are in general the same as those which limit our own search for truth: even if an argument is sound (that is, even if its premises are true and logically imply the stated conclusion), its effect will be conditioned by the knowledge of the hearer, especially in cases where he does not know that the premises are true, or in cases where his conviction of their truth is for some reason weak or hesitant. Furthermore, in the case of the hearer, as in our own, there are numerous non-rational factors (that is, factors which influence belief but are not objective grounds for the reasonableness of belief) which both motivate and obstruct belief-commitments. To some extent the influence of these factors can be offset or neutralized by the discipline of watchful-mindedness; but that corrective is only partly effective even in the case of those who are explicitly and keenly aware of these non-rational influences; and many persons to whom arguments are addressed have scarcely begun to glimpse the reality or extent of these influences, so that the corrective will have little effect on their belief-commitments. More bafflingly still, it seems often to be the case that, in varied and unpredictable ways, non-rational factors motivate individuals to believe propositions which actually are true and which contribute importantly to the enrichment of their lives, although those same factors may have the opposite effect as well —namely, the effect of depriving them of truths which they need to know.

> 2. To some extent non-rational factors which limit objectivity can be offset by careful attention; *a.* but that process is only partly effective,
>
> *b.* and sometimes these factors actually motivate persons to believe what is in fact true.

All this may make the business of philosophizing more modest than we might wish; but we may as well accept the situation as it is and proceed to expend our best efforts at that modest task. And if, as I believe, it is more important that individuals accept the truths they need than that they do so for philosophically adequate reasons, we need not hesitate to employ any tool of persuasion that will open them to these truths, provided only that we do not violate their intrinsic personal worth through the use of methods that are deceptive or otherwise immoral.

> 3. The role of philosophy is therefore modest, but that is no motive for carrying out that role with anything less than our best efforts.

Hallmarks of Oriental Thought

It is not difficult to understand why all philosophy, both Western and Eastern, is religious in its basis and motive, at least as philosophy was originally and traditionally conceived. Religion may be broadly characterized as the total life response of man to what he comes to regard as ultimately and decisively significant for human destiny, and to whatever he views as depending on this sense of significance or as symbolizing it in some important way. Of course, a man responds to any provocative situation not only in biological ways that he shares to some extent with other orders of living beings, but also in ways that are distinctively human. This characteristically human

response is basically threefold: a man responds to a situation *intellectually* with a set of beliefs; *volitionally* with a set of decisions and their implementation in action; and *emotionally* with a variable complex of im-

pulses, feelings, inclinations, and attitudes. What makes a response religious, in these three aspects, is the object toward which that response is directed and the qualitatively distinct modes of awareness with which a man confronts and reacts to that object. The object is the ultimately and decisively significant: whatever is regarded as making the final difference between an authentic, meaningful life in the fullest sense and a basically inauthentic, relatively meaningless and directionless life. On the subjective side (that is, the side of the person responding), a response is religious if it is pervaded by ultimate, unlimited, unconditional concern, in contrast to the limited and conditional urgency that characterizes other types of human awareness. And since there is something that, either consciously or unconsciously, matters ultimately to each human being, it would seem to follow that, in this broad sense, every man responds religiously to reality as he understands it.

Philosophy, on the other hand, has traditionally concerned itself with a relatively explicit and systematic attempt to formulate a scheme of beliefs that provide a general explanation of the meaning of reality and of its bearing on the significance of man in relation to that reality. And since philosophers increasingly tried to save their theories from sheer arbitrariness, they also developed a strong interest in arguments for their views and in the general logical characteristics which they supposed would make those positions and arguments appear reasonable to others beside themselves and those who accepted their presuppositions. But of course they were not merely interested in *metaphysics* (the explanation of reality) and *epistemology* (the clarification of the origin, nature, and limits of knowledge, and of the nature and tests of truth-claims); they were also concerned with *ethics*—that is, with beliefs about values and moral obligations as these related to their understanding of the nature of man and his place in the scheme of things.

Now it is probably correct that, originally and historically, philosophy grew out of, and was naturally correlated with, the intellectual aspect of man's religious response. It is true that in the West philosophy gradually strove to achieve independence from this religious root—not because its concern with beliefs was essentially different from that of religion, but because philosophers came to feel that organized religion tended at best to substitute authority and tradition for objective reasonableness as a ground for belief-commitment. This substitution, they thought, not only hampered the philosophical search for truth, but it reinforced the almost natural lethargy of established views. In the East, however, the original affinity of philosophy with religion continued undisturbed right down to the present, so that all the systems of classical oriental philosophy are religious in nature, context, and objective. The historical reasons for this unbroken affiliation are no doubt very complex: although the power of established tradition was strong, perhaps there was not as much restraint brought to bear on individuals who developed seemingly novel interpretations within the tradition; again, since empirical science did not, until very recently, become a

1. Its over-all purpose.

2. Its main concerns or subdivisions.

c. Relation of philosophy to religion in its intellectual aspect.
1. Why western philosophy attempted to divorce itself from religion,

while oriental philosophy did not.

2. Explanation of this difference.

primary concern of oriental peoples, perhaps the sense of an unresolvable conflict between the truth-claims of traditional religion and the apparent implications of empirical science simply did not emerge. But for whatever reasons, classical philosophy in the orient has almost always proceeded by reconstruction from within the religious context, rather than from a reaction that tended to externalize that philosophy into an independent tradition in its own right.

2. Generally inclusivist attitude of oriental philosophy: tolerant openness to alternative viewpoints.

It is possible that the religious motif of oriental philosophy may be partly explainable in terms of a second feature of Eastern thought: namely, the generally inclusivist quality of its attitude. Certainly the East has had its share of individual dogmatists who claimed exclusive truth for their own positions; but in general the intensity of such individual claims has been tempered by a tolerant openness to other views beside one's own, and even by a tendency for viewpoints originally very different to merge together in many of their positions on particular points. Partly for this reason, for example, classical Taoism and idealistic Neo-Confucianism are very close in outlook; and Hinduism was able to absorb the main insights of Buddhism so successfully that the latter virtually died out in its native India. Even the Christian truth-claim is often tolerantly received by oriental philosophers, so that Jesus Christ is welcomed as one of the incarnations of the Hindu Brahman or one of the human manifestations of the Buddhist Dharma-Kaya (the Buddha's body of pure being). To some extent this tolerant non-exclusivism grows out of the tendency of oriental thought to encourage widely divergent perspectives within each of its main religious traditions—the "orthodox" schools of Hindu philosophy, for example, are doctrinally as different from each other as any of those schools are from traditions outside Hinduism. On the other hand, it may be that this openness to various perspectives reflects a pervasive oriental presupposition to the effect that no one viewpoint, projected as it is by individual thinkers however capable,

a. Some examples and effects of this attitude.

b. Resultant diversity of viewpoints within the same tradition.

c. Possibility that this feature reflects a recognition of the relativity of particular viewpoints.

can do more than approximate an understanding of certain limited aspects of the ultimate truth. And perhaps even more fundamentally the receptiveness of oriental thought may reflect a suspicion that in some sense analytically precise and conceptually formulated philosophies are more likely to cramp an adequate understanding of reality than to liberate it.

However that may be, there is a further characteristic of oriental thought which would at least be consistent with the possibility just raised—namely, that the style of exposition in Eastern philosophical treatises is comparatively unsystematic in form, although this feature is considerably less characteristic of Indian philosophy than of other oriental traditions. To a Western student trained on the exemplary clarity of a G. E. Moore or a George Santayana, the classical tomes of Eastern philosophy exhibit a rambling style and a relatively disorganized structure that are the occasion for the frustration and even despair of more than one such student in his attempt to comprehend the viewpoints elusively lodged in such a setting. With rare exceptions, these thinkers tend to express a series of comparatively unconnected bursts of fertile insight which aim more at provoking a moral and spiritual response than at displaying any model of conceptual clarity and analytic precision. The closest parallel to this style in Western thought would be a writer like Ludwig Wittgenstein, to some extent in his *Tractatus Logico-Philosophicus,* and especially in the *Philosophical Investigations.* To a certain degree this stylistic contrast with Western philosophy is a matter of tradition; but it may also reflect the supposition that a mode of exposition characterized by organized precision might seem implicitly to claim a greater grasp on objective truth than would be becoming to the humility appropriate to any finite attempt to understand the absolute. And this presupposition has two cutting edges: on the one hand, it recognizes the limits imposed on any thinker by the individually and culturally relative circumstances that pervade even the

3. Comparatively unsystematic form of oriental philosophical treatises.

a. Aim at fertile insight rather than clarity and precision by Western standards.

b. Some possible reasons for this feature:

1. limitations on the aim at rational objectivity;

2. basic distrust of discursive intellect as a means of insight.

most courageous attempt to achieve objectivity; on the other hand, such an assumption discloses a basic distrust in the competence of discursive intellect and conceptual analysis to attain anything approaching an adequate insight into ultimate truth. But whatever the reasons for the rambling, aphoristic style of most orien-

c. Elimination of this style in the present work.

tal philosophy, I myself have found this style to be more a stumbling-block to understanding than a provocation to appropriate humility. For this reason I have completely dispensed with the classical form of exposition and sought to express the content of the viewpoints I discuss in the organized way which, for me at least, occasions the clearest understanding I can achieve on such subjects.

4. Generally non-personal view of the ultimate reality.

A final quality of oriental thought has to do with the view that prevails in these perspectives about the ultimate object of religious and philosophic pursuit. To many westerners a religious world view would entail as such that the highest object of religious concern be a supreme moral and spiritual personality of some sort: and there certainly are oriental views that reflect this outlook—in the *bhakti* or devotional tradition of Hinduism, for example. But this outlook is far from typical: some of the most impressive perspectives of

a. Some reasons for this outlook.

oriental philosophy (impressive in their comprehensiveness and impact) regard the category of personality as a limiting and restricting quality that is not finally satisfactory as a clue to the nature of ultimate reality. Hence, advocates of this insight regard the absolute reality as non-personal, not in the sense that it is less than personal, but in the sense that its infinite reality lies beyond every attempt to characterize it through particular, determinate qualities. And some traditions find it

b. Views which dispense with the notion of ultimate reality.

possible even to dispense with the notion of an ultimate, changeless reality altogether—Hinayana or Theravada Buddhism, for example. I myself do not suppose that this basically non-personal view of the ultimate religious object makes the positions that embody this assumption any less religious, much less non-religious: uncritically to define religion itself as requiring a distinctive assumption of our own tradition (namely, that the ultimate must be a changeless, personal reality) would be an unwarranted bias at best, and one that could well restrict arbitrarily the sort of full understanding that one ought to seek about such momentous and decisive questions.

c. Caution against unwarranted bias.

Part One

Classical Chinese Perspectives

1 / Confucianism:
A Philosophy of
Ethical Idealism

Background and Basic Concepts

Apparently the sixth century B.C. provided the setting for the emergence of the two distinctively Chinese religious-philosophical traditions—for that was the century of the great sage Confucius, or K'ung-fu-tzu (551–479 B.C.), and also, at least traditionally, of the legendary and elusive founder of philosophical Taoism, Lao-tzu, reportedly an elder contemporary of Confucius. But even though these men and their later successors forged the distinctives of the traditions they represent, they did not of course create those traditions out of nothing—they were more like the scholars and interpreters of a long-established framework of notions than like the seminal originators, much less the fiery prophets, of some new religious-philosophical stance.

1. Relation of Confucius, Lao-tzu, and others to the development of Chinese thought.

a. Their position as interpreters of tradition.

From a literary point of view, Confucius presumably began the work of collecting and editing the scattered writings and orally preserved expositions of the religious tradition that came to bear his name. Of the five classics of Confucianism (the Books of History, Poetry, Changes, and Rites; and the Spring and Autumn Annals of the State of Lu), only the last embodied any substantial contribution by Confucius himself, and the others were crystallizations of earlier tradition which reached their final form considerably after Confucius' day. Of the four Confucian books, so-called, the *Analects* is indeed a collection of the sayings of Confucius and the

b. Confucius and the Confucian classics.

c. Later Confucian thinkers and the periods of Chinese philosophy.

chief primary source of our knowledge of his teachings; two others, the Great Learning and the Doctrine of the Mean, are expanded chapters from the earlier Book of Rites; and the last is the Book of Mencius, a fourth-century (372–289 B.C.) disciple, commentator, and teacher of what we may characterize as classical Confucianism. These nine works (the five classics and the four books which provided them with supplementary commentary) came to be regarded ultimately as the authoritative expression of the Confucian religious philosophy in classical times. The two principal later contributors to this same development were apparently Hsün Tzu (298–238 B.C.) and especially Tung Chung-Shu (179–104 B.C.). And we may refer to this whole period from about 600 to 100 B.C. as the period of the philosophers (that is, of the formulators of the tradition), in contrast (but only moderate contrast at first) to the period of classical learning which extends from about 100 B.C. down to about 1800 A.D., when a period of interaction with Western religious and philosophical influences began in earnest.

2. Basic concepts of the traditional Chinese outlook.

From a doctrinal and conceptual point of view, Confucius, Lao-tzu, and later reinterpreters began with a context of traditional ideas within which they developed their distinctive emphases. These ideas presumably formed a part of the ethnic religious heritage of China, although any attempt to describe them in their pre-Confucian and pre-Taoist form is bound to be highly speculative and controversial, since our knowledge of these concepts is refracted through the form given to them by these later interpretations. However, it seems to me to be reasonable to attempt such an analysis, however tentative and debatable, since this heritage clearly provides the background for later developments.

a. Concept of the Tao:

as ultimate reality

Perhaps the most basic of these early notions is the concept of the Tao (pronounced *dow*): literally, the term means a way or path, but it came to stand vaguely for a variety of related ideas. On the one hand, it alludes to the ultimate reality, without any precise resolution of the question whether this ultimate reality is a sort of changeless absolute of which all the objects of common experience are so many surface (perhaps superficial) manifestations—that interpretation was the direction taken by the classical Taoist philosophers—or whether the concept, as referring to ultimate reality, expresses the notion that reality, as basically Tao or way, is essentially characterized by change, process, and transition in its most original, fundamental form—that was the interpretation taken by the classical Confucian philosophers. On the other hand, the idea of the Tao naturally comes to stand ethically for a way that is right or correct as directed toward a meaningful or significant goal—and hence the Tao comes to stand for meaning, right order, and the universal harmony of being.

(differently interpreted in Taoism and Confucianism),

and as right order and universal harmony.

And it is a short step from this basic notion to the thought that every level of cosmic reality has its appropriate or right order—Heaven (T'ien), Earth, and Man are all distinctive spheres that exhibit Tao or right order in ways that are expressive of the nature of each. To some extent the actual worship of the major nature powers in popular religion doubtless provided a background and context for this whole complex of ideas— and in this early period there was even the personalized (possibly anthropomorphic) notion of Heaven as a sort of Supreme Ruler. But these aspects of popular religion tended to become decisively secondary for the sixth-century philosophers. In any case, the idea of a Tao or right order for man began to take on the connotation of an ultimate moral or ethical order to which human life was subject; and man himself came to be regarded as a sort of microcosm or little world ideally exemplifying this right order through his capacity to understand the Tao and then either to respond to, or resist, its ethical implications, although probably my way of stating this aspect of the Tao is too precise and sophisticated for the thought of this early period—the direction of these ideas is there, but the goal is not actualized until considerably later.

1. Application of the notion of order to different levels of reality.

2. Emergence of the notion of moral order and its relation to the concept of man.

b. Yang and Yin as the two basic aspects of the Tao.

However that may be, the Tao was regarded as having two basic aspects or forms of expression in the structure of things: the positive, active, and even aggressive aspect (Yang); and the negative, passive, receptive aspect (Yin). And the right order of the universe involved the proper correlation and balance of these two manifestations of the Tao, although it was left to later thought to work out the detailed ethical implications of this correlation for human life.

c. The family as the basic social unit: the role of respect for ancestors.

A final ingredient of this early cluster of ideas grows out of the social extension of the notion of right order: the family was regarded as the basic social unit within which were to be developed the models for broader social relations. And the family embraced not only its living members, but also the whole line of its deceased ancestors; hence, there naturally emerges a tradition of rites for expressing respect and affection toward these departed ancestors. We might call this practice ancestor worship, I suppose, except that the word *worship* has such a strong theistic ring in Western ears that we are inclined to misinterpret this ancestral respect as a form of idolatrous perversion. To some extent, of course, these rites may vaguely have possessed this significance in the popular mind; and the whole practice may have had its origin in earlier animistic notions about the mysterious potency of vaguely apprehended spiritual forces as pervading the whole natural order of things. But we should remember that the ultimate significance of a practice is not limited necessarily to the circumstances of its origin; and we should bear in mind that, just as we would not want the ultimate significance of one of our own religious practices to be judged by the standard of its popular perversions, so we should not judge the final meaning of some practice other than our own by that standard either.

The Classical Expression: Confucius, Mencius, and Tung Chung-Shu

It was against the background provided by such a religious outlook that Confucius and his principal early interpreters began the task of forging these embryonic elements of previous religious tradition into a unified and developing philosophical world-view. And as I understand that maturing perspective, its most fundamental insight was the notion that the inclusive totality of the natural order of things (the Great Whole constituted by the dynamic, interacting unity of Heaven, Earth, and Man, as pervaded by and exemplifying the principle of cosmic order or Tao) is the embodiment and progressive actualization of an objective moral realm in which everything has its appropriate place and function. That the universe is such a moral order involves a network of implications: for one thing it means that the principles of natural order and moral order are basically the same, that the various levels of natural order exemplify in their harmonious unity the sort of principles that ought to characterize right order in human life, and that it is by progressively achieving integral oneness with the various natural (including social) spheres to which a man belongs that the individual realizes his own true good—a good that is ultimately fulfilled through creative and spontaneous oneness with the natural universe as a whole. In this way, following the decrees of Heaven, as Confucius put it, does not mean obeying the revealed commands of a Supreme Lawgiver, but it means understanding and exemplifying in oneself the principles of order which the harmony of the heavens symbolizes and embodies as a model or exemplar, yet in a specific way that is relative to, and expressive of, the distinctive nature of Heaven, on the one hand, and of Man, on the other.

That the natural order is a moral order therefore also means that the moral law is the law of human nature,

1. The Great Whole of the universe as an objective moral order of being.

a. Principles of natural order as guides for ethical living directed toward integral oneness with that order,

but in a way that is expressive of the distinctive nature of each natural level.

b. The moral law as an essential

ingredient of
human nature.

1. Rejection of
radical ethical
relativism:

a. although
moral beliefs
may be
relative,
b. the moral
law itself, as
the law of
objective
reality, is not.

2. Assertion of
rigorous moral
objectivism,

but qualified
by situational
relativity.

c. Virtue and
vice as
respectively
their own
reward, and
the consequent
rejection of
any hedonistic
view of
rewards and
penalties.

that it is an element in man's original constitution as
man, and that man therefore can come to understand
and recognize that law as the obligation to become in
moral character and practice what he is in principle as a
human being. Nor can the ethical ideal implied by the
moral law be regarded as the individually and culturally
variable projection of transitory states of opinion,
belief, feeling, or response. Moral beliefs themselves
may be variable and relative in this way, but the moral
ideal, which those beliefs at best aim to approximate, is
not relative in the same way. For the moral law is the
law of objective reality, and as such its status as law is
independent of what we may happen to think about it.
The defining properties of human nature, for example,
retain an objective constancy of character, however our
opinion about that nature may vary. And from this
point of view, classical Confucianism is one of the
strongest expressions of the theory called moral objectivism. Still, the way in which the objective principles of
moral order apply to human life in general, and to
variable circumstances of the human situation in particular, is relative to all the morally significant facts
about man and his situation; so that, in contemporary
language, moral objectivism in Confucian thought is
not only consistent with situational relativity, but actually requires it.

Finally, the identity of the natural order and the
moral order means that the natural processes of the
universe will ultimately reward true virtue and punish
vice. Nor does this notion mean primarily the thesis that
in the end the virtuous will find fulfillment in proportionate pleasures, while the immoral receive their rec-
ompense in appropriate pains. Some passages in Confucian literature might be interpreted in this way, but
the main thrust of this concept is that the virtuous man,
in actualizing his moral nature, is becoming a better
man—a man pervaded by harmony, order, and integrative personal and social wholeness; a man who belongs
to the world and has found his true place in it. The

basically immoral man, on the other hand, is literally
falling apart, gradually bringing about the disintegration of his true moral and spiritual nature, and pitting
his energies against that moral and natural order in relation to which alone he might have realized his true good.
It is in this sense ultimately that for Confucian thought
virtue becomes its own enduring reward, and vice its
own worst punishment.

The application of the concept of objective moral
order to individual and social existence implies, especially through the eyes of later interpreters of the tradition, the notion of a series of spheres of ethical
existence—a sphere being a context of individual and
social relations pervaded and constituted by a determining motivation or prevailing attitude. A person who, in
a relatively unself-conscious frame of mind, simply allows the bent of his life to be governed by the combined
impact of instincts, desires, emotions, and customary
habits of response, may be said to carry on his life in the
natural sphere in the sense that he unreflectively follows
the spontaneous and frequently chaotic inclinations that
stir and motivate him. But if, motivated by an explicit
and conscious egoistic drive, the individual aims always
to realize his own self-seeking advantage, so far as he
can determine it, then he occupies the *utilitarian* sphere,
in which the prevailing attitude is that of personal
profit. In contrast, if he begins to glimpse a larger social
and human totality, in relation to which his own true
well-being can alone be implemented, and to the genuine good of which he is morally obligated through principles of duty that are incumbent upon him irrespective
of his personal feelings and opinions, then he has, in
that very recognition and commitment, risen above the
natural and utilitarian spheres to find his place in the
moral sphere, in which the determining motive of decision is directed toward the various social wholes or
groups to which the individual belongs. And if a man
goes on to envision society itself as an integral part of
the Great Whole of the universe, in harmonious union

2. Spheres of
ethical
existence.

a. The spheres
or levels
described:

1. natural
sphere

2. utilitarian
sphere

3. moral
sphere

4. transcendent
sphere.

with which society can alone find its well-being in turn; if, seeing this, the individual develops a mature ethical character which spontaneously and progressively understands and embodies the principles of Tao or right order that pervade that Whole, then he has moved into the *transcendent* sphere, in which the over-riding aim is the realization of the good of all reality, regarded as an inclusive, harmonious moral order. It is not, then, that there are different worlds: there is only one world, but individuals may, and do, belong to it in radically different ways, depending partly on the degree of their self-awareness in relation to the true nature of that world, and partly on the extent of their moral commitment to the principles of right order that pervade it. It was left to the Neo-Confucian thinkers of a much later period to develop in detail a theory about spheres of being corresponding to these spheres of ethical life, though the beginnings of such a metaphysical corollary can be detected from the start. For Confucian thought generally, ethics is not foreign to metaphysics; it *is* metaphysics, in one of its aspects.

b. Development of the doctrine of spheres by later Confucian thinkers;

illustrated in the ethico-metaphysical views of Tung Chung-Shu.

Tung Chung-Shu (179–104 B.C.), for example, views the universe as an organized structure of component parts, pervaded by the distinction between Yang (active energy) and Yin (passive receptivity), which in all their expressions constitute together the dynamic process and basic structure of the natural universe and at the same time explain all the transformations that take place within it. Man himself is the universe on a small scale (and vice versa): he finds his proper place in the universe by incarnating in himself the principles of cosmic order. Just as, for instance, the active energy (Yang) of the universe provides structure, direction, and limits to its passive aspects (Yin), so man, by active moral commitment, should exercise the same sort of control over his own passive nature—his emotions, affections, and desires.

But of course the whole idea of a progression of ethical spheres entails, for the classical Confucian thinkers, an ideal of moral virtue that is embodied in the habitual character of the truly good man in the moral and transcendent spheres. To a thinker like Mencius, who dwelt on the fact that man by nature has within himself all the resources for the good life, it seemed in this sense that man was characterized by an original and natural capacity for the realization of the ideal of goodness. But to other thinkers, who measured the moral state of the average man by the standard of goodness exemplified in the sage, with his spontaneous balance of wisdom and ethical responsiveness, man seemed on the whole to be naturally prone to vice and moral lethargy. Yet for both views the actual achievement of the highest moral life in practice required an enormous and enlightened effort of self-discipline which gradually matured into spontaneity.

And Confucian thought proceeds to elaborate on the aspects of this high ideal of virtue. In a sense, we can think of these aspects in the plural as so many virtues or qualities of good character; but they belong together and are simply inconceivable as separate achievements. Just as one cannot acquire any complex excellence (like musical skill, for instance) by parts, but only through the gradual development of all the parts in an expanding unity, so the virtues are realizable only through the gradual maturing of a whole of ethical character.

Perhaps the most fundamental aspect of virtue is *yi* or righteousness. As a principle, *yi* means objective, absolute, and therefore unconditional moral obligation—*objective* in the sense that its status as a requirement for moral beings is independent of culturally and individually variable states of opinion, preference, feeling, or response; *absolute* in the sense that it extends throughout the whole sphere of moral obligation and therefore cannot be suspended or overruled by any more basic or ultimate moral principle with a wider range of applicability; and *unconditional* in the sense that its being a moral obligation on persons does not depend on the fulfillment or non-fulfillment of any set of facts or

c. Ideal of moral virtue in the concept of the truly good man or sage.

3. Main aspects of ideal virtue, intelligible only in their reciprocal relations to each other;

a. *Yi*—righteousness as unconditional moral obligation.

circumstances which may or may not happen to occur—
facts, for example, about our desires, aspirations, or
goals in acting one way rather than another. Such a
principle stands in contrast to moral beliefs which may
vary from individual to individual, group to group,
culture to culture—in fact, those beliefs are themselves
to be evaluated by the standard embodied in that principle. And again, the obligation to fulfill that principle is
quite distinct from what we may call prima facie requirements which hold within certain limits but may be
set aside by the requirement of logically more inclusive
obligations which go beyond those limits—in fact, it is
ultimately by an absolute appeal to such a principle that
we can reasonably justify at times the suspension of
more limited and restricted obligations. Finally, the
principle of righteousness, as an unconditional obligation, stands logically over against any sort of utilitarian,
prudential, or self-seeking motive which would depend
on our having certain desires or aims which might or
might not be present—in fact, the liberty to respond to
such conditional and variable motives can itself operate
with moral legitimacy only within limits prescribed by
such an unconditional principle of moral obligation
itself.

Of course, the ultimacy of the principle of righteousness is quite consistent with the notion that what the
obligation to it requires in detailed practice will be
dependent on all the morally relevant facts about a particular case of moral requirement. And it is further the
case that the unconditional character of that principle
does not mean that conforming to it subserves no end
other than conscious commitment to that law itself: it
rather means that it subserves no primarily utilitarian
end directed toward the fulfillment of individual desires
which are grounded in a morally misguided self-prefer-
ence. In fact, Confucian thinkers commonly point out
that the goal of the unconditional principle of righteousness is the profit of society, not in the sense of the collective realization of individual, self-seeking desires, but

1. Relation to
a. moral
beliefs,

b. prima facie
moral
requirements,

c. and
prudential
motives.

2. Compatibil-
ity with

a. situational
relativity,

b. and the
pursuit of both
individual and
social well-
being.

rather profit in the sense of the true moral well-being of all members of the social order, including that of the individual bound by the requirement in the first place. Hence, it is clear that an individual who consciously recognizes and accepts the unconditional obligation to righteousness not only does not set aside the pursuit of his own true good, but actually aims at implementing it in the context of an aspiration to universal human well-being—a context which provides, in the end, the only dependable framework for effective moral self-realization.

The notion of aiming at universal human well-being naturally leads to a further but closely related principle, which identifies the substance or content of the absolute moral law as *jen* (pronounced *wren*) or love in the ethical sense—a sense which does not, for Confucian thought, exclude affectionate fellow-feeling, but rather extends beyond it to the recognition of, and respect for, persons as ends characterized by intrinsic or self-contained worth, instead of merely as means for the achievement of one's own selfish ambitions. *Jen* means, then, a sort of inclusive or all-comprehending human-heartedness, embodying the proper way for any man to treat another human being *as* man. And it involves a principle of moral reciprocity (*shu*) or exchange which requires an individual to act toward another person in accordance with principles which he could, with moral justification, expect that other person to exhibit toward him if the roles were reversed. By a sort of stunted, legalistic shortsightedness, a person must recognize the formal requirement of righteousness without his response to that requirement embodying the love which *jen* involves; but no one could embody that ethical love itself in his character and conduct without doing so in the context of a settled commitment to the unconditional law of righteousness.

In actual human society, the individual does not find himself confronted with the task of building from scratch, as it were, a stable structure of moral respon-

b. *Jen*—ethical love as recognizing and respecting the intrinsic worth of persons.

1. Love as involving *shu*—moral reciprocity.

2. Relation of love to righteousness.

siveness under the sole guidance of the general principles of righteousness and love, any more than a specialist of any sort, with rare exceptions, finds it necessary to construct the whole edifice of principles governing his specialty out of nothing. In both cases there is an established and accumulating tradition of propriety (*li*)—a framework of principles for guiding one in the fulfillment of the unified obligation to righteousness and love, so far as that framework has been more or less defined by customary insight and practice. And it is the mark of a truly good man that he understands and accepts this standard of propriety, not as an absolute finality, but as a moral map on which he will make revisions under the direction of his own developing knowledge of what righteousness and love require of him in the changing circumstances of his moral life. A moral tradition ground out on the whetstone of prolonged human experience is, in general, a more reliable guide to moral practice than would be the free creation of novel, individual imagination, even when that imagination is itself conditioned by moral sensitivity; creativity is certainly not irrelevant here, but its effectiveness depends on the propriety of its materials. The individual is furthermore provided, in a well-ordered society, with an instructive model of this propriety in the moral relations of persons to each other in a family, the context, in any case, which provides our first opportunity for moral instruction and self-expression. It is in this environment that the virtue of filial devotion (*hsiao*), especially as exemplified in the correct moral relation between father and son, finds its most striking and basic illustration. And what that virtue means, here as elsewhere in society, is the obligation of due respect and appropriate obedience to those above one in the social order, with the reciprocal responsibility of condescension, justice, and love for those who, in turn, are subject to one's own moral instruction and direction.

But of course, the moral ideal embodied in these exemplary virtues and principles implies a self-conscious

c. Li—propriety as an established structure of tradition for ethical guidance.

1. Relation of this guidance to individual moral insight.

2. The family as a model of propriety and school of moral training; the concept of filial devotion as a principle of social order.

awareness of these principles and what they require in practice; and that insight, as an enduring quality, is itself the virtue of wisdom or understanding (*chih*). Nor is it enough that a man's character traits and actions, through appropriate moral conditioning, merely conform to what the moral law requires of him: to embody true virtue a man's moral response must be pervaded by conscious knowledge and moral commitment; otherwise he has only the empty shell and not the true essence of virtue.

d. *Chih*— wisdom as the self-conscious awareness of, and commitment to, moral law.

The truly good life, then, involves the enlightened and habitual disposition to the expression of the unified ideal involved in the harmony of these virtues or moral excellences. And if, in actualizing such an ideal, an individual sees himself against the backdrop of this objective concept of moral character not only as contributing to the well-being of human society, but also as embodying in himself the principles of harmony and order that pervade the Great Whole of the universe, then he has not merely entered the moral sphere, but has passed over to the Great Beyond of the transcendent, so as to become truly a sage.

4. The good life in retrospect.

The Neo-Confucian Reconstruction

Classical Confucianism did not proceed in its subsequent elaboration as a religious-philosophical worldview without the chastening and provocative influence of contrasting positions with which it jostled through the centuries. Taoism was also, in its classical form as represented by the Lao-tzu and Chuang-tzu books (fourth century B.C.), an attempt to re-interpret the concepts of the earlier Chinese religious tradition, although it moved in a different direction by interpreting the Tao as the ultimate, featureless reality of which the ordinary objects of experience are so many surface manifestations at various levels of being. And in the first century A.D. or thereabouts Buddhism trickled over into China from India with a further alternative for understanding

1. Development of Confucianism through ongoing interaction with Taoism and Buddhism.

a. Emergence
of Neo-
Confucianism.

the meaning of existence. It was therefore through a continuous dialogue and interaction with these other developing positions that Confucian thought moved gradually toward the unfolding of an inclusive world-view in the Neo-Confucian reconstruction which began with Chang Tsai (1020–1076 A.D.), reached a peak of fulfillment in the impressive but contrasting interpretations of Chu Hsi (1130–1200 A.D.) and Wang Yang-ming (1473–1529 A.D.), and then reached across the centuries to significant contemporary representatives like Fung Yu-lan (1895– A.D.) and Hsiung Shih-li (1883–1968 A.D.).

b. Effects of
reciprocal
criticism.

Interpretations differ markedly, but my impression is that the long-range effect of these two millennia or more of gradual interaction was that all three traditions—those of Confucianism, Taoism, and Buddhism—tended to incorporate some of the basic elements of the other two in the process of achieving comprehensive, systematic philosophical form; contrasts of emphasis, and even of viewpoint, remained, as will become clear, but in the main these traditions tended to turn the edge of external criticism by incorporating the thrust of that criticism into their own understanding of reality. As it turns out, the most disarming response to a critic is an invitation for the critic to join the object of his criticism as a qualifying paragraph within it.

2. Relation of
Neo-
Confucianism
to classical
Confucianism.

It would probably be a mistake to interpret Neo-Confucian thought as no more than a development of ideas implicit in classical Confucianism from the first; but it would, I think, also be a mistake (perhaps a more serious one) not to realize that the Neo-Confucian thinkers viewed themselves as interpreters of the classical tradition, and that they provided for the core of that tradition the same sort of systematic, sophisticated philosophical context that Western thinkers like Augustine and Thomas Aquinas provided for Christian thought.

a. Philosophi-
cal contrasts
supplementing
the concept of
ethical levels.

For one thing, this metaphysical context was provided through the gradual clarification of a series of philosophical contrasts which were correlated with the spheres of ethical life as developed in earlier Confucian thought. The realm of ordinary experience and its objects (what Western philosophers sometimes refer to as the natural, empirically discernible, phenomenal realm) is called the realm of *shapes and features:* it includes all the distinctions and contrasts that characterize the things of common experience—chairs, tables, trees, and stones, for example. This realm as a whole stands in contrast to the *transcendent* or *sublime* level of being—a realm that includes whatever possesses real being, in the sense that it has an objective status that is independent of what we may happen to think about it, but does not have the sort of actual existence possessed by an ordinary object of everyday experience. Interpreters of different schools differ about what is included in this transcendent realm, but a clarifying example, for one such interpretation, would be a necessary principle of logic (the principle of contradiction, for instance). Such a principle has a status in reality that is quite independent of, and even impervious to, our thought about it, though our thought must conform to that principle to be intelligible; but on the other hand, we certainly would not expect to stumble over it in a dark room, much less catch a glimpse of it, as an object among others, in a lighted one.

1. The realm of shapes and features as related to the transcendent realm.

Corresponding to this metaphysical difference between the transcendent and the phenomenal is what we may call an epistemological difference between the types of concepts we use in thinking about these contrasting realms. A *positive* concept is the concept of a thing or type of thing which either does or might actually exist in the realm of shapes and features; whereas a *formal* concept is the concept of an object or referent which is real in an objective sense, but can not be intelligibly conceived as a thing at all, and therefore can not actually exist as a particular object.

2. The epistemological distinction between positive concepts and formal concepts.

And from an ethical point of view, a person who lives in the natural or the utilitarian sphere is primarily preoccupied with the realm of shapes and features, while one

b. Role of these contrasts in the understanding of ethical life.

who lives in the moral or transcendent sphere is attempting to guide his life through principles and insights whose objective status is clearly transcendent or sublime. Such a man will *act* in the realm of shapes and features, but the grounds on which he acts, and the context in which he lives, will transcend that realm: he will be a king in the wise direction of his worldly affairs, but he will be inwardly a sage in the source of life from which that wisdom flows.

c. The foundation of Neo-Confucianism in Chang Tsai.

The maturing of these ideas clearly begins to emerge in the thinking of Chang Tsai (eleventh century A.D.), who envisions oneness with Heaven and Earth, or union with the Great Whole, as the moral and spiritual goal of human life. The natural universe in its entirety is the embodiment of Tao or supreme harmony as actualized in the differentiation of *ch'i* (matter, or the basic stuff of the physical universe) into the things and processes of the world through the interaction of Yang (active force) and Yin (passive receptivity). The difference between man and other manifestations of the Tao is that man uniquely has the self-conscious capacity to recognize, and respond to, his oneness with the whole of being. By enlarging his mind to include this totality, the individual moves through the moral sphere to the transcendent, and at the same time achieves an indifference to the accidental circumstances of life, so that in this way he synthesizes the sublime and the common: in other words, to borrow a contemporary phrase, he "gets it all together."

d. Division of Neo-Confucianism into two main schools:

1. rationalism

With the amazing Ch'eng brothers, the Neo-Confucian reconstruction both begins the achievement of its fullest expression and divides into two distinguishable perspectives: Ch'eng Yi (1033–1108), by emphasizing a transcendent realm of formal principles which the actual world to some extent exemplifies, becomes the founder of the *School of Li* (form, or ideal pattern)—a perspective which I will call *rationalistic* Neo-Confucianism; while his brother Ch'eng Hao (1032–1085), by emphasizing the undifferentiable oneness of all things in the Tao—a oneness actualized in human life by universal love (*jen*), and apprehended by thought as an all-inclusive Mind, becomes the founder of the *School of Universal Mind*—a perspective which I will call *idealistic* Neo-Confucianism. The rationalistic school was extended and further elaborated by Chu Hsi (twelfth century) and is currently represented by Fung Yu-lan, the best known of contemporary Confucian philosophers in the Western world—principally because a number of his books have been translated into Western languages. The idealistic school had a long line of distinguished representatives after the time of Ch'eng Hao—especially Lu Hsiang-shan (twelfth century), Wang Yang-ming (fifteenth and sixteenth centuries), and contemporary thinkers such as Hsiung Shih-li.

I refer to the School of Li as *rationalistic* because basically it explains the actual world through a transcendent realm of rational principles or ideal patterns (*li*) which that actual world partly exemplifies by what we might call, reminiscently of Plato, participation. Particular things are instances of the *li* or ideal forms, but that latter realm is logically (though not temporally) prior to, and metaphysically independent of, the realm of shapes and features in which particulars exist. And the realm of form includes all logically possible essences or pattern-types, rather than merely those types that happen to be actualized in the phenomenal world. Thus a given *li,* such as the ideal pattern of manness, is a standard or perfection point (*chi*) of a class of actual or possible things or relations in the existing world; and at the same time that *li* is the object or referent of a corresponding concept in our knowing minds, so far as we are, or can become, aware of that form. All the *li* are present in all things, according to this perspective, but the discernible nature of each class of thing is determined by the predominance of certain forms over others in that class. Analogously, all the *li* are implicitly present in the mind of man, but they become explicit objects of consciousness only through an effort that moves

2. idealism.

3. Doctrines of the two schools.

a. The realm of ideal forms and its relation to particular things.

1. Particulars as instances of forms, but not fully exhausting the formal realm.

2. Concepts as apprehending forms.

3. All forms as implicitly present:

a. in all things,

through the particulars of experience to a recognition of the ideal forms embodied in them. In this sense, and using Western terminology, the concepts of transcendent forms are *a priori*—they are in the mind as implicit contents prior to actual experience with objects.

But of course the *li* alone do not explain the actual world. A particular natural object must have a capacity or potentiality for participating in, or exemplifying, the forms which are predominant in the class to which the thing belongs; and there must be an active cause of that participation as well. These two roles are attributed to *ch'i*—the basic and dynamic physical and substantial force of the natural universe. In more familiar terms *ch'i* is both the matter or stuff of things and at the same time the efficient cause of their participation in the transcendent patterns. The concept of *ch'i* in its material aspect is of course relative: pure matter could not conceivably exist as such, since particular existence is only possible by a thing's being of a certain nature or character, and hence exemplifying a form; but formed matter of a certain type may itself be the matter of some further form. The wood in a tree has a nature of its own, but it is by having that nature particularized that it can become the matter for the form lumber; and lumber itself may in turn serve as the matter of a house.

The Great Whole, as the all-inclusive totality of being, includes both the transcendent realm, with its explanatory principles and ideal patterns, and the realm of shapes and features, as embracing all the things and processes of the phenomenal world. And it may be that early Neo-Confucian rationalists, impressed by the unity of being in the Great Whole, sometimes failed to distinguish with full clarity between the real being of the transcendent as apprehended through formal concepts, and the actual existence of particular things and processes as apprehended through positive concepts. But however that may be, both the unity of being in the Great Whole and the distinction of the two realms are clear enough in general, and it would be nit-picking to

b. in knowing minds (hence *a priori*).

4. Ch'i or matter as both the stuff of things

and the efficient cause of their participation in form.

a. Relativity of the concept of matter.

b. General nature of its relation to form.

5. The Great Whole as the inclusive totality of being.

be more than moderately critical of whatever confusion had not yet been fully eliminated.

The path to ethical and spiritual liberation, for the rationalists, begins with the recognition of things as actual instances of the ideal forms and ultimately culminates, through great effort in the extension of knowledge, in a sort of transforming vision in which the individual apprehends the whole of being through the *li* as a universal, fully intelligible order. The moral result of this vision is that the person engages in all of his activities in such a way as to exemplify in them the ideal patterns and thus to express through love his harmonious oneness with humanity and his growing participation in the Great Whole. To become a sage in this way does not in itself mean that a man achieves full technical competence in practical affairs; but it does mean that he acts from an inclusive unity of vision which synthesizes into an integral whole the sublime, or the transcendent, and the fully meaningful performance of common tasks.

I refer to the School of Universal Mind as *idealistic* because it emphasizes the oneness of all things in an ultimate Mind within the unity of which the distinctions and contrasts of the ordinary realm (the realm of shapes and features) tend to break down and merge in a transcending oneness. For this view, as elaborated by Ch'eng Hao and others, the achievement of undifferentiable oneness with all things does not mean the obliteration of all differences, but it means the recognition that everything is inwardly and essentially connected with everything else in the Great Whole and is therefore embraced by the inclusive grasp of *jen* (universal love, or comprehending human-heartedness). For the vision of a man pervaded by such love the distinction between self and not-self, between internal and external, between one man and another is engulfed by an inclusive unity that transcends all such contrasts: thus selfishness is either eliminated, or else expanded to include all being as impartially the object of one's concept—I love my neighbor because, in the depth of

6. Ethical self-realization as the progressive actualization of the ideal forms in the universal harmony.

b. Idealism.

1. The oneness of all being in universal Mind.

a. Not the obliteration of differences, but their essential, inward relation to each other in the Whole.

b. Ethical application of this concept in the ideal of love.

reality, I am one in being with him and with all things. Nor does this realized oneness render one indifferent to particular tasks; instead there emerges a synthesis of inner stillness with a pattern of external activity which responds openly to all things out of a unified balance of character.

2. Intuitive knowledge of the innate moral law, as correlated with the spontaneity of virtuous character and conduct.

Especially for Lu Hsiang-shan (1139–1193) and Wang Yang-ming (1473–1529), the virtuous man's knowledge of the good was a sort of habitual, intuitive grasp of that good as an innate or inherent constituent of human nature; and such a man's response to that inner moral ideal would not involve a laborious struggle with temptation to evil—it would instead be a natural and spontaneous expression of realized oneness with all things.

a. Contrast with the rationalistic view.

To these idealists, such a spontaneity of virtue seemed to stand in contrast to the complicated method of moral instruction and the gradual accumulation of righteousness through strenuous moral self-discipline that was emphasized by the rationalists. It is only when the mind is clouded by selfish lust that one's inner vision is obscured and fails to reach expression in that appropriate action which is the extension of true moral knowledge and indivisibly one with it. But if all this comes off, so to speak, correctly, as the habitual and insightful manifestation of well-formed character, and as embracing the oneness of all things through universal love, then that is what the Great Learning (one of the traditional Confucian books) refers to as "revealing shining virtue" or as "manifesting the clear character"; and it is in that manifestation that the learning of the great man truly consists.

b. The essence of true learning.

Critical Problems of Confucian Philosophy: A Personal Response

1. Impressive significance of Confucian moral and metaphysical insight.

Frankly, I am powerfully impressed: for the most part, Confucian thought embodies a firm confidence that the structural principles of reason, which are basic to our own capacity for intelligible thought and knowledge, are also characteristic of the objective nature of reality itself, and that therefore the principles of reason, rightly exercised, constitute an adequate formal instrument for knowing reality at every level. Girded with such a buoyant epistemological optimism, Confucianism clearly sees that the natural, empirically discernible realm of everyday common experience (the realm of shapes and features) is neither self-existent nor self-explanatory, but ultimately depends, both for its existence and for its final explanation, on a transcendent realm which, though characterized by real being, does not possess actual existence in space and time in the way that objects of experience do. And human nature itself is regarded, at its best, as both exemplifying the transcendent principles of order and harmony that pervade the universe at large and progressively achieving moral self-realization through the recognition of a rigorous ethical objectivism grounded in the nature of reality and through an enlightened response to that moral claim by the disciplined formation of an ideal of virtuous character which sees itself as one with the whole of being.

It is of course possible to reject such a firm confidence in reason—and the subsequent analysis of alternative systems of oriental thought will amply illustrate that rejection. In my introduction to this whole project, I have already given some account of the basis of my own confidence in the ultimacy of rational categories. Most such rejections are either based on a misinterpretation or else are the arbitrary projection of an ultimately groundless decision of will. It is a misunderstanding, for example, to suppose that if reason is ultimately adequate as an instrument, it should follow that a finite rational mind ought to be able to wield that instrument with invariable correctness and therefore to claim virtual infallibility for its results. For the best of instruments can be put to a wrong use, and even the best use of such an instrument need claim no more than some degree of approximate correspondence with ultimate truth in its results. Furthermore, those who reject

a. Combines:
1. confidence in objective reason,

2. dependence of the empirical, natural realm on the transcendent, and

3. a vision of man's true good as harmony with the objective moral order of which he is a part.

b. A response to those who reject this confidence in objective reason.

1. Such rejections commonly based on misinterpretation.

2. The rejection either arbitrary or else appealing to the very rational grounds it purports to deny.

reason commonly provide a series of rational grounds for doing so; and if they are not joking, they seem clearly to be using the sword of reason to dull its own edge in combat against itself. On the other hand, if they provide no such grounding, their rejection of reason will be simply the extension in propositional form of an arbitrary act of will which cannot even make its own choice intelligible without employing the very categories of the reason which that choice purports to call into question.

c. Reasonableness of belief in the transcendent realm.
1. The natural order contingent and therefore not self-explanatory.

Again, plenty of critics have regarded all this talk about a transcendent realm of being as a metaphysical version of whistling in the dark. But if I understand the issues clearly, there is a lot more to it than that: if every state of things in the natural order is indeed contingent in the sense that it can be explained only through causal conditions outside itself, then it will follow that the collection of all those states, each of which is contingent in the same way, does not explain itself either, since that collection, as thus constituted, will be neither self-existent nor self-explanatory by virtue of the contingent parts of which it is composed. The transcendent realm,

2. Transcendent principles self-grounded and self-explanatory, and thus independent of their empirical illustrations.

with its status of real being independent of the space-time order, provides precisely the sort of explanation required. For transcendent principles are indeed, if they are real at all, self-grounded and self-explanatory. Particular objects of experience may variously illustrate those principles, but the principles themselves have a status, as characterizing reality, which is independent of those accidental examples. No object of experience can conceivably exist unless all its qualities are logically consistent with each other: but this transcendental requirement itself has an ultimacy that does not depend on the existence of objects that conform to it in the empirical

3. Even the doctrine of real essences plausible.
a. Particulars unintelligible without such essences.

world. And I myself am quite comfortable here with the thesis of rationalistic Neo-Confucianism to the effect that this transcendental realm is, to a very significant extent, a realm of real essences or ideal patterns which existing things in varying degrees exemplify. If there were no such entity as the essence or nature of a certain type of thing, how would the existence of a thing of that type even be conceivable? Nor do I think it reasonable to suppose that these essences, apart from things, exist only as concepts in finite knowing minds: for in that case, what would the object or referent of such a concept be? Much less do I suppose it reasonable to think that there *are* no real essences anywhere and that general words are merely tags to group things with a view to practical convenience: for in that case, what would be the objective basis for such a classification or assignment of tags? And furthermore, is the notion of a tag or identifying mark itself merely another tag or identifying mark? And if so, to what should one proceed to attach it? It begins to look as if it *takes* a real essence to dispose of the *notion* of real essences, and that seems clearly absurd.

Well, moral objectivism has been subjected to vigorous criticism too. And that critique, in the sweep of Western thought, has for the most part rested on the supposition that moral beliefs and moral principles, if not identicial, nevertheless share the same fate; and since it is historically obvious that moral beliefs vary from person to person, group to group, and culture to culture, the double conclusion is drawn that moral beliefs are relative and changing expressions of these variable factors, and that moral principles or truths must therefore be equally relative and objectively incorrigible. However, it seems clear, to me at least, that beliefs or tenets are quite distinct from the truths which they aim to express (that lesson I learned, once and for all, from George Santayana), and that even the most radical variations in beliefs *about* a given subject have not the least tendency to show that the truth about that subject is itself relative to those variations, much less to indicate that there is no objective and non-relative truth about that subject at all. Hence, the evident fact that moral beliefs vary provides no reasonable basis whatever for the supposition that there are no objective

b. Inadequacy of:

(1) conceptualism

(2) nominalism (which in fact seems incoherent).

d. Soundness of moral objectivism.

1. Rejection of moral objectivism usually based on the supposition that the relativity of moral beliefs implies the relativity of moral truths or principles.
a. But beliefs are clearly distinct from truths,

b. so that variations in belief do not imply any necessary variations in the truths beliefs aim to express.

moral truths or principles, although that fact may indeed reveal that at best our moral beliefs about those truths are no more than an approximation of the objective principles themselves.

2. Other critics argue that moral beliefs, like all others, are determined by non-rational factors, so that their approximation to objective truth cannot be determined.

Clinging still to the identity of beliefs and truths, critics of moral objectivism have sometimes proceeded to argue that moral beliefs cannot have the required rational objectivity, since those beliefs, along with all others that an individual may accept, are clearly the determined product or effect of non-rational emotive, biological, and environmental conditioning factors which are, as a rule, only dimly glimpsed by the individual in question and which, in a complex of variable combinations, cause the person to have whatever conscious beliefs he happens to accept at a given time. If beliefs are determined in this way rather than on objective rational grounds, then there is no way of determining whether they approximate objective truth, even if there should be such a realm. However, it again seems clear that this whole argument depends on the evidently spurious identification of moral beliefs and moral principles—a fallacy which became obvious in the previous argument. Furthermore, this whole line of reasoning, involving psychological determinism as it does, turns into a veritable monster of Frankenstein by proving too much: for if all beliefs are causally determined, then the belief that they are so is just as determined and just as lacking in the requisite objective reasonableness as any other beliefs; and in that case the belief in psychological determinism becomes self-contradictory in the sense that its own objective truth-claim is inconsistent with the doctrine it asserts about beliefs, since it is itself also a belief. On the other hand, if there is some way in which a psychologist (or anybody else) can become increasingly aware of non-rational factors in his own situation, so that he is able to compensate for their possible influence on his thinking and thus also able to aim at a goal of objective reasonableness in his own theories and results, then that same way toward objectivity

a. But this argument again fails to distinguish between beliefs and truths,

b. and in any case, this argument would, if accepted, destroy the objective reference of all beliefs and would therefore contradict its own truth-claim.

c. If there is any way at all to approximate objective reasonableness in any of our theories, that way is as open to the moral objectivist as to anyone else.

is in principle equally open to the moral objectivist in aiming to approximate objective moral truth in his beliefs. It appears, then, that this criticism of ethical objectivism, like the previous one, leaves things as they were; and I cannot avoid quietly recalling a well-worn remark of William James to the effect that even the most radical attacks on our habitual modes of thought leave most of the old order still standing. And I mean that sword to cut in two directions, since I fully expect psychological determinists also to go right on with their old order, however shaky its foundations may appear to some of the rest of us.

Now if a critic goes on to press for a radical ethical relativism which claims that there are no objective moral values, truths, or principles at all, irrespective of whether or not such principles share the fate of moral beliefs, then I think there is a way of responding to that suggestion as well. In effect, such a critic is arguing that nothing is objectively more or less valuable than anything else; and it will follow that the belief in ethical relativism is no better objectively than any other belief about moral values, and hence that there is no objective reason why the relativist, or anyone else, should believe this or any other theory about this or any other subject. Now if the critic accepts this consequence, his objection clearly becomes irrelevant, since it will itself become the subjectively relative projection of his own preference; and there is no apparent reason why the variable preference of a given individual should be regarded as a standard for all individuals. But if the critic argues instead that there is some objective basis for relativism, such that an individual ought to believe it (for example, because he supposes it to be true); then that critic is appealing to the very sort of objective standard that his theory denies, so that here too there is an existential contradiction.

Supposing, then, that a moral objectivism of some sort is both reasonable and practically indispensable, we are left with the problem of identifying the precise na-

3. If nothing is objectively any better than anything else, then ethical relativism is no better as a belief than any of its alternatives.

a. No reason to take the preference of certain individuals as a standard for all.

b. Any evasion ends by appealing inconsistently to the standard it purports to deny.

4. Confucian view of precise nature of moral worth

also reasonable,

a. since it appeals to integrative harmony and order,

without which no significant activity toward an end is possible,

b. and regards personal being as the intrinsic good to be actualized through ethical love,

so that the moral law is the obligation to fulfill man's own true nature.

(1) For this view, character formation is an unending approximation to an ideal of goodness,

ture of objective moral worth. And Confucian thought proposes a solution to that problem which, as far as it goes, seems generally sound. From a formal, structural point of view, no state of things can reasonably be regarded as objectively good unless it is characterized by integrative harmony and unifying order: whatever else the good is, it is a goal or standard to be actualized in the activity and character of moral beings; but it is of the very nature of a goal-seeking process that it should embody unified harmony and wholeness of response, since lack of harmony and order is precisely the disruption and disintegration of significant activity toward an end. Now for Confucian philosophy the intrinsically valuable end that is implicitly presupposed and explicitly actualized by the progressive formation of a character habitually capable of this sort of integrative and unified response is personal being, both in the individual who is involved in this process of realization. and in other individuals who are to be equally regarded as ends of significant moral activity. The concept of *jen* (universal ethical love) decisively embodies this principle of intrinsic personal worth, since ethical love is precisely the unrestricted recognition of that worth and the persistent moulding of thought and activity to its implementation. Personal being is therefore the intrinsic or self-contained moral good: and the objective law of moral obligation is thus objective not by being an external constraint, but rather by being the internal obligation to fulfill man's own true nature, irrespective and independently of variable opinions or beliefs about that obligation.

Nor is the process of character formation, which aims to incarnate the principles of right order imbedded in man's nature (and all nature), a mere instrument of personal worth as an end—a useful ladder to be dispensed with when the transcendent height has been reached. Instead that process of achieving integrative wholeness is the very essence of actualized personal worth; so that the good is viewed, not as a line to be crossed in some concluding triumph, but rather as an expanding ideal to be aimed at relentlessly, though never fully achieved. Still, as character steadily matures, the moral nature of the individual does indeed achieve a constancy of habitual response and a creativity of adaptability to situations, all of which transform virtue into a spontaneous and intuitive expression which leaves the constraint of external rules far behind. And that appears to be the true meaning of Lu Hsiang-shan's notorious counsel: "Have faith in yourself, and let everything else take care of itself!"

The intrinsic reasonableness of this comprehensive moral ideal begins to dawn clearly, at least for me, as I see that the whole notion of pursuing an ethical ideal, since it involves the enriching of personal life, presupposes the implicit recognition of intrinsic personal worth: if the point of morality is not to become a better person (that is, a more fully actualized person) and to act in ways that make it dependably possible for others to do so in a harmonious and ordered fashion, then morality would appear to have no point at all. And in general, the true, objective good of anything cannot consist in a goal that is totally foreign to its nature but must consist primarily in actualizing that nature itself. And if all that sounds not only like the essence of Confucian moral thought but also like a compilation of results from a Western tradition which stretches all the way from Plato and Aristotle to John Dewey, then surely truth is no less objective in status for being universal in extent; in fact, it would be surprising indeed if that were not so, and if the essential truth were not as close to each man as his own front door.

But the cognitive and ethical comfort of this appealing Confucian stance is nevertheless not quite universal for me. As I compare the rationalistic and idealistic versions of Neo-Confucianism, with their emphasis on a transcendent realm that is not only a sphere of ethical life but a level of real being, it seems to me that each could benefit from the fundamental insight of the other.

(2) but it can achieve a mature stage in which rules give way to spontaneous and intuitive expression.

c. This view seen to be reasonable through the recognition that the very notion of pursuing an ethical goal implies personal enrichment as its main point.

2. But there are also critical shortcomings, from the author's point of view.
a. Idealism and rationalism could well supplement each other by combining

The idealist emphasizes the inclusive unity of that realm so fully that he regards the concept of universal mind as the most adequate means of grasping that unity; but in his preoccupation with unity he tends toward a viewpoint in which all distinctions tend not merely to synthesize, but actually to break down and, as it were, dissolve. The rationalist, on the other hand, sees that difference characterizes not only the realm of shapes and features with its plurality of individual objects, but also the transcendent realm with its logically ordered realm of real and ultimate essences in which those individual objects participate; but in his preoccupation with the ultimacy of real and essential differences, he fails clearly to grasp the implications of the integrative unity of that realm, a unity best conceived as the structure of ultimate mind or eternal reason. If these two notions are put together, then what emerges for thought is the unity of an absolute mind that embraces difference without obliterating it, and yet the rich complexity of an organic whole which preserves unity without tending to transform it into undifferentiated formlessness. The obliteration of difference would in the end lead to scepticism, since knowledge is possible only through a conceptual framework that involves difference; still, an ordered realm of essences is itself fully intelligible in its unity only if it is envisioned as the structure of inclusive, ultimate mind.

For Confucian thought, the realm of shapes and features is eternal, in the sense of having always existed, and nevertheless dependent or contingent in the sense of being able to exist only through participating in the principles of the transcendent realm of necessary and real being. Furthermore, the active or efficient cause of the embodiment of the ideal patterns in particular things is *ch'i* or matter, which is the other constituent of those things in addition to the patterns themselves, which, as such, have no causal power. If now we consider any given state of the natural order, it seems clear that each such state is the effect of a previous state and so on to infinity; so that the past history of the universe constitutes an actually infinite series of successive states of the universe, each of which is itself the effect of a prior infinite series of such states without any possible limit. Now this whole complex notion raises in my mind a number of closely related problems which I am unable to resolve within the framework of that notion. First, since matter or *ch'i,* as the principle of potentiality, can only possess actual existence in a determinate state of things that already participates in the ideal patterns (by hypothesis, that is, there can be no pure, formless, or unqualified matter), and since it requires actual existence to produce any further state of actual existence, I fail to see how matter can, as such, be the principle of efficient causality: only that which is itself determinate can produce an effect that is determinate, since if the cause were not determinate, it would have no specific nature by which to act or produce an effect. On the other hand, the forms or ideal patterns themselves are also devoid of causal power; and it is difficult for me to see either how two principles (matter and form) which are as such incapable of efficient causality could become related so as to explain the existence of particular things, or how any active causal power could characterize those things if they did come into existence in this way.

Again, I am constrained to raise the question whether any state of the natural order, even if it does depend by participation on the realm of form, is actually given a logically adequate explanation in causal terms by being regarded as the effect of previous states which themselves require explanation in the same way. It seems as if a cause that is genuinely efficient or active cannot itself be wholly the passive effect or product of something else, since that would leave its active causality unexplained; such a "cause" might pass on an effect that it had itself received, but it could hardly be itself an active, efficient cause. It would appear to follow that an explanation, in terms of efficient causality, is only ade-

1. If matter can exist only by participating in form, how can it be the efficient cause of the embodiment of forms in particular things?

2. Since the forms also lack efficient causality, how explain their coordination with matter in producing particulars, or the possession of relative efficient causality by particulars?

3. Can any adequate causal explanation of things be given by regarding them as effects of other things which in turn and without limit require explanation in the same way? *a.* An instrumental cause not truly and fully an active, efficient cause.

b. The only adequate efficient cause would be a transcendent reality that possessed actual existence as a ground of its causal role.

quate and complete when it comes to rest, as it were, in an active cause that is self-existent and self-determining, so that it requires no further explanation of the same kind. And of course, such a cause, though it would have to possess actual existence and determinate nature through which to produce an effect, could not itself belong to the realm of shapes and features, since it would itself be the cause of that realm as a whole; this ultimate efficient cause then would belong to the transcendent realm and it would itself be an exception to the view that nothing transcendent possesses actual existence—in fact, it would itself be the active agent through which alone the transcendent principles could come into dynamic relation with the realm of shapes and features.

4. Is the concept of an actually infinite series of successive dependent states logically intelligible?

A final suspicion clinches this point for me: I wonder if the concept of a realm that consists of an actually infinite series of successive states, each of which is itself the culmination of an equally infinite series of the same kind, is even logically intelligible or consistent. If this series is, in any state of itself, already actually infinite in the number of its previous states, how can such a series, which by definition already includes all possible states, conceivably be further extended to include additional states (which is exactly what would be happening in a universe conceived along these lines)? Nor does it seem plausible to me to cite mathematical examples of the infinite series to relieve this anxiety: for the mathematical illustrations are not infinite in the same way, since, although they have no definitely assigned last member (there can be, for example, no highest number), they nevertheless have a determinate starting point; while the series here contemplated for reality has neither a starting point nor a definitely assigned last member—a conjunction of properties which makes the cases strikingly different. Well anyway, I am certainly not the first one to become the victim of this kind of bewilderment, nor do I regard the problem as merely an idiosyncratic difficulty of my own individual psyche.

And if I follow the lead suggested by this difficulty, it turns out that the realm of shapes and features is not eternal, and that its origin and existence require explanation in terms of the very sort of ultimate efficient cause whose role we have already been led to contemplate.

The Confucian thinker apparently regards individual human beings as purely mortal, with a destiny that is, for each person, completed in the present scene of things: at best a man may hope to become a pleasant, respected, perhaps even revered memory in the minds of his living descendants. Yet Confucian thought recognizes, at the core of each individual, a principle of essential, spiritual selfhood, constituted through transcendent principles of harmony and reason, characterized by objective and intrinsic worth, subject to the inescapable moral requirement of being itself, and capable of progressively actualizing an ideal of moral virtue. Is it reasonable to take the individual's spiritual selfhood so seriously if that individual has no destiny that transcends the present order of things? Can I really be an intrinsically valuable person subject to objective moral requirement, if in the end the universe is to write a cipher both as the sum of all my works and as the final epithet of my being? If I am not to persist as the subject of enduring moral responsibility, is that obligation really incumbent upon me in the final analysis? I see no reason why essential, spiritual selfhood either should, or could, be dissolved in the ocean of time, and every reason why, for a moral objectivism like that of Confucian philosophy, it ought to endure.

This last problem leads, in turn, to another, which is perhaps the reverse side of the same coin. Personal being is intrinsically valuable, and the locus of ultimate, intrinsic worth; while love, as recognizing and implementing the actualization of that worth, is the essential principle of ultimate moral requirement. But it seems clear both that finite persons are contingent and dependent in their existence, and that the good itself must be

c. The high Confucian view of the moral and spiritual selfhood of man seems incongruous with the supposition that man is to be viewed as having a merely mortal destiny.

d. Is the concept of intrinsic personal worth given an ultimately satisfactory explanation in Confucian thought?
1. Finite persons contingent and derivative,

self-contained and independent in its status, if it is to be truly objective and ultimate. Finite individuals therefore must have an intrinsic worth, as persons, that is derived and secondary. But in that case, in what does the ultimate embodiment and objective reality of intrinsic personal worth consist? The Tao, as the transcendent principle of right order, is impersonal; so also is the universal Mind of idealistic Neo-Confucian thought. How can an impersonal ultimate incarnate the absoluteness of underived and intrinsic (or self-contained) personal worth? And if love is, as such, an interpersonal relationship, while at the same time, as a principle, it is the unconditional moral requirement, can the final direction and ground of that love be reasonably regarded as itself less than ultimate personal being?

2. while the absolute reality, on which ultimate value depends, is viewed as impersonal.

3. Results of our criticism summarized.

If now, finally and in retrospect, we assemble the pieces of our critical inquiry, we might begin to glimpse an objective moral order of being, grounded in the absolute worth and primordial causal power of a transcendent Personal Mind, consisting in eternal reason as the culmination of ideal form or essence; a Mind, furthermore, from whose creative ultimacy finite individuals derive both their being and their intrinsic worth as persons. In this fulfilling vision we will not have left the dynamic thrust of Confucian thought behind; we will rather have gone beyond its explicit limits by following the lead of its own intrinsic notions in the direction of a still greater relevance and coherence; and we may, for all that, find ourselves closer to ultimate truth.

Suggested Readings

Historical Background

Chan, Wing-tsit. *A Source Book in Chinese Philosophy.* Pp. 3–13 (chap. 1).
Fung Yu lan. *A History of Chinese Philosophy.* I, 1–42 (chaps. 1–3).
———. *A Short History of Chinese Philosophy.* Pp. 1–29 (chaps. 1, 2).

Classical Confucianism

Chan, Wing-tsit. *Source Book.* Pp. 14–135 (chaps. 2–6); 271–88 (chap. 14).
Fung Yu-lan. *History.* I, 43–75 (chap. 4), 106–131 (chap. 6), 279–311 (chap. 12); II, 7–87 (chap. 2).
———. *Short History.* Pp. 38–48 (chap. 4); 68–79 (chap. 7); 143–54 (chap. 13); 166–77 (chap. 15); 191–203 (chap. 17).

Neo-Confucianism

Chan, Wing-tsit. *Source Book.* Pp. 460–691 (chaps. 28–35); 751–72 (chaps. 42, 43).
Fung Yu-lan. *History.* II, 407–629 (chaps. 10–15).
———. *Short History.* Pp. 281–318 (chaps. 24–26).

2 / Taoism:
A Philosophy of
Mystical Oneness
and Self-Transcendence

Early Roots: Yang Chu's Philosophy of
"Selfishness"

The explicit beginnings of philosophical Taoism seem to be shrouded with a considerable degree of mystery. Lao-tzu, traditionally regarded as the founder of the movement, was presumably an older contemporary of Confucius (sixth century B.C.) and author of the principal classic of this school, namely, the *Tao Te Ching* (*Classic of The Way and Virtue*), commonly referred to as the *Lao-tzu Book*. But historical critics usually regard this book, at least in its final form, as the product of the fourth century B.C.; and the *Chuang-tzu Book* itself refers reminiscently to the views of an earlier exponent of Taoism, a thinker identified as Yang Chu and regarded by scholars as himself falling between Confucius and Mencius—which would put him in the late fifth and early fourth centuries B.C. For our purposes, however, there is no need even to suggest a resolution to these historical issues; what does seem clear is that Yang Chu was viewed as providing a provisional stage for the emergence of the classical Taoism of the *Lao-tzu* and *Chuang-tzu Books,* although our only knowledge of his existence and ideas comes from scattered, and sometimes inconsistent, references in these and other writings of the same general period.

Yang Chu was apparently a recluse who, both in lifestyle and in teaching, was regarded, by Mencius for instance, as a dangerous opponent of Confucian moral

1. Difficulty of giving an accurate historical account of the early phases of Taoism.
a. Literary sources.

b. Role of Yang Chu in the history.

2. Summary of Yang Chu's impact.

55

a. Personal
self-interest as
the basic
motive of life.

philosophy with its central emphasis on the social context of the good life. The gist of the teaching seems to have been a sort of *utilitarian egoism* which recommended that the individual prize life for himself and aim at the implementation of his own personal self-interest.

1. Not
hedonistic,
however,

Nor does this seem to have been a piece of hedonistic advice which urged man to the greatest possible fulfillment of his desires; in fact, it was held that a man could best implement his self-interest by becoming indifferent to external things, either as objects of desire or as obstacles to its fulfillment. In this way, he might aim at occupying the balanced perspective of a state between desire and renunciation, between having and not having special qualities, though even the approximation of this goal might not guarantee the complete fulfillment of self-interest. In the end this sort of "selfishness," or calculating self-advantage, since it turned out to be both unrealiable in practice and counter-productive in effect, could only attain its true objective by sacrificing a cramping self-centeredness for a transcendent self-realization through oneness with the Tao conceived as undifferentiated, absolute reality: and that is exactly the step that took place in classical Taoism.

2. but rather
directed at a
balanced or in-
between state.

b. Transition
to classical
Taoism.

The Classical Expression: Lao-tzu and Chuang-tzu

1. The *Lao-tzu*
and *Chuang-tzu* books as
primary
sources.

The *Tao Te Ching* is one of the most striking pieces of literature in the whole treasure house of world philosophy: even in English this brief treatise—which occupies about forty-two pages of an average printed text—impresses one as an incomparably beautiful philosophical poem which gathers into its provocative metaphors and rhythmic phrases all the main elements of an inclusive philosophical world-view. If it is not the work of a single fertile mind, it is nevertheless so pervaded by singleness of thought and purpose that it merges naturally into a model of the ultimate oneness of Being which the book envisions. Yet with all its unity of insight, its aphoristic form and remarkable brevity leave it largely without either adequate elaboration or reasonable basis: it is a visionary sketch waiting to be completed by the rich color and solid texture of some later philosophical artist with a passion for substance and detail. Nor was this fulfillment, at least within the Taoist tradition, long in coming; for the fourth-century philosopher Chuang-tzu (369–286 B.C.) brought to the exposition and defense of the Taoist vision the whole acumen of his unparalleled dialectical skill. The *Lao-tzu* and *Chuang-tzu* books together make up the full expression, in classical times, of this significant alternative to Confucian philosophy in Chinese thought.

I have called Taoism a philosophy of *mystical oneness* and *self-transcendence;* I might, in fact, have referred to this classical expression of it as a form of *pantheistic mysticism,* though the terminology could be misleading in either case. If by *pantheism* we mean in general any outlook for which all that is real is, in some sense, essentially one in being with (or an aspect of) the sole ultimate and therefore self-existing reality, then the Taoist vision of the oneness of all things in the all-inclusive but undifferentiated Tao is indeed pantheistic. And if by *mysticism* we mean any epistemological perspective for which that ultimate reality is grasped by the individual through a directness of conscious oneness with its object which largely, if not totally, transcends the mediation of discursive intellect and fixed concepts with a determinate meaning, then the Taoist notion of the recognized oneness of the individual with the Tao as object of knowledge—a oneness in which separate individual selfhood is transcended by being discarded as an illusion—is indeed mystical.

But the monism of this view requires careful elaboration so as not to be misunderstood. In contrast to early Confucian thought, the Tao is not merely the principle of right order proliferated at various cosmic levels—Heaven, Earth, and Man; the Tao is rather the all-inclusive, absolute reality itself. Rightly understood, the Tao does indeed constitute a standard of ideal morality; but

of ideal
morality
through its
metaphysical
status.
2. Oneness of
all things with
the Tao, but
explained as
involving two
levels.

a. Appearance—
the realm of
ordinary
experience
characterized
by striving and
reversal.

b. Reality—the
absolute level
devoid of all
differences and
qualities.

(1) Undifferen-
tiated oneness.

(2) Concept of
phenomenal
illusionism.

c. Rejection of
conceptual
reason and
discursive
intellect as
adequate
instruments for
knowing
absolute
reality.
1. Basis of this
rejection.

that aspect of it is merely an implication of its status as the changeless, indeterminate, qualityless, and ultimate being which the Tao is, and of which all ordinary objects, without any goal-directed activity or striving on the part of the Tao, are the manifestation. Hence, it is not things as they are for common experience that are collected up into a kind of encompassing hodge-podge of togetherness in the Tao. No—we must distinguish here between appearance and reality. At the level of appearance (which is the level of ordinary empirical experience), separate, individual things are real enough, and they follow in general a principle of reversing in which change is explained as an interaction of various opposing forces, a process in which things, though progressively striving to preserve themselves against other things, nevertheless gradually turn into their opposites in the sense of constantly becoming what previously they were not. But these differences are not ultimate: at the absolute level, distinctions are viewed for what they really are, that is, as so many illusory manifestations of a reality (the Tao) which is, as such, devoid of all differences and therefore also of all qualities or attributes; it is only in undifferentiated oneness with the Tao thus understood that things have any genuine reality at all. And I refer to any such view as *phenomenal illusionism,* since it takes the objects of experience as they appear (phenomena) to be, as such, ultimately illusory and unreal.

The other pieces of this bold picture may be quickly fitted together. While the Confucian tradition relied heavily, at least in its main thrust, on reason as an adequate tool for apprehending ultimate truth, it is not difficult to see why the Taoist could not share this optimism: conceptual reason and discursive intellect are by nature fitted to understand reality in terms of differences and determinate qualities—the concept of anything *is* the understanding of it as a definite object with determinate qualities which, taken together, distinguish it from all else. But if the ultimate object of true awareness (namely, the Tao) is devoid of all such quality and difference, then concepts will be worse than useless in apprehending that object, except so far as they chasten the mind by their very inadequacy. All conceptual knowledge is therefore relative to the phenomenal realm of shapes and features—a realm which itself has a merely provisional reality at best. And the futility of trying to understand reality through rational concepts is strikingly depicted in the indissoluble conflict of opposing philosophical viewpoints which those concepts generate: each proponent finds some bastion of opinion which he arbitrarily selects as his fortress, and no proponent is reasonably able to settle the conflict either in favor of himself or against his opponents. Nor is this philosophical stalemate really surprising, since for each participant in the struggle the very standard of reasonableness he accepts is itself a part of the fortress he attempts to defend. What is needed here is a stance of direct, intuitive awareness in which all conceptual viewpoints are transcended—left behind because one has passed through them and clearly discerned their futility. And this stance is the Tao Axis from which one apprehends all things as indistinguishably one with the Tao—including the self of the one who apprehends: this is the no-view viewpoint which is not a viewpoint, it is the post-gained no-knowledge, the ultimate ignorance which alone apprehends truth.

2. Relevance of conceptual knowledge to phenomenal realm.

3. Philosophical conflicts as irresolvable by reason or intellect.

4. Concept of the Tao Axis as an intuitive awareness that transcends all viewpoints.

The ethical implications of this vision are clear enough: if the Great Tao is the ultimate exemplar or standard of rightness and goodness, and if It is without either determinate quality or goal-directed activity, then the basic virtue will accordingly be a sort of inaction or non-action through which, without competitive struggle, the individual realizes his true good in oneness with the Tao. From this point of view, it seems necessary to unlearn much that seemed basic to Confucian moral philosophers. The accumulation of righteousness through rigorous moral self-discipline is itself viewed as a disguised form of aggressive self-seeking—one should

3. Ethical ideal of Taoism.

a. The Tao as the model of true goodness by inaction (or non-striving).

b. Futility of ordinary moral self-discipline.

c. Virtue the expression of spontaneous oneness with the Tao.

realize one's virtue naturally and spontaneously through the renunciation of all forms of striving and trust others ultimately to do the same, however often they may disappoint one because of the bondage of their ignorance. Through such an outlook, for which even the notion of inaction must itself be continually extended and transcended, the virtue of realized oneness with the Tao may become actualized in human experience.

The Neo-Taoist Reconstruction

1. Basis of the reconstruction. a. Reaction to concept of the Tao as ultimate Being or Non-Being.

For classical Taoism the Tao might be referred to indifferently as either ultimate *Being* (because it is the only true reality) or ultimate *Non-Being* (because, as absolutely unqualified reality, it has no determinate characteristics and is therefore nothing in particular); in either case, the Tao is nameless in the sense that no conceptually meaningful term can designate its true nature, since the latter is wholly without qualities.

b. Reaffirmation of the relative incompetence of conceptual reason.

In the age-long confrontation of succeeding Taoist thinkers with their Confucian and Buddhist counterparts, representatives of this tradition found no reason to qualify the negative disenchantment of classical Taoism with conceptual reason or discursive intellectual viewpoints grounded in its exercise: Wang Pi, Hsiang Hisu, and Kuo Hsiang (fourth century A.D.), the principal representatives of Neo-Taoism, were in fact fond of pointing out that the one thing that rationalistic philosophers of different persuasions could agree on was that each was himself right in his views, while his opponents were clearly wrong. But the chastening influence of interaction with other views, coupled with the corrective of self-analysis, did lead these thinkers to a radical revision of the notion of the Tao and to a profound reinterpretation of the ideal of ethical inaction.

2. Reinterpretation of the concept of the Tao.

They agreed with their predecessors that the Tao was Non-Being: but, for the main thrust of Neo-Taoism, instead of meaning by such a designation that the Tao was qualityless and therefore nameless, they meant by Non-

Being that the Tao was literally nothing at all from a metaphysical point of view. Hence, they held that there was no transcendent realm of undifferentiated unity, and that the inclusive totality of the realm of shapes and features was the only genuine realm of being. For this type of thinking, the notion of the Tao is not merely a formal concept (probably Lao-tzu and Chuang-tzu would have approved that idea), but it is a sort of metaphorical symbol or religious figure of speech. To say that all things came from the Tao is actually to say that they came from things like themselves, that each determinate state of things emerges naturally from previous determinate states, and so on to infinity. In fact, nothing can be prior to determinate things, since it will either itself be determinate and therefore a thing, or else it will be nothing at all. And of course it follows that there is no reason to regard the realm of shapes and features as an illusory appearance: rightly understood, it is reality itself. The reference of things to the Tao, therefore, may be a helpful motive for transcendent ethical life: but it is in no sense an extension of our knowledge of reality. I think of such a view as a variety of what I will call *naturalistic symbolism—naturalistic* because it regards the natural order as the only reality there is, *symbolic* because it interprets transcendent metaphysical terms as metaphorical symbols or figures of speech.

As for the reinterpretation of the ideal of inaction, earlier thinkers had tended to interpret that standard as involving the cessation of emotional response, the passive acceptance of circumstances, and the renunciation of all deliberate activity toward ends. But for the Neo-Taoists, inaction means not the suppression of emotion, but an emotional responsiveness in which one nevertheless retains one's freedom and independence by not being "caught in the toils" or allowing oneself to sink into emotional bondage. Nor does the good life entail a passivity of attitude which imitatively reincarnates the aloofness, or even the moral rules, of previous sages: it

a. Denial of the Tao as ultimate Non-Being or Being.
b. Exclusive reality of the natural order.

c. Notion of the Tao as a metaphorical religious symbol.

d. Rejection of phenomenal illusionism; realistic view of natural order.

e. Terminology for describing this view.

3. Revision of the ethical ideal of inaction.

a. Inaction consistent with emotional responsiveness.

b. Moral ideals subject to informed revision

as an expression of creative spontaneity.

c. Deliberate activity also compatible with true inaction.

d. Summary of the revised moral order.

requires instead a sensitivity to social changes and a flexibility of adaptiveness which is continuously revising subordinate moral principles in the context of altered circumstances. To be unwilling to change in this way would be to cramp the natural spontaneity of creative response which is involved in the ideal of inaction itself. And that ideal further implies not the renunciation of all deliberate activity, but the developing fulfillment of natural abilities and propensities: it is only what is incongruous with the nature of man, or of the individual, that is truly artificial and therefore opposed to inaction properly conceived. And if, in summary, a man allows his nature to fulfill itself spontaneously through the actualization of his abilities and capacities; and if he does so with a wise adaptiveness to altered conditions, while trusting his fellows to do the same; and if he can respond to all things as contributing to the natural evolution of being, yet without becoming slavishly dependent on any of those things; then such a man has achieved that transcendently perfect happiness and freedom which are the essence of inaction and the enduring substance of the truly good life.

Critical Problems of Taoist Philosophy: A Personal Response

1. Positive value of the Taoist outlook.

a. The corrective effect of the recognition that belief commitments are influenced by a complex of factors.

1. Sincere opposition of viewpoints.

Every serious-minded individual needs the corrective and chastening that come from being reminded that in adopting his ultimate beliefs, however firm his commitment to them may be, he is being influenced by a virtually incalculable and largely inexplicit complex of variable conditioning influences that range all the way from the structural features of his cultural and historical situation, through the biologically rooted balance of his impulses and desires, to the sheer uniqueness of his personal idiosyncrasies; and he needs as well the humbling impact of the realization that others feel the urgency and reasonableness of their beliefs, however different or even contrary they may be, as deeply as he does his own.

With such an awareness, one can hardly avoid a sympathy with the Taoist disillusionment with discursive reason as the interpretive instrument through which these opposing viewpoints are both defined and argumentatively defended. And he may respond favorably as well to the appeal of the Tao Axis as a stance in which the endless wrangle of conflicting philosophies is transcended.

2. Understandable disillusionment with discursive reason.

Still, the no-view viewpoint is itself also a viewpoint after all, since it stands in contrast to whatever views and attitudes it purports to leave behind. Nor is this the first context in which I have pointed out that the awareness of conditioning influences on one's thought makes it possible, in part at least, to compensate for those influences and thus aim at a closer approximation to objective truth than would otherwise be possible. But in this process a man *does* not (perhaps he *can* not) discard all determinate viewpoints; he rather exchanges a less adequate position for one that promises to be more adequate, and thus moves from a narrower vision to what he sincerely believes to be a fuller one. To suppose otherwise is quite possibly to become unwittingly the victim of a self-deception, more subtle than that of the optimistic intellectualist, indeed, but for that fact no less deadly. The over-all tentativity of philosophical positions should not plunge us into disenchantment with the whole notion of philosophy: it should instead help us to see more clearly what a philosophy really is—namely, an expanding, continuously revisable vision of the meaning of reality which provides a correspondingly enduring framework for significant life. Such an attitude combines openness to truth with a growing stability of enlightened confidence: to expect more is to misunderstand our human situation.

3. Yet the Taoist stance is itself also a particular viewpoint.

a. Possible to compensate (in part) for the effect of non-rational factors on our thought.
b. And this means not discarding all viewpoints but progressively aiming at a more adequate one.

As far as the concept of reality is concerned, I have already explained, in critically responding to Confucianism, my commitment to the notion, shared by classical Taoism, that the natural order of things is neither ultimate nor self-explanatory, but requires ex-

2. As for the concept of reality,
a. classical Taoism right in holding that the natural order depends

on the transcendent realm, but Neo-Taoism also right in rejecting the concepts of *1.* ultimate Non-Being, *2.* and phenomenal illusionism. b. If the Tao is not the same as the natural universe, both must have determinate qualities to distinguish them. *1.* Nor can this point be rebutted by the notions of an unqualified Tao and an illusory world (so that there is no real difference to explain). *2.* For *a.* no way to explain our awareness of such a reality, or the origin (basis) of such an illusion;

b. but this question to be reconsidered in Buddhist and Hindu contexts.

planation in terms of a realm of transcendent being. On the other hand, I share also the Neo-Taoist suspicion that indeterminate, unqualified Being (or Non-Being) is literally nothing, and that therefore the phenomenal universe cannot be reasonably regarded as no more than an illusory appearance of an ultimate reality so construed. If the natural universe, with its determinate qualities and recognizably distinct things and processes, is not *as such* the same as the Tao, then it must in that sense be different from the Tao; and if two realities can reasonably be regarded as different only on the ground that each possesses qualities and/or relations that distinguish it from the other, then the Tao must have determinate qualities which involve that difference. Now if, to escape this conclusion, a proponent should argue that the Tao is different not through possessing qualities but by being devoid of all of them, and should then go on to maintain that since phenomenal qualities are illusory there really is no difference to be recognized, then in that case I would be provoked to raise a whole complex of questions. For example, in what state of awareness could a person be conscious of such an indeterminate reality? How could such a pervasive illusion originate, since it is at least real as an illusion? Surely the illusion of the natural order could not have arisen from the Tao, since by hypothesis the latter has no determinate nature which would prompt it to act in one way rather than another, or even to act at all. At the very least, if the notions of a qualityless absolute and of an illusory world can be supported by any reasonable dialectical analysis, that basis is not provided by classical Taoism in anything more than an embryonic and vaguely suggestive form. And since an explicit effort in this direction *is* attempted by both Mahayana Buddhism and Non-dualistic Hinduism, any further attempt to grapple with these issues is best deferred for later contexts.

Happily, it is not necessary at this juncture to choose between a formless absolute in which all difference is, as it were, dissolved, and an eternal order of difference for which no reasonable explanation seems possible. There is, in my opinion, no reason in principle why we cannot combine a *cosmological realism,* for which the natural order of things and events is genuinely actual in a non-illusory sense, with a *transcendental monistic absolutism,* for which that natural order is creatively dependent, in its existence and character, on a realm of transcendent principles of value and being which constitute, in various ways, the structure and nature of universal self-existent Mind, of whose self-activity the world order is a meaningful product. Such a synthesis would tend both to turn the edge of Neo-Taoist suspicion about the earlier classical view and at the same time resolve, at least provisionally and tentatively, the difficulties inherent in the Neo-Taoist's own concept of a presumably self-explanatory natural order of being, all the successive phases of which are nevertheless contingent and dependent.

If the ultimate Tao is reinterpreted in the way I have suggested, the result, in ethical outlook, will be a revamping of the ideal of inaction along lines already developed by the Neo-Taoist reconstruction. For if the Tao itself, instead of being a qualityless ultimate, is rather the transcendental basis and ground of the rich and varied fabric of existence itself, then the activity of the Tao will naturally be understood as the creative manifestation and active extension of its own ultimate nature. And if further that Tao is regarded as the exemplar or model of the moral ideal for man, then the good will consist in the progressive manifestation of true human nature in self-development and moral activity: only those forms of activity and patterns of character which lead to individual and social disintegration will be artificial obstructions to the good life. In this way, inaction will indeed be not the cessation of all emotional response and deliberate activity, but the concrete actualization of true being, a fulfilment which, though not without the discipline of struggle against destructive forces, will ultimately burst into

c. No reason why cosmological realism and transcendental monistic absolutism cannot be combined.
1. Meaning of this synthesis.

2. Such a view would be a partial solution for the critical perplexities of both Taoist traditions.

3. Neo-Taoism essentially right in its ethical reconstruction.
a. But needs supplementation by a revised concept of the Tao as both transcendent and determinate, so that the world is its creative expression.

b. And the good for man will be the realization of a stable character in which he realizes his true nature and achieves a rapport of oneness with the Tao in the moral sense.

the spontaneity of a stable moral character that expresses a rapport of ideal oneness with the Great Tao. And for me, at least, it is difficult to see how this transcendent ethical ideal can even be intelligible, much less thrive as a live option, without such a grounding in the transcendent absolute of Being.

4. Consequence of our critical work as pointing toward a developing unity of Confucian and Taoist thought.

In over-all retrospect, if the critical directions I have sketched are allowed to provide guidance for our thought, then we can glimpse a kind of developing unity between Confucian and Taoist thinking about the meaning of existence and the nature of the good life, for each tradition tended, in the long haul of historical interaction, to absorb certain central emphases of the other—Confucianism, for example, placing increasing emphasis on the relation of the natural order of things to a transcendent realm (an emphasis that Taoism embodied from the first), and Taoism placing increasing emphasis on the reality and significance of the natural order and man's moral place within it (an emphasis that Confucianism had perennially maintained). Nor is it surprising that reflective traditions which have grown up together should come, each in its own way, to share a participation in the solid core of truth. No doubt there are many inadequate philosophical mergers which provide no more than a temporary ground on which to stand before sober thought moves relentlessly on toward some higher plane. But if truth itself is, as I believe, ultimately one, then the sincere among us should expect to discover increasingly a root of intellectual and spiritual unity which will expose our petty differences and superficial squabbles for what they really are.

Suggested Readings

Classical Taoism

Chan, Wing-tsit. *A Source Book in Chinese Philosophy.* Pp. 136–210 (chaps. 7, 8); 305–313 (chaps. 17, 18).
Fung Yu-lan. *A History of Chinese Philosophy.* I, 132–43 (part of chap. 7); 170–91 (chap. 8); 221–45 (chap. 10).
———. *A Short History of Chinese Philosophy.* Pp. 60–67 (chap. 6); 93–117 (chaps. 9, 10).
Legge, James. *The Texts of Taoism.* 2 vols. Contains the Lao-tzu Book and the Chuang-tzu Book.

Neo-Taoism

Chan, Wing-tsit. *Source Book.* Pp. 314–35 (chap. 19).
Fung Yu-lan. *History.* II, 168–236 (chaps. 5, 6).
———. *Short History.* Pp. 217–40 (chaps. 19, 20).

Part Two

Classical Indian
Perspectives

3 / Buddhism: A Philosophy of Enlightenment

Background and Basic Concepts

The primoridal religious origins of philosophy are no less elusive in Indian history than in Chinese. What is clear is that the fundamental ideas and concepts variously interpreted by the later traditions of Indian thought began to emerge significantly in a long period extending from about 2000, or somewhat later, to about 500 B.C.—a stretch of time commonly referred to religiously as the Vedic period, the word *Veda* being the general term for the body of sacred literature which came to assume definite written form during that era. It was roughly in the first millennium of this period that the Vedas proper came to be accepted as authoritative; and they in turn were subdivided into two parts, namely the Mantras, or hymns to the gods associated with various nature powers (for example, the sky, fire, and even intoxicating drink), and the Brahmanas, or ritual documents prescribing various modes of worship under the leadership of the Brahman or priestly caste, whose spiritual and even political-social leadership had by that time become deeply entrenched.

Sometime after 1000 B.C., and at least by around 700 B.C., there began to appear a second, recognizably distinct body of literature called the Upanishads, presumably the product of the spiritual vision of a series of religious seers of that and earlier times. While the term *veda* means "knowledge," there is no general

1. Historical background and literary expression of the basic concepts.

a. The Vedic period.

1. The Mantras and the Brahmanas.

2. The Upanishads.

71

a. Basically philosophical postscripts to the earlier scriptures.

b. Transition from polytheism to a monistic view of the religious Ultimate.

b. The distinction between scripture and traditional interpretation.

2. Analysis of the basic concepts.

a. Brahman as the all-inclusive absolute Reality.

agreement about the precise significance of the word *upanishad,* though it literally means "that which lies, or is situated, under" something. Whether the term has this reference or not, the documents themselves are philosophical postscripts, as it were, to the earlier Vedas; and they purport to explain the inner or secret meaning of that earlier literature. On the surface of it, the Mantras and Brahmanas seem to involve a kind of departmental polytheism not wholly unlike those of ancient Greece and Rome in the West; but there are vague hints which, interpreted in a certain way, might suggest that the different gods of the Vedic literature were really not separate beings, but so many distinguishable manifestations or expressions of a single, underlying, absolute Reality. However that may be, it was this suggestion that was taken up and developed by the various Upanishadic seers.

The Vedas and the Upanishads together (sometimes referred to collectively as the Veda) came to be regarded as possessing an ultimate spiritual authority which became the touchstone of orthodox Hinduism. These writings were called *sruti* (things that were heard by the ancient seers), and stood in some contrast to the body of interpretive tradition that grew up around them; the latter writings were referred to as *smriti* (things to be remembered) and did not have the same degree of authority as *sruti,* or scripture, itself. But this distinction was often blurred; and even the widely respected *Bhagavad Gita,* though invested in the devout mind with an authority virtually tantamount to that of *sruti* itself, was, strictly speaking, a part of *smriti* or traditional comment.

The over-all outlook and basic concepts of the Upanishadic literature became the crucible in which were blended together the ingredients of virtually all the main traditions of classical Indian philosophy. The most pervasive of these notions was the concept of Brahman, construed as a single, all-inclusive, spiritual (but non-personal) Reality, of which all the things and processes of the experienced world are so many parts, aspects, or manifestations; but a Reality which, though including the world, nevertheless is not exhaustively actualized in that world, but, as one of the seers puts it, extends beyond it by ten fingers' breadth! Many terms were used as epithets to designate this absolute reality, but the most significant philosophically is perhaps the term *Atman* or Self. To many of us such a word might tend at once to suggest the idea of personal, self-conscious being; but such an inference would probably be misleading, since Indian thought had no trouble conceiving the selfhood of Brahman as non-personal or impersonal. In fact, personality came to be regarded as a limiting category, applicable indeed to individual, finite minds like ourselves, but not straightforwardly applicable to the unlimited, infinite Consciousness of Brahman. Of course, since all reality without exception is included in the Absolute, it follows that the finite self is, at base, one with the Self of Brahman; but still the distinction must be made, at least provisionally, and to keep this difference clear the finite self is commonly referred to as *jivatman* (individual self), *jiva,* or *purusha* (soul). The further clarification of the relation of separate selves to each other, and to the absolute Self, was left for later interpretive traditions to elucidate in a variety of clearly distinct ways.

But however that relation was subsequently understood, the self, in whatever sense it was real, was regarded as without temporal origin and, in that sense at least, eternal. And since the present, this-worldly career of any such self does seem to have a temporal origin, the notion of reincarnation naturally suggests itself so that phenomenal existence is viewed as a beginningless cycle of births (*samsara*) succeeding one another more or less uninterruptedly. This cycle or *samsara,* however, did not proceed in any random fashion: the total life-situation of any given individual in any given birth was viewed as the cumulative effect of his choices and deeds in previous lives; and this principle of causal con-

1. Commonly referred to as *Atman* or Self, but

a. impersonal in nature,

b. and at least provisionally distinct from finite selves.
2. Further clarification in later perspectives.

b. Reincarnation and the cycle of births.

1. Viewed as without beginning,

2. but determined by the force of *karma* as connecting deeds with their effects in a causal pattern.

nectedness, this law of the deed and the effect, was called the principle of *karma* (deed, or action). In later thought, the concept of causal order involved in the idea of *karma* was extended to the causal framework of the entire universe or cosmos; but at this early stage, its main connotation was moral or spiritual in emphasis.

c. Salvation or *moksha* as involving release from the cycle of births.

Bound thus to the cycle of births by the inevitable consequences of his previous *karma,* an individual would understandably come to view the realm of *samsara* as a condition of bondage from which escape was to be sought at various levels. Hence, there emerges the concept of *moksha* (escape, salvation, or deliverance) as involving release or liberation from the bondage of birth. The provisional and transitional level of this

1. Achieved by progressive improvement of successive incarnate states,

deliverance would consist in an improved life-situation in succeeding births as a consequence of the wise and morally sound use of one's present circumstances, however hampering and oppressive they might be: good deeds and noble character would have their inevitable karmaic effect as well. But in the end this process of im-

2. and eventually by breaking the bondage of the cycle altogether.

provement was itself to be transcended, and the ultimate spiritual goal, on its negative side at least, was regarded as involving some sort of final release from the cycle of births itself. And the whole body of notions embodying all these doctrines and prescribing laws or principles for achieving release was collectively referred to as *dharma*

d. *Dharma* or religion and the task of philosophy.

(doctrine, law, religion, etc.). In this context of thought, the obvious task of a philosophical system would be to provide a comprehensive explanation of existence that would reasonably clarify the nature of man and his place in the scheme of things in such a way as to elucidate a path to release: and that was precisely the task that the traditional Indian philosophical schools attempted.

3. Subsequent development of the main systems.
a. Historical periods.

The explicit formative development of these various interpretive traditions occupied something over a millenium which extended from about the sixth century B.C. to the sixth century A.D.; and this period of literary and systematic crystallization was in turn followed by another equally long era in which, at the hands of remarkably able thinkers, the implications of these views were endlessly elaborated and dialectically argued. If a tradition purported to accept the ultimate spiritual authority of the Vedic literature and at least attempted to show that its own developed doctrines were not inconsistent with that authority rightly understood, then such a tradition was generously regarded as an expression and extension of orthodox Hinduism. But if, though preoccupying itself with classical notions as elucidated above, a tradition did not acknowledge the ultimacy of Vedic authority, it was assigned a place outside of orthodoxy and regarded as heterodox. By far the most influential of the heterodox schools, of course, was Buddhism.

b. The distinction between orthodoxy and heterodoxy.

Siddhartha Gautama (560–480 B.C.) came on the historical scene in the religious-philosophical context of Hinduism that we have been describing; and although it would probably be impossible to exaggerate the extent and significance of his ultimate impact on the religious development of human thought, still the emergence of his own mature insight was the outcome of an extended personal struggle. The relevant particulars of his personal life may, for our purposes, be quickly reviewed. Born as the son of a rich Hindu rajah or ruler of the Shakya clan in north India, he grew to young manhood in an environment of splendid luxury and, while still in his teens, was married to a neighboring princess named Yashodara, by whom, after an interval of ten years, he had a son who was inexplicably named Rahula (a fetter or tie). Like all such young nobles, Gautama was largely shielded from the unpleasant dimensions of human existence; but he could not remain completely aloof from the ravages of old age, disease, and death, which, though they had yet to touch him personally to any significant extent, were nevertheless virtually rampant around him. Tradition has it, in any case, that he was eventually shaken to the core by the inescapable, disturbing presence of these human conditions; and that when

4. The career of Gautama (the Buddha).

a. His personal life.

b. His spiritual quest.

his inner turmoil about all this was climaxed by the sight of a holy man who seemed to have an enduring confidence in the midst of it all, Gautama's spiritual search began in earnest. In the dead of night, we are told, he rose from his bed, took a final look at his wife and child as they quietly slept, rode to the edge of his father's kingdom with his favorite servant, donned the garb of a holy man, and went off to seek spiritual enlightenment. Nor should we boggle at the moral propriety of such a radical change of life style: the temporary or even permanent renunciation of family life for the pursuit of spiritual realization was a standard pattern of behavior for householders who had fulfilled their family obligations by providing for the security of its members.

For six years Gautama wandered about, consulting with various spiritual savants and even gathering a handful of equally searching disciples about himself. For a considerable time they practiced the methods of self-denying asceticism: but Gautama found neither peace nor insight in that way, and so decided to give it up—a decision which motivated his disciples to desert him. Undaunted by this solitude, he continued his search alone, until finally he sat down, presumably in the lotus position, under a fig tree in the little village of Gaya, about one hundred and fifty miles east of Benares, the holy city of Hinduism. There, as he rested and meditated, he entered into a transforming experience of enlightenment in which he achieved at last an illuminating understanding of man's moral and spiritual predicament, its cause and its ultimate cure. Nor was this radical change a merely intellectual one: for in it he himself, in his whole being, was transformed so that he entered into a state of wisdom, joy, peace, insight, and out-going love, through which he became the *Buddha* (the Enlightened One) and the *Tathagata* (the Perfect One, He who has fully come through). Though momentarily toying with the thought of withdrawing into the pure self-enjoyment of the

c. His enlightenment.

1. Aspects of the experience.

2. Consequences of its motivation.

release he had thus attained, he quickly put aside that notion as spiritually incompatible with the deeply urgent love for humanity that had been generated by the enlightenment itself. And his first step in self-giving led him to seek and find his former disciples at Benares: there, according to tradition, he preached to them his first, and perhaps greatest, sermon, in which he summarized the fundamental substance of his new-found insight. Profoundly moved, this handful of men immediately accepted the good news, began to share the Buddha's enlightenment, and became the nucleus of the first monastic order. Buoyed up by the seemingly inexhaustible energy of his experience and by the uncompromising confidence of his insight and love, Buddha spent the remaining forty-five years of his life (from age thirty-five to age eighty) literally evangelizing the whole of India and organizing groups of disciples which later became the foundation of the Buddhist Orders, or, as it was called, the Brotherhood.

d. The subsequent activity of Buddha.

I have tried to capture the motivating power of Gautama's experience in a ballad of the Buddha that I call *Up the Ladder of Joy:*

e. Poetic summary.

i

In kingly robes he drifted as a young man:
But earthly pleasures never brought him peace;
He left it all and sought long for the pure land:
His ev'ry effort bent on true release!

ii

In patience through the years he searched for wisdom:
The scriptures and the seers he gladly heard;
With heavy heart he saw at last the truth come:
Beneath the Bo-tree light his soul had stirred!

iii

The light of true compassion led him onward:
The cause of human ills all must discern;
Root out desire and listen to the pure word:
The fire of love within your heart must burn!

iv

Through strength of will, O wand'rer, tread the pathway:
With watchful eye on word and work stand fast;
In singleness of mind live out your short day:
The morning of release will dawn at last!

(Refrain)

O, he went up the ladder of joy, and found truth within his
soul:
Waves of wisdom, peace, and love began to roll;
The cycle of rebirth at last was broken;
The chains of passion dropped—He was made whole!

(November, 1972)

5. The division of the Brotherhood.

Buddha had of course envisioned for his followers a unity of brotherhood from which sectarian squabbles would be largely eliminated by the sheer unifying dynamic of truth and love as he understood them. But as with all things human, divisions of opinion and interpretation, along with the changing effect of varied cultural settings (especially in China and Japan), ultimately led to the proliferation of Buddhism into a considerable variety of different sects and schools.

a. The distinction between *Hinayana* and *Mahayana*.

Philosophically the most significant division was that which ultimately emerged between *Hinayana* (the Lesser Vehicle, but less prejudicially called *Theravada* or the way of the elders) and *Mahayana* (the Greater Vehicle). This cleavage appeared in India itself: the Hinayana then spilled over into Ceylon, Burma, and Indo-China, while the Mahayana engulfed practically all the forms of Buddhism in China and Japan.

b. The literary expressions of the two vehicles.

Both traditions accept as religiously authoritative the body of slowly accumulated discourses and doctrinal treatises basic to the Hinayana and called the Tripitaka (or Three Baskets, so called because of the cases of basket-work in which one collection came to be stored), along with the *Dhammapada* (Way of Virtue)—a traditional anthology of Buddha's sayings. In addition, the Mahayana spawned a succession of other treaties embodying the special doctrines of that Vehicle—such as

The Lotus of the True Law and *The Questions of King Milinda.*

The complex doctrinal differences between the two Vehicles must engage us shortly. Meanwhile, a difficult but inevitable decision must be made: most critical scholars regard the doctrines of the Hinayana as the most reliable guide to the original teachings of Gautama, while Mahayana scholars, though freely acknowledging a doctrinal development in the various branches of their Vehicle, sincerely believe that the essential ingredients of the Mahayana were communicated by Buddha to those among his disciples whose spiritual maturity made them eligible to benefit by those ideas. Now I see no reason to even suggest a settlement of this controversy, since we know about Buddha's teachings only through these Vehicles. However, in what follows it will be convenient for me to discuss the views of the Hinayana as though they at least approximated the thinking of Gautama himself; but I will build no substantive conclusion on this point, and it is primarily with the viewpoints themselves that I am concerned, rather than with their relation to the historical Buddha.

6. A decision about interpretation.

The Essence of Original Buddhism: Hinayana

Buddha's thinking was initially a reconstructive reaction to traditional Hindu concepts and their implications for human society. Perhaps the stratification of Indian society into rigid hereditary castes was originally grounded in the reasonable thesis that by nature and endowment individuals are suited to the performance of quite different social functions which, taken collectively, would serve the whole spectrum of human needs. Unhappily, however, these diverse capacities are seldom defined by purely hereditary lines of descent; and even as early as Buddha's time a discerning eye could interpret the caste system as an oppressive and unyielding social mechanism which contributed more to the disori-

1. Buddha's reaction to Hindu concepts.

a. Rejection of the caste system.

entation of genuine human well-being than to its implementation. In any case, Gautama saw it that way and therefore rejected the whole system, thus providing one of the grounds on which his religious teachings were regarded as heterodox and placed outside the pale of Hindu orthodoxy.

b. Reinterpretation of the authority of the Veda.

But other facets of tradition were equally disturbing to Buddha. He respected the Vedas and the Upanishads and drew deeply on their insight; but he thought it unreasonable to subscribe to their ultimate spiritual authority beyond the extent to which their teachings commended themselves to the reason and experience of a sincere and enlightened individual. What basis, in principle, could there be for regarding the vision of the ancient seers as any more normative for spiritual understanding than the sober reflective insight of any spiritually restored person? In the end, the relevance of tradition could be germane to an individual's thinking only so far as his own careful consideration had accredited it as reasonable. On grounds like these, Gautama could not subscribe unqualifiedly to the ultimate spiritual authority of the Veda, and by this disclaimer he provided the other basis for his outlook's exclusion from orthodoxy.

c. Rejection of the concept of *atman* as permanent being.

1. Aspects of the doctrine.

Still, it was Buddha's conceptual reinterpretation that provided the most radical point of departure from Hindu tradition. The Upanishadic seers had strongly emphasized the notion of enduring and permanent selfhood (*atman*) both for the individual self (whose soul was viewed as persisting virtually unchanged in its essence through successive lives) and for the Absolute Self of Brahman (who, one way or another, was regarded as the ultimate, changeless cause and true underlying reality of all things); in fact, the notion of substantial permanence was even extended to the things and processes of the experienced world. Now Buddha

2. Denial of permanence in things and individual persons.

saw no reason, in experience as he viewed it, for clinging to this concept of permanence in any of these senses: all around him things and processes seemed characterized by sheer flux and transitoriness—he could identify no quality or aspect of things as enduring unchanged; and sober introspection of the stream of conscious experience disclosed only transitory psychological states which emerged only to pass into memory, never to be recovered in the same form. There was of course a kind of fluid continuity in things, and there was also a dynamic interconnectedness among the mobile elements of experience; but he discovered no permanent thinghood without and no changeless selfhood within.

As for the notion of a changeless Absolute Self or Brahman, Gautama found no adequate basis for that conception either. How such a changeless cause could be construed as intelligibly related to the radically changing world, as its ground and true being, seemed an insoluble problem to begin with. How could Brahman be the cause and locus of a changing world without himself being essentially qualified by change as well? Nor was it easy for Buddha to understand why, if God did originate the world in some sense, He could not have invested that world with absolutely unambiguous marks of its divine origin, instead of shrouding the whole problem of reality with mystery and perplexity. And if, further, the absolute divine causality is taken as all-inclusive and all-explanatory, does that determining causal efficacy not deprive individuals of moral responsibility, and render ethical self-realization both impossible and pointless?

3. Agnosticism about the concept of Brahman as the changeless Absolute.

Over against this whole fabric of notions Gautama pitted the thesis that, judged by the standard of a reasoned interpretation of experience, everything is impermanent or no-soul (*non-atman,* or *anatman*). The real, empirical world, both within and without, is in a state of beginningless flux or change: the term *atman,* so far as it has any useful and non-misleading application, is a name for the overlapping continuity of transitory conscious states in the stream of experience. These complexes, in turn, are of five basic types, ranging from various states of sensory awareness through those of

2. Doctrine of impermanence.

a. Meaning of the concept.

b. Reinterpretation of atman as implying enduring continuity.

feeling, conception, and volition, and culminating in consciousness as a sort of general capacity for awareness which, wrongly interpreted, leads to the notion of permanent selfhood.

c. Resultant view of reincarnation.

On this basis, one might suppose that Buddha would go on to challenge the notion of reincarnation itself; but that would be a mistaken inference. There is, of course, no permanent individual self that persists to be reincarnated; but in the experience of any given phenomenal human person there is an accumulating effect of previous psychological states in the momentary complex of such states at any given time. And according to Gautama, this cumulative achievement, at the time of the death of any such person (when the complex continuity of his on-going states passes into dissolution), can reasonably be viewed as a starting point for the experience of some other such person. Just as the burning of a candle at any given moment is the cumulative effect of the previous process of burning, so with the psychological states of a person at such a moment; and just as the wick of a new candle can be lit from the dying flame of the old without the transfer of any enduring substance, so the moral and spiritual (and generally the personal and psychological) achievement of one person can become the flame from which a new center of personal continuity springs to light. Should anyone object that in that case the real person does not actually become reincarnated, then it is incumbent upon such an objector to identify reasonably that facet of real personhood which is not carried over in the dynamic transfer of the unfolding effect of previous experiences; and Buddha was confident that no such facet could be recognized, much less intelligibly related to the ever-changing core of successive psychological states.

1. Compatibility with the denial of permanent selfhood.

2. The candle analogy.

3. Answer to objection that the real person is not reincarnated.

d. *Karma* and the principle of dependent origination.

The whole continuity and relation of such processes follows, for this view, the principle of *karma* or causality, so that each momentary complex of conscious states is the ordered consequence of previous complexes of the same sort. So Buddha could hold, with unassailable orthodoxy, that the total life-situation of any given person is the consequence of previous *karma*. And this causal relationship was itself regarded as one illustration among others of a principle of dependent origination which pervades the whole fabric of the experienced world: "This being given, that arises"; and thus the whole state of the universe at any given moment embodies uninterruptedly the operation of the principle of *karma*. The whole of existence therefore is rather like a wheel which, in its turning, exhibits both the interdependent connectedness of its parts and the causal continuity of its motion.

To understand the frailty of human existence in this way, and to apprehend clearly how human involvement in the inexorable rolling of the wheel constitutes a condition of moral and spiritual bondage, is at the same time to realize that human well-being involves escape from this cycle of births and that true enlightenment begins with the identification of this predicament as suggesting its own solution. It was this inclusive insight, or something like it, that Gautama saw clearly for the first time under the fig tree, and through which he himself is said to have achieved release. The ethical dimension of all this constitutes the most familiar (but often misunderstood) stretch of Buddhist thought, and is explained through the analysis of the four noble truths and the eightfold path.

The very impermanence of existence and its conformity to the law of *karma* together entail a passivity of personal being which involves subjection to pain, sorrow, suffering and misery. But these consequences of passivity constitute a condition of bondage precisely because men are generally ignorant of impermanence and causality, and therefore become the victims of a selfish craving grounded in a mistaken belief in their own permanence and a misguided notion of happiness in which well-being is wrongly identified with the possessive acquisition of transitory objects of desire that are inevitably fated to disappear even if they come

3. Deliverance from the cycle of births:

the four noble truths and the eightfold path.

a. The *first* truth: existence involves subjection to suffering and misery.

b. The *second* truth: ignorance and selfish craving are the causes of this predicament.

momentarily into our grasp. The predicament therefore from which man needs deliverance is one that emerges from the conjunction of an ignorance of the true nature of reality with a bondage to selfish craving and all its effects in frustration, alienation, and disappointed desire. Nor does this analysis mean to affirm the obviously false proposition that those in such a state are as miserable in every respect as they could conceivably be; it rather affirms that even the most fortunate among us cannot escape misery altogether, and that even the fleeting happiness which we seek by trying to do so turns out in the end not to be genuine happiness at all.

c. The *third* truth: these causes can and should be eliminated. *1.* No deliverance through satisfaction of selfish craving.

The solution that Gautama propounds recommends that through enlightened insight and firm resolve selfish craving be eliminated. Coddled by Western affluence, we might be tempted to suppose that the way to deliverance is through the complete satisfaction of selfish craving, on the supposition that the best way to escape the frustrating effect of temptation is to yield to it without compromise. But that numbing proposal is clearly misguided: many desires, like the longing to live forever in the prime of vigorous youth, cannot be satisfied at all in this world; still other desires involve, in their actualization, a competitive and inevitably alientating struggle with our fellow human beings, with all the further misery entailed therein. And in any case, satisfying desires of this sort, rather than delivering a man from emotional bondage, merely shackles him more tightly with its chain. Besides all this, identifying well-being with the satisfaction of desire presupposes, as we have seen, a mistaken view of personhood. Nor is Buddha recommending that men enter into a state of lethargic indifference to all forms of goal-directed activity: instead he is recommending that we renounce those forms that lead to bondage and recognize those that lead to spiritual liberation and release.

2. Reorientation of goal-directed activity.

d. The *fourth* truth: deliverance is possible through the eightfold path.

The eightfold path of this realization strikes a mean and opens a door between an enslaving indulgence of fleshly appetite and a self-denying asceticism of the sort that Gautama himself had found unworkable. In essence the way to release involves an openness to truth supported by firm resolve, matched by a balanced lifestyle that incarnates this seriousness of purpose, and climaxed in a discipline of mind and body that itself culminates in a liberating enlightenment which both recognizes the whole of truth and accepts it with transforming moral commitment. More specifically, the way begins in (1) an openmindedness which suspends all previous presuppositions and is supported by (2) an unwavering intent to follow the path to its culmination—there is no room here for the merely curious who wish only to dabble in oriental thought. And of course this beginning must be correlated with a life-style pervaded with a rigorous self-discipline of (3) speech, (4) action, and even (5) personal vocation: all of these must display a character that is fitted to the earnest pursuit of the spiritual goal, so that no word, deed, or occupation which thrives in any way on the avoidable miseries of others can possibly qualify. Yet these five steps merely lay the groundwork and provide the context for spiritual deliverance: to succeed one must go on with (6) an unyielding effort to eliminate all distracting influences which might tend to turn one away from one's goal, and must exercise (7) an unrelenting control over the wandering tendency of the mind itself. Through this demanding ladder of spiritual ascent one may at last break over into (8) that controlled attention which consists in complete identification with, and acceptance of, the truth. On its psychological side this last step is *samadhi* or fully unified concentration; and on its moral and metaphysical side, it is *nirvana* or that extinction of selfish craving which, for that individual, stops activating the wheel of existence, promises final deliverance from the cycle of births, and leaves the person in a state of living release in which, through out-going love and unmistakable example, he can help others to achieve salvation as well. Of course, the way is not easy, and in any given age few, doubtless, will accede to its

1. The essence of the path.

2. Steps of the path briefly described.

3. The culmination of the path in the extinction of selfish craving and in enlightenment: *nirvana.*

4. Rigor and difficulty of the path.

a. An open
possibility for
all.

demands; but the rest of us can at least hope to have enough insight to recognize and accept these spiritual giants for what they are, and to realize that the transformed life which they exemplify is an open possibility for each of us whenever we wish to pursue it.

b. Problem of
unanswered
questions and
Buddha's
attitude about
them.

This challenging vision of Buddha leaves many unsettled questions for the systematic philosopher; and there is good reason to believe that he himself was quite aware of the most baffling of these questions: Is the concept of an eternal universe of successive, momentary states really intelligible? Will the state of final release that follows the death of an enlightened person involve his continued existence in a positive state of being? And so on endlessly. But perhaps he thought that excessive preoccupation with such problems was itself a distraction from the spiritual goal: when the house is burning, that is not the time to discuss the nature of fire; and if we postpone spiritual commitment until all such problems are solved, we may also relinquish all chance of

c. The path as
involving a
continuing
risk.

genuine release. That stepping onto the eightfold path involves an initial risk never fully eliminated until one reaches the goal is not denied; but to regard the alternative to that step as the perpetuation of bondage and personal disintegration is already to have begun the arduous ascent.

The Emergence of the Mahayana

1. Difficulties
in the
Hinayana
outlook:
proliferation of
distinct schools
of thought.
a. The Realist
school.

Over the centuries the Hinayana tradition itself spawned, for many thinkers, the grounds for its own transcendence in doctrinal variations which appeared within its ranks. So strong was the emphasis of tradition on the momentary status and relative discontinuity of successive elementary states of being that some followers, fearful that causal continuity and the real existence of the elements might be lost or consigned to illusion, propounded the realistic doctrine that all the states—past, present, and even future—were genuinely actual; in this way they sought to preserve a stable framework of being for the operation of the principle of *karma*—itself essential to the notion of the accumulation of moral effects through the successive and variable states. Others still, fearing that personal identity and moral responsibility might be dissolved in the complex of changing psychological states which constituted the phenomenal individual in the traditional view, argued that although there was no eternal self or *jivatman* that persisted unchanged from life to life, there must be, within each such life, a relatively enduring personal agent or *pudgala* which accounted for the continuity of individual experience and at the same time provided an object for the self-giving love that Buddhist ethics recommended as an expression of true release. In the end, however, these critical descendants of the Hinayana all died off and left the so-called Theravada or Way of the Elders as the only surviving school within the Lesser Vehicle.

b. The Personalist school.

In the meantime, partly on critical grounds like these and partly for reasons growing out of a different view of Buddha and his relation to reality, a powerful and rapidly growing alternative to the Hinayana had begun to emerge and define its tenets. By about 100 A.D., after a series of historical transitions best left to the critical scholar, the philosopher Ashvaghosha could speak quite appropriately of the "Awakening of Faith in the Mahayana," and in doing so become one of its first great proponents. For the Hinayana, the historical Buddha was primarily an example and evidence of the sort of individual self-discipline and enlightenment that could lead to release; and others could achieve similar results by launching out independently on that same path—a path on which, though motivated by the example and love of others, each person must ultimately make his own way and find his own release, thus becoming a separate or individual Buddha (*pratyekabuddha*).

2. Emergence of the Greater Vehicle.

a. Altered view of Buddha and enlightenment. *1.* Hinayana concept.

But the Mahayana began to take an increasingly different view of all this. Why, they asked in effect, if separate release for each person is the goal, should an

2. Mahayana reinterpretation.

a. Critique of the individualist view.

b. Outgoing concern and love as an essential expression of enlightenment.

c. Nirvana reconsidered. (1) Identity of *nirvana* and *samsara.*

(2) The *bodhisattva* ideal.

b. Metaphysical implications of the revised view: the triple body doctrine. *1.* Concept of the Buddha essence.

enlightened person (Gautama, for example) not find the most appropriate expression of his new state of living release in a life of withdrawal and meditation, rather than in a life of compassionate love and devotion to others still in a state of ignorance and bondage? For the Buddha, such outgoing concern seemed to be an *essential* expression of enlightenment, rather than merely an open possibility: though it is the responsibility of each person to seek deliverance, the release that comes broadens his vision to see that his new state of freedom is precisely a bondage of love, so that he does not regard the promise of *nirvana* as an individual goal, but as a destiny that one achieves in loving unity with all suffering beings. From this point of view, the *nirvana* that one enters alone is, in the last analysis, not the true *nirvana:* in fact, the notion ultimately dawns that *nirvana* is not separation from *samsara* (or the cycle of births), but instead it is the realization of devoted oneness with others in an inclusive outreach for which the ethical difference between *nirvana* and *samsara* simply dissolves. Such a person is a *bodhisattva*—an individual whose true being consists in a pure enlightenment that is pervaded by universal love and grounded in firm resolve. Unshackled by the chains of *karma,* the *bodhisattva* may even accumulate a fund of merit which can in turn be channeled in love toward the well-being and ultimate deliverance of all sentient creatures.

But of course this transformed ethical perspective carried with it a parallel transition in the way Mahayana thinkers understood reality and the knowledge of true being. The historical Buddha came to be viewed as the individual human manifestation of an underlying, all-embracing Buddha essence, of which all phenomenal things and processes were a sort of provisional expression. In this vein, Buddhahood is seen as the true reality of everything at its core. Eventually, for this tradition, there emerged the doctrine of the triple body (*trikaya*) of Buddha: three distinguishable, but closely related, levels of the Buddha essence. Accessible to ordinary experience is the body of transformation (*Nirmanakaya*) which can be understood by the discursive intellect and which corresponds to the empirical world order; and it is also, ethically speaking, the realm of bondage and ignorance in which the principle of *karma* is universal—in other words, it is *samsara* or the cycle of births.

In a sense, the body of transformation stands in sharp contrast to the Buddha's body of pure being (*Dharmakaya*), since this highest level of the Buddha essence is wholly devoid of all the multiplicity, variability, and individuality which characterize the phenomenal world. The *Dharmakaya* is pure, unqualified, indeterminate, and absolute suchness (*bhutatatnata*): as such, it is of course unknowable by conceptual reason or discursive intellect, since these means of knowing depend, as we have seen previously, on the reality of that very sort of difference that is wholly inapplicable to the absolute reality. Yet this ultimate of being is knowable by a sort of completely perfected awareness in which the knower is apprehended as undifferentiably one with the object of knowledge. And from all this there arises the supposition that, strictly speaking and from the absolute standpoint, the *Dharmakaya* alone is genuinely real, while the *Nirmanakaya* is to be regarded as an illusory appearance, apprehended through the relative, intellectual awareness that characterizes ordinary experience but must at last be left behind. In fact, the enormous cosmic blunder involved in mistaking the realm of change and process for the real world is itself an intrinsic aspect of the ignorance that enlightenment purports to dispel. In another sense, therefore, there really is no difference between the absolute realm (the *Dharmakaya*) and the empirical realm (the *Nirmanakaya*), since the latter is ultimately illusory; and this identity parallels the thesis that in reality *nirvana* is not separate from *samsara,* since the cycle of births is in fact a process of that finally illusory empirical world.

So once again, as in classical Taoism, we find ourselves in the context of monistic absolutism and phe-

2. Body of transformation: realm of ordinary experience and bondage.

3. Body of pure being: realm of absolute suchness.

a. Known

(1) not by conceptual reason,

(2) but by undifferentiable oneness.

b. The sole reality in contrast to the ordinary realm as illusory appearance.

c. But no ultimately real difference between the two realms:

consequent identity of *nirvana* and *samsara.*

d. Contrast with the Hinayana view: (1) clear difference, (2) but understandable transition from elements in the original teaching of Gautama.

nomenal illusionism; and just as importantly, we find ourselves in a context that seems, in any case at first glance, a far cry from the cosmic realism and confidence in reason that characterized original Buddhism, at least as viewed by the Hinayana. And yet it is not difficult to see how this bold and comprehensive metaphysical vision could expand to its present current of fullness from the trickle of light that flowed from Gautama's original insight: a world of incessant flux and fleeting momentary states easily gives way to an understanding which views that world as merely relative and ultimately unreal; a conceptual reason which both requires a realm of difference as its object and yet aims at something more stable than ceaseless change easily falls away in the brilliant light of intuitive oneness; and a state of release in which one achieves deliverance from the transitory cycle of births quite naturally passes into a transforming oneness with being for which love achieves its highest fulfillment in identity. So perhaps, as Mahayanists believe, it really was all there to begin with in the person and teaching of Gautama: there are, after all, no eyes so blind as those that are determined not to see.

4. Body of bliss as intermediary between ordinary and absolute realms. *a.* Controversy about its meaning.

Meanwhile, there is an intermediary body of the Buddha between the extremes of conceptual ignorance and completely perfected awareness, though controversy embroils the understanding of this third realm. It is called the body of bliss (*Sambhogakaya*) and is commonly spoken of as a varied manifestation of true being for the pure self-enjoyment of one who has achieved Buddhahood. Yet it is difficult to see how anything determinate, however splendid, could be a true representation of absolute suchness. For this reason, Mahayana thinkers often came to regard the term *sambhogakaya* as an inclusive way of referring to successive stages of understanding correlated appropriately with the spiritual condition of a person on the path to more complete enlightenment. To each such individual the Buddha essence is revealed in a provisional stage of insight that best communicates the reality of that essence to one

b. Symbolic reinterpretation.

(1) Relativity of insight to spiritual progress.

who is at that particular stage of development; and each such stage is itself to be transcended for a more adequate one until complete and final insight is achieved and all distinctions of viewpoint have been left behind. That ultimate truth accommodates itself to these transitional stages of thought is an expression of the principle of means (*upaya*), according to which every possible incentive to spiritual progress should be employed, provided only that such means are free from deception and whatever else may be incompatible by nature with the goal to be achieved.

(2) The doctrine of means or *upaya.*

Quite consistently with this concept of *upaya,* the philosophers of the Mahayana developed an impressive structure of dialectical arguments which, employing every weapon in the arsenal of conceptual reason and discursive intellect, purported to show that the distinctions and relations of the experienced world as ordinarily understood were all self-contradictory and therefore violated their own standard of intelligibility and reasonableness. None of these arguments, rightly understood, were intended to show that any particular conclusion could be demonstrated: after all, they were based on principles of reason which the Mahayanists themselves regarded as suspect. No, the whole of philosophy here is a sort of out-going expression of self-giving love in which the Buddhist philosopher, as a *bodhisattva,* is using the best means at his disposal for influencing the rest of us to set foot on the eightfold path; in fact, in that sense, philosophy is the manifestation of both the love (*karuna*) and the wisdom (*prajna*) of the blessed *Dharmakaya* itself.

(3) Correlation with dialectical arguments:

instrumental view of the nature of philosophy.

The finest expressions of Buddhist dialectical thought developed within the framework of two different schools of Mahayana philosophy. The key thinker in the first of these perspectives was the Indian Buddhist Nagarjuna, probably of the second century A.D., whose *Verses on the Middle Way (Madhyamika-karika)* became the basic treatise of this position; but almost equally significant were Nagarjuna's fifth-century

3. The principal Mahayana schools.
a. Historical representatives.

1. Nagarjuna and the Voidist school.

disciples, Chandrakirti and Shantideva, who expounded and further argued the ideas of the founder. The school itself was called by various names: *Madhyamika* (the Middle Way, so called, perhaps, because it was doctrinally mid-way between the realism of the Hinayana and the sort of self-destructive nihilism for which there was no genuine reality at all) and *Shunyavada* (the Way of Emptiness or Voidness; so called both because it regarded the *Dharmakaya* as "empty" in the sense of having no determinate qualities and because it viewed the empirical world as "empty" in the sense that it was ultimately illusory and unreal) were the most common of these designations. I myself will refer to this school as *Voidism*—a term in fairly wide use in this connection.

2. Chief thinkers of the Idealist school.

The principal philosophers of the second school, in India at least, were Maitreyanatha and the two brothers Asanga and Vasubandhu—all of approximately the fourth and fifth centuries A.D. A Chinese thinker of the seventh century, whose name was Hsuan-Tsang, after years of study in India, produced what is perhaps the clearest and most thorough classical expression of this view in a work entitled *Treatises on the Establishment of the Doctrine of Consciousness Only*. Again, the school itself was called by various names: *Vijnanavada* (the Way of Consciousness; so called because true reality was identified with pure, undifferentiated consciousness) and *Yogacara* (the Way of Yoga or Unity; so called because it emphasized the techniques of yogic meditation for achieving conscious oneness with the absolute reality) were the most frequently used titles in this case. My term for this school will be *Idealism,* a word commonly used in the Western world for any view which holds that reality is basically mental or conscious in nature.

b. Basic doctrines of the two schools. *1.* Their common ground.

The mere explanation of the names of these two viewpoints has of course already provided some clue to their philosophical content. Both subscribed to the main Mahayana doctrines that I explained previously, holding, for example, that ultimately only the *Dharmakaya* is fully and genuinely real, while the world of ordinary experience is ultimately unreal. The fundamental differences between the two views are mostly at two levels: for the Voidist, no quality or attribute which has a conceptual definition can appropriately be applied to the absolute reality or suchness, since every such property would constitute a limit of being by excluding from the absolute whatever did not have that property; Idealists, on the other hand, held that consciousness was the one meaningful attribute that did not imply such a limitation, and that therefore it was both appropriate and necessary to view the *Dharmakaya* as pure, undifferentiated consciousness itself. At the level of ordinary experience, further, the Voidists held that the objects of awareness had a provisional reality status that was independent of our consciousness of them—in other words, they subscribed at this level to a qualified realism about the objects of perceptual experience, more or less like John Locke in the tradition of British empiricism; but the Idealists were more like Bishop Berkeley, Locke's famous critic, since they held that the being of perceived objects consisted merely in their being perceived by the mind, or, as they put it, the objects of determinate consciousness were nothing other than transformations of that consciousness itself. But it must be understood that both views are, in the end, worlds apart from either Locke or Berkeley, since they are agreed against these Western thinkers that the whole realm of ordinary experience, however understood, is ultimately illusory and therefore merely provisional.

Now if the bold dialectic of the Mahayana is to become anything more than a strange pipe dream for us, it will be necessary at least to illustrate by developing specific arguments. Otherwise, the ultimate rejection of the ordinary realm will be at best an empty threat to our earth-bound confidence, and at worst a frenzied product of sophisticated madness brought on by the enervating heat of the Indian sun! To make his outlook reasonable on dialectical grounds, the Voidist is

2. Their fundamental differences.

a. The Absolute as above all qualities (Voidism) vs. the Absolute as Pure Consciousness (Idealism).

b. Qualified realism about the objects of ordinary perception (Voidism) vs. qualified subjectivism about those objects (Idealism).

c. But a common illusionism about the ordinary realm as a whole.
c. The dialectical arguments of the two schools.

1. Voidism.

presumably required to show (1) that the principles through which the realm of ordinary experience is conceived are riddled with self-contradictions by their own standards of meaningfulness; (2) that since the nihilistic doctrine that nothing exists is also self-contradictory, true reality must be absolute and unqualified Being or "Emptiness" beyond all intellectual distinctions; and (3) that Voidism itself is not a distinct view over against others, but is instead a way of pointing to a level of Reality in which all views and distinctions are tran-

scended. Sorting all this out is, for the Buddhist, rather like a game of condescension in which he agrees to meet us on our own terms; and furthermore the game is enormously complex and involved, demanding the sharpest exercise of our wits. But the stakes in this game are so high that only a fool could refuse to try his hand.

(1) The things and processes of ordinary experience, then, are understood by reason through various interpretive categories, the most basic of which are substance and causation. A substance is any identifiable object of experience—a chair, for instance—which, though it has qualities or characteristics which define it, cannot itself be a quality of anything else, though it can be related to other things. However, the whole notion of a substance as qualified by attributes is self-contradictory: for an attribute or quality cannot be a quality of nothing, and yet it is logically impossible to identify any substance except by referring to its attributes. Of what then are these attributes the qualities? They cannot be qualities of substance, since substance is nothing apart from its attributes; they cannot be qualities of themselves, since to be an attribute is to be a quality of something else, namely, a substance; and they cannot be qualities of each other, since they are by hypothesis different qualities distinct from each other. The whole affair is an insoluble muddle: and yet we cannot even begin to talk meaningfully about the experienced world without gullibly imbibing this very muddle.

Furthermore, we normally view the objects of experience as causally related to each other, at least in the sense that a given thing exists as it does because its being and character are the effect of other, usually previous, things of the same sort requiring a similar explanation. But there is no clear and consistent way to elucidate the principle of causation either. Since any given cause, so-called, is in turn an effect itself, it cannot be a real cause the being and activity of which adequately explain its effect: at best, such a "cause" can only be the instrument of some other cause to infinity, so that no real cause can be identified at all. Besides, either a thing exists at any given moment or it does not: if it exists, then it has real being and requires no cause; but if it does not exist, it is nothing and cannot even be conceived to have a cause, since a producing cause cannot be regarded as producing that which is not. Finally, suppose again that a given thing exists as an effect of something previous: then at the very moment that the effect is produced, the cause no longer exists, unless of course the cause continues to exist, in part or whole, as identical with its effect, in which case there is no distinction between cause and effect at all. Again, it begins to appear that a category which is indispensable to our ordinary understanding of the world is itself hopelessly incoherent.

(b) Causation.

Now the crucial thing to realize here is that the difficulties associated with the notions of substance and causation merely illustrate the sort of difficulties and self-contradictions connected with *all* conceptually defined objects of thought; and, more bafflingly still, the principle of coherence or contradiction, which is basic to these arguments, is no externally imposed standard of criticism: it is the very principle on which distinctions within experience are supposed to be grounded, since it is through this principle that we understand things by means of definite concepts that exclude what is distinct from them. If we respond by arguing that it is unreasonable to criticize the distinctions made *through* the discursive intellect on the basis of a

(c) The principle of contradiction.

principle recognized only by that same intellect, then the Voidist's answer is that he is not trying to establish any conclusion at all: he is only trying to expose the muddle from which we need to be delivered altogether.

(2) If then it is absurd to suppose that the ordinary world with its distinctions exists, it is equally absurd to suppose that nothing at all is real. For such an assertion would clearly be an existential self-contradiction in the sense that what was being asserted would itself be inconsistent with the fact that it was being asserted. After all, if nothing existed, then the theory and claim to that effect would itself not exist. It follows obviously that the opposite thesis, namely, that something exists, is logically and existentially indisputable. Now then the Voidist has already exposed the incoherence of supposing that anything with determinate qualities exists. And

it follows that the real must be wholly indeterminate, undifferentiated, and qualityless: and that real is precisely the absolute, transcendental emptiness, or, in

religious parlance, the blessed *Dharmakaya*. Should the knower at this point suppose that even he himself is cognitively distinct from and over against the real so that he is apprehending its qualityless status as a discernible object of his own thought, even that inference would be unwarranted, since the true knowledge of the real (or the Real) is an intuitively discerned, un-

differentiated Oneness from which the distinction between subject and object has been finally and wholly dispelled by being consigned to the illusory ignorance of which it is an aspect.

(3) In this realm of absolutely non-differenced Being, Voidism, as itself a distinct view, is also transcended: if there are no differences here, then all views are identical, and no particular stance can even be identified, much less contrasted with other perspectives. And of course, everything else falls into place too: *nirvana* and *samsara* are identical, the absolute Reality and the empirical world are the same, each person is indistinguishably one with every other; all this because none of these

terms can stand for anything determinate or distinct in relation to its supposed opposite. From an ethical point of view, the love which energizes the *bodhisattva* is precisely the realized expression of this absolute Oneness.

(b) Love as absolute Oneness.

The Buddhist Idealist has an even heavier burden to bear in his attempt to engulf us with love through dialectic, more or less analogously to the way that Berkeley, with his mentalism, puts a far greater strain on our common-sense credulity than does Locke, with his perceptual realism. For while the Idealist accepts as provisionally effective the arguments which purport to show that the realm of ordinary experience is ultimately illusory, he also maintains that common sense fails to see things correctly even at the empirical level. So the attempt to make his outlook reasonable apparently requires him to show (1) that even at the empirical level objects have no status except as determinate phases or transformations of the consciousness of the knowing subject; (2) that the distinctions within individual conscious subjects, and even between one such subject and another, are ultimately self-contradictory and unreal, so that true reality is precisely pure, non-individuated Consciousness; (3) and that Consciousness thus apprehended neither limits absolute Reality nor stands in any sort of contrast with anything else.

3. Idealism.
a. Requirements of its dialectic.

(1) Relation to the Voidist view.

(2) Its phases.

(1) Seasoned students of philosophy will breathe more easily here when they recognize, in support of the thesis that objects of thought exist only within thought, the familiar arguments of Berkeley and Leibniz, although they may be surprised to realize that the Buddhists had thoroughly discussed all these dialectical turns a millennium or more before they appeared in definitive form in Western philosophy. Like Berkeley, the Idealists argued that we identify perceived objects through enduring clusters, as it were, of sense qualities; that we have no reason for supposing the object to be numerically distinct from such a group of qualities; and that since all these qualities are relative to our subjective,

b. Development of the dialectic.
(1) Subjectivity of the objects of perception.

(a) Relativity to sensation.

sensory awareness (every quality is experienced *as* a sensation), it is totally reasonable to suppose that the objects have no independent existence apart from the conscious awareness of them. It is often said, of course, that external objects exist because we have an immediate experience of them as separate and distinct from our consciousness. But such a claim is clearly unreasonable because so-called immediate experience is itself nothing but a series of conscious states. Besides, in dreams we have the same strong feeling of independent objectivity, but awake to discover that the whole succession of experiences was wholly subjective. How then can any conscious experience even render plausible the notion that anything other than conscious states exists?

(b) Concept of literal extension self-contradictory.

Like Leibniz, the Idealists also argued that the notion of the existence of external objects that were literally extended in a spatial continuum was self-contradictory. If my guitar, for instance, is literally extended, then it must be composed of parts which are literally extended also, since otherwise they could not, when put together, constitute an object that was itself extended. But then every such part would in turn have to be composed of still further extended parts for the same reason and so on to infinity. And that notion is self-contradictory since no composite thing at all could come into existence if it must have been preceded thus by an infinite series of such composite steps. If, to avoid this, one argues that there are ultimate extended units that have no composite parts, then that supposition is also self-contradictory, since for every determinate magnitude of extension a finite force sufficient to resolve it into further elements can clearly be conceived. And if to avoid this, finally, anyone argues that there are ultimate parts of larger composites, but that these parts are not themselves extended, then there is no conceivable way in which such parts, when assembled in however great numbers, could compose even the smallest extended thing. Hence the Buddhist argues here that the very spatial extension required by the notion of objects that are external to consciousness is ultimately self-contradictory. Yet no such logical conundrum of this sort attaches to the doctrine that perceived objects are merely transformations of individual consciousness, since states of consciousness are clearly not to be conceived as spartially extended in any literal sense. And if someone should object that it seems exceedingly odd to suppose that spatial extension is merely a form of perceptual appearance and not a property of the objects perceived, then I think that the Buddhist would smilingly concede with Bishop Berkeley (slightly revised) that in these things one must speak with the vulgar, but think with the enlightened.

(c) Relative consistency of the subjectivist doctrine.

(2) Heavy as this dialectical dose may be already, we have at best swallowed only the first teaspoon of our purgative medicine, although the rest may well go down more easily now that the palate is so thoroughly lubricated. In any case, we must take the further step of seeing that though consciousness itself is indisputably real, nevertheless the distinctions within any given consciousness are themselves ultimately relative and therefore unreal. And that is not difficult to see since any perceived object, to be distinct from other such objects, must have qualities that are themselves distinct from each other, and from those of other objects, in the same way. But at least two kinds of insuperable obstacles confront us here: for the object and its qualities can be conceived as distinct only in comparison with other objects and their qualities which have the same sort of conceptual dependence on the original object; and hence there is no way for such differences to emerge, since each such object would presuppose the logically prior being of other objects which in turn equally presupposed it. Worse still, perhaps, for one object to be different from others it must have different qualities which can themselves be different from each other only by some further difference and so on to infinity. So it appears that the supposition of there being different objects within the same individual consciousness is absurd.

(2) Ultimate unreality of distinctions

(a) within any given consciousness,

(b) between each conscious subjects and its own objects of thought.

But so also is the difference between the knowing, conscious subject and all those objects construed as identical with each other. For an object can be an object only for some knowing subject, but such a subject can be a subject only in relation to an object: neither is conceivable without the other, and so how can either exist as distinct from the other? Hence, all that remains is the self-identical individual consciousness. Yet by a precise piece of parallel reasoning, one individual consciousness, however identical with all its states as objects, cannot be conceived as distinct from any other individual consciousness: for anything that would establish this difference would itself have to be a distinct quality or state within such supposedly distinct consciousnesses; and the notion of any such distinct quality has already been shown to be absurd.

(c) and between each such subject and every other.

(d) Resultant reality of pure, undifferentiated consciousness.

It therefore follows that true reality is pure, undifferentiated consciousness transcending all distinctions between subject and object, or between subject and subject. To clinch this insight, one has only to see, introspectively as it were, that every apparent distinction within consciousness takes place in a more inclusive whole of awareness which therefore transcends all such supposed differences, even the differences between one conscious subject and another. To an Edmund Husserl, this is the discovery of the transcendental ego or the transcendental inter-subjectivity; but to the Buddhist Idealist it is realized Oneness with Pure Consciousness or the blessed *Dharmakaya*.

(3) Pure Consciousness as beyond all limitations.

(3) And it will now be easy to see how Pure Consciousness, as absolutely real, does not involve any limitation of being, as Voidist critics incorrectly supposed: for a thing or reality can be limited only by standing in contrast with other things; but since Pure Consciousness, as transcending all differences, stands in contrast to nothing and has no quality but the self-illuminative quality of consciousness, it is absolutely Real without limit. And it is commonly supposed by Buddhists themselves that at this arid and relatively un-

3. Ultimate non-difference of the two outlooks.

populated dialectical height, dwarfing infinitely even the unimaginable majesty of the Himalayas, there could really be no difference worth discussing between the transcendental Emptiness of Voidism and the Pure Consciousness of Idealism. Are they not indeed two faces of the same metaphysical clock, which after all cannot itself have either a plurality of faces or a distinction of parts?

And now the dosage is complete in principle, although the bewildering intricacy of Buddhist dialectic far exceeds in scope and depth the merely illustrative sample of spiritual medicine offered here. And if anyone is unmoved even by the whole of it, then it need not ultimately matter, since the inclusive love involved in the *bodhisattva* ideal will endeavor to find some other means for arresting us in our ignorance and bondage, until at last all have been delivered.

4. Alternatives to the dialectic.

A Zen Postscript

Girded with so much advance preparation, we may perhaps understand why the Chan sect in China and the Zen sect in Japan (both expressions of the Mahayana) took the position that there really was nothing much to Buddhist philosophy: the Zen masters had travelled all the barren stretches of the dialectic and had come out the other end. Theirs was not the disdain of ignorance but the chastened insight which, turned back from so many blind alleys of speculative reason, clearly recognized the self-contradictions of dialectical philosophy for what they really were—insoluble conundrums which pointed the mind in a wholly new and transforming direction.

1. Attitude toward Buddhist philosophy.

The basic ideas of Zen were supposedly brought to China by the Indian scholar Bodhidharma in the sixth century A.D. In essence, the fundamental principles of this transplanted version of Buddhism did not differ markedly from those of the classical Indian schools; but significant differences of emphasis developed and

2. Main emphases of Zen.

became the stock in trade, as it were, of a long succession of Zen masters which extends to the present day in both China and Japan. Like all Buddhism, this version emphasized the decisive importance of rigorous self-discipline and fully-controlled contemplation (*dhyana*) as means of achieving enlightenment. But in view of the uselessness of conceptual reason for apprehending the *Dharmakaya* or Buddha-essence of all reality, the Zen masters downrated the significance of speculative philosophical studies and speculative arguments. Even pre-established techniques for cultivating spiritual insight through meditation were discouraged. Preoccupation with these aspects of Buddhism would, they supposed, tend to leave the earnest seeker still bound by the chains of misguided intellectualism. A man need consult no book or treatise of philosophy to find the truth; it is only necessary instead to look with the right eyes into his own heart to discover the undifferentiable oneness of all reality with the Buddha-nature. True knowledge is a kind of post-critical vacancy from which the distinctions of analytic reason have disappeared; and the true method of spiritual cultivation is an openness to truth which has surrendered all bondage to prescribed techniques.

So the Zen teachers often used strange tools of instruction, providing apparently irrelevant and even harsh answers to the questions of inquirers and proposing some unanswerable questions of their own. Such puzzling answers and questions were commonly (in Japan) called *koans,* and an equally perplexing dialog or story was called a *mondo.* The whole intent was neither to confuse the disciple nor to answer his agonizing (but ultimately spurious) questions; it was rather to encourage such enquirers to give up the whole business of questions and answers, arguments and counter-arguments, in order to open themselves to the absolutely undifferentiated One.

There is, for this position on the whole, no such thing as the gradual occurrence of final enlightenment or

---

a. Self-discipline and contemplation as essential.

b. Qualified irrelevance of technical philosophy,

and of prescribed techniques.

c. Introspective awareness as the true method, leading to post-critical mental vacancy.

d. Role of *koans* and *mondos.*

e. Concept of sudden enlightenment.

satori: there may be long and seemingly futile preparation; but when, ultimately and unexpectedly, enlightenment itself occurs, the whole experience, being intrinsically indivisible, takes place instantaneously—in a flash. Nor is there any guaranteed way of insuring that this sudden bolt of spiritual lightning will strike at a particular time, however meticulous and painstaking one's preparation may be. And anything at all (or even nothing at all) may trigger this revolutionary experience: the chiming of a distant gong, the plopping of cow dung, or even the soft tinkle of a spoon in a cup of tea. The difference is all in how these experiences are taken; yet there will be no mistaken identification here, for when the true light dawns, the opened eye will see with a self-illuminative certainty that reduces all else to the nothing which it actually is.

1. The experience as indivisible.

2. Absence of guaranteed results.

3. Variety of occasioning circumstances.

4. Self-evidence of the result.

Critical Problems of Buddhist Philosophy: A Personal Response

It is, of course, enormously difficult for me to disentangle from any attempt at forthright critical evaluation my own profound admiration and respect for a man so pervaded by love and unquestionably genuine moral commitment as Gautama. But however difficult the task may be, there is every reason to try and no reason to hold back: sincere and informed criticism will ultimately leave truth undisturbed and authenticity unchallenged, while blowing from our minds the dust of ignorance and misunderstanding that so easily and unwittingly misleads us. There are, of course, many possible wrong turns: but that should impel the serious-minded among us to expend even greater diligence in finding the right way.

1. Enormous difficulty of critical response.

Assuming again that the views of Gautama are most closely approximated in the Hinayana tradition, I am frank to urge that there is an impressive cluster of truths here that no seeker can afford to overlook. Truth itself will certainly remain the same objectively, whatever our

2. Reaction to Hinayana (understood as Gautama's original view).

a. Enduring positive significance. *1*. Epistemological ultimacy of the interpretive principles of reason.

settled opinion and reasoned judgment about it may be; but Gautama seems clearly right, at least in principle, when he maintains that, so far as the method of knowledge is concerned, it is unreasonable for a man arbitrarily to accept, as logically prior to the interpretive principles of reason incarnated in his own mind and supported by his own fullest experience, the authority of any body of propositions external to that context, whether or not those propositions purport to stem from prophetic vision. Any argument either way about this question will in the end have to appeal to that very context of reason and experience which Gautama takes as decisive here, if that argument is to resound with the ring of plausibility. In effect, Buddha is appealing here to the principles of rational coherence and experiential relevance which I myself have recognized as criteria of evaluation from the outset of this whole journey through the Eastern mind.

2. Impermanence of the ordinary realm and of the immediate objects of ordinary experience, yet the pervasion of both by causal connectedness.

It would also be difficult to contest the thesis that the world of our ordinary experience is essentially characterized by impermanence—all the complex states and processes of that world are pervaded by ceaseless flux, change, and transition. And yet a string of causal connectedness runs through the whole and makes of it not a senseless chaos, but an ordered realm accessible to reason and intelligible to thought. Impermanence and dependent origination: both are empirically indisputable, and any live and momentous philosophical option will at least have to begin by taking them as provisionally real. For experience generally, this flux of the cosmos is amply paralleled by the swift flow of introspective awareness; the most overwhelming impact of consciousness is sure to give way in moments to its equally short-lived successor.

3. The human moral predicament as at least partly one of emotional

The ethical corollary of impermanence seems likewise to be basically sound: man's moral predicament is at least in part a bondage to unwarranted selfish craving which is destined to be frustrated on every front, since man, in his ignorance, mistakenly identifies his well-being with a concentrated effort to grasp, as permanently satisfying, objects and experiences that change to ashes in his hands. And so the law of moral causality inevitably brings such a person back around the wheel of existence for another try at the impossible and the ultimately worthless. Nor is it difficult to agree that the solution, at least to a considerable extent, must lie not in the doubling of our efforts to satsify selfish craving, but in the renunciation of those efforts for an enlightening liberation which sees selfish craving as subtly but surely destructive of man's true good. And even the eightfold path is a fascinating challenge: on the whole it is a spiritual summons and an ultimatum which, when we finally weary of the competitive and unhappy struggle with our equally selfish counterparts, calls us to undertake the path to spiritual fulfillment with an uncompromising seriousness of purpose and an unqualified external and internal discipline of experience. What is that call but the promise that those who genuinely open themselves to truth and meaning will ultimately not be disappointed?

But there are limits even to the fullest and most inclusive human vision: and I should be the first to admit that my own critical judgment here is itself subject to that same restraint. So I must honestly say that, as I understand it, the principle of impermanence in Hinayana Buddhism presents us with a vivid illustration of a limited and important truth which, when universalized, runs rampant and ends up threatening, if not destroying, much that it sought to preserve as significant. In critically discussing rationalistic Neo-Confucianism, I have already explained my belief that the particular things and processes of the world have a stable being and intelligibility best accounted for by the supposition that they participate in and exemplify real essences or natures which, as transcending these particulars, possess a fixity and permanence that are immune to change. If I am right about this, then this fact provides a limit to the principle of impermanence: indeed, the continuity of re-

bondage grounded in ignorance.

4. Deliverance as requiring the elimination of selfish craving.

b. Critical shortcomings of this outlook.
1. Limits of the principle of impermanence.

a. Real essences as a ground of the continuity and causal order of the empirical world.

lationships and the causal order of the empirical world become intelligible in this way. It is difficult to see how there can be any continuity or causal order at all if the whole reality of things consists in momentary states which appear only to pass into immediately succeeding non-being. It seems to me that any kind of pattern or order accessible to rational insight requires a continuity of permanent being. And this continuity is important to the Buddhist ethic through the idea of *karma:* if nothing persists through the succession of moments, how can deeds performed now have a recognizable retributive effect at a later time, much less provide an explanation, through reincarnation, of the external and internal conditions with which a phenomenal human being starts his earthly sojourn?

The limits of the idea of impermanence become more pointed still when that notion is applied to the individual conscious person. After pondering all the questions of King Milinda (in the traditional Mahayana treatise which bears that title), together with their answers, I still see no way to explain personal continuity, memory, and the like, if there is no enduring self that persists through the succession of transitory psychological states. Otherwise, who is it that discerns these states as momentary, or recognizes some present state as the memory of a previous one? The Personalist school seems clearly on the right track in urging that all this requires a pure subject of experience (I would say: a transcendental ego) which stands over against all its momentary objects in awareness and is therefore immune to the flux that pervades them. Ethically, the crisis

is even more severe: how can an overlapping continuity of transitory states be the enduring subject of moral responsibility or accumulate a stable framework of moral character unless something persists as the locus of this mounting effect? Who can either exhibit or be the appropriate object of self-giving love, if the person is no more than a cluster of fleeting states? And waiving all

this, is it reasonable or just to suppose that another

phenomenal human person, however conceived, should be stuck with the cumulative effect of my moral choices? That I should bear the consequences of my own free and responsible moral decisions seems plausible enough; but that a phenomenally distinct individual, who by hypothesis can claim no firm link to me, should be bound by those decisions seems unthinkable. Yet without such a moral transfer, without the fire passing from candle to candle, the whole notion of the cycle of births, and of a way of release from it, collapses. From this point of view, it is hardly surprising that Mahayana thinkers not only sought for a principle of permanence but in the end were willing, by identifying the true reality of all things with the absolute Suchness of the *Dharmakaya,* to consign the whole empirical world, with all its distinctions, to sheer illusion in order to safeguard that permanence.

reincarnation as construed here.

(3) The Mahayana search for permanence.

But we are not ready for that lofty insight until we examine critically a final implication of the doctrine of impermanence for Hinayana thought. So all-encompassing did transitoriness appear that the concept of a transcendent, essentially changeless cause of the world (in Hindu thought, *Brahman* or *Atman*) seemed out of the question. The probes, traditionally ascribed to Gautama, about this whole notion are painful indeed; but they may not be irremediable, if we chasten our understanding of the relation of such an absolute Ground of Being to ourselves and our world. If, as I have suggested, changes within the world are fully intelligible only through a stable framework of permanence, it is at least not unreasonable to suppose that the whole contingent world itself is fully intelligible only through a transcendent, changeless Ground of Being, whose very immunity from process enables it to be fully present and operative in the full compass of that contingent realm itself.

d. Reasonableness of the concept of a changeless Absolute.

(1) Empirical world fully intelligible only through such a Ground.

If, furthermore, we should suppose, with Gautama, that a truth so momentous as the being of the Absolute should be unambiguously evident to all, then we might

(2) Implausibility of Gautama's objections.

ask in turn why truths as liberating as those of Buddhism should be obscured by the enslaving ignorance of all those who need salvation? Now whatever the answer to this question, it will provide at least an equally plausible explanation for the profound human ignorance of the ultimate, changeless Reality. And there is, finally, no reason to match what I have termed the unrestraint of the principle of impermanence in the Hinayana with a parallel unrestraint in our concept of the divine causality: the reality of an absolute Cause need not be extended to a productive efficacy so universal that it either destroys personal freedom or renders the pursuit of virtue pointless. Indeed, there is every reason to suppose that if Divine wisdom had any point at all in creating the world, such a wisdom might have found its highest creativity in bestowing on rational, moral beings like ourselves the opportunity for genuine ethical self-realization. In any case, it was, among other things, the disturbing accumulation of questions like those I have been raising that provided much of the motivation for the Mahayana reconstruction.

2. Transition to the Mahayana reconstruction.
3. Reaction to Mahayana in its various forms.

Turning, then, to that reconstruction itself, I for one find myself confronted with one of the most impressive products of human philosophical ingenuity that has ever come to my attention. Nor is it necessary to stumble and boggle over the thorny historical and critical question as to whether the main insights of the Mahayana, at least in embryonic form, go back to the esoteric teachings of Gautama himself. Either way we are still left with a thoroughly systematized philosophical tradition that it would be folly to ignore, especially since this tradition is grounded in an engulfing moral concern for human well-being and directed toward the sort of understanding of the human situation which promises universal deliverance from human bondage and ignorance.

a. Intrinsic reasonableness of the Mahayana outlook.
1. Empirical order as

It will already be evident, from my critique of the Hinayana, that I find myself irresistibly drawn to the Mahayana interpretation on many points. That the empirical world order as commonly understood is not self-existent or self-explanatory and therefore requires explanation in terms of a transcendent, absolute Ground of Being which is both; that the root of reality in the depth of each phenomenal human person is a transcendental and permanent principle of pure subjectivity beyond all differences within individual consciousness; that self-giving love which extends itself to the whole of being as its object is the essential, and not merely an optional, expression of true spiritual enlightenment, so that any spiritual release which one enters alone is something less than the fullest and most authentic deliverance; and that the qualities of wisdom, love, and resolve which characterize such enlightened persons are both an expression of, and a clue to, the Absolute Reality itself—all these points I have previously raised and argued in one context or another.

The remaining question is, quite simply: How much further does it seem to me reasonable to go with the Mahayana? Well, I am first of all convinced that it is essentially sound, on moral grounds, to see the most significant function of philosophy as providing a persuasive device or tool (*upaya*) for spiritual commitment, and that such a role provides the main, if not the only, ground for regarding the pursuit of philosophic study as any sort of moral duty or obligation. No doubt there are other motives for the study of philosophy: that it satisfies intellectual curiosity, that it involves one in a competitive struggle of viewpoints that is intrinsically exciting (like a contest of skill and dexterity in any field), that it provides the highest exercise of a man's rational faculties, or even that it is just intrinsically enjoyable ("a positive gas," as they say). All these are true of myself; but it would be unthinkable to regard such motives as making philosophy any sort of duty for anyone at all, much less for all serious-minded persons. In fact, if these motives or others like them were the whole justification of philosophy, it would be, in my opinion, no more significant to human destiny than a game of chess or even a Kierkegaardian outing in the Deer Park!

requiring transcendent explanation.
2. Permanent principle of pure subjectivity.

3. Self-giving love as an essential expression.

4. Qualities of spiritual character grounded in the Absolute.

5. Philosophy as primarily a persuasive device for motivating sound spiritual commitment.

a. Other motives for philosophical study.

b. The moral
justification of
philosophy.

But that philosophy may both enrich one's own under-standing of spiritual self-realization and at the same time provide a context of persuasion through which those in moral bondage may take a step of commitment that starts them on the road to freedom and true self-hood in the ethical sense—all that is quite different, and it provides for philosophy a moral justification which extends just as far as its effective instrumentality in prompting such results. And that is, on the whole, the attitude of the Mahayana philosopher toward his voca-tion; it happens to be mine as well. Philosophy is either a tool of love, or it is worse than useless; since it would, in that case, superficially appear to promise so much, while actually delivering so little.

c. But
inadequacy of
thesis that all
viewpoints
either can, or
should, be
transcended.
(1) Much
philosophy
may be a
distortion,
(2) or better, a
view relative to
spiritual
progress.
(3) Yet the
ultimate truth
is not beyond
conceptual
reason.
(a) Philosophy
is enormously
difficult, and
subject to all
sorts of error.

On the other hand, I do not fully agree with the con-victions that underlie the attitude of the Buddhist here, for he regards philosophy as a tool of love precisely because, from the dizzying height of undifferentiated Oneness, he has turned his back, as it were, on all view-points and arguments as inevitably distorting the ulti-mate truth in one way or another. Now I am prepared to admit that much philosophy is in fact such a distortion; and I find a profound insight in the Buddhist thesis that there is a hierarchy of symbolic representations of the Absolute, a sort of philosophical ladder whose rungs cor-respond to stages of spiritual development. But I cannot view the ultimate truth as beyond the distinctions of conceptual reason and discursive intellect; and I cannot therefore regard viewpoints and arguments as cogni-tively pointless in principle. The reasons why so much philosophy distorts the truth are enormously complex: the whole project of philosophy is so intricate that the possible starting points for error are virtually without number; none who pursue the philosophic task are, in the end, motivated solely by the uncompromising will to approximate objective reasonableness; and most mature persons, even assuming sincerity and integrity, do not decide ultimate belief-commitments on objective philo-sophical grounds, partly because they are not confidently aware of them, and partly because they commonly do not follow them when they think they are.

All these considerations make philosophy difficult; and they should move each serious thinker to a humility which views his own best efforts as no more than a stage of approximation to the ultimate truth. But this does not mean that the philosophic enterprise has to collapse into cognitive irrelevance. If, as the Buddhist believes, there is a ladder of intellectual stages, the higher rungs of which more closely approximate the absolute truth precisely because they match corresponding stages of spiritual development, then it follows that not all viewpoints are equally distortions of the ultimate, and conversely that the Absolute Reality itself is in principle accessible to philosophical insight. If this last point were not essentially sound, then no viewpoint would be any more (or less) of an approximation to the Absolute than any other, since, as utterly devoid of all determinate qualities, that Absolute would be equally and infinitely remote from them all. Now I believe in the hierarchical ladder of philosophical ascent. But when I see that, on a given rung, I am still not at the top, I do not regard the whole climb as pointless; instead, I am moved to step upward, confident that in this way I am occupying a new rung which, though still not the last, really lifts me closer to the ultimate truth.

But I am ready to take still another step, with the Mahayana Idealists in this case, though again with some qualifications. Even at the level of ordinary awareness, the Idealist thinkers reject the notion of a realm of literally extended physical objects standing in various spatial relations to each other. As I see it, their most effective argument for this rejection is the contention, already explained, that the concept of objective, literal extension (of objects, for example, which are themselves literally extended, and which are composed of literally extended parts) is self-contradictory. Reared, as I have been, in the school of Leibniz and others like him, I find this contention eminently reasonable. But what disturbs

(b) This should provoke humility and the recognition that results are no more than approximative, (c) but the very notion of intellectual stages implies that in principle ultimate truth is accessible to rational thought.

6. Qualified soundness of the Idealist thesis that the concept of literal extension is self-contradictory.

a. But no reason to believe that objects are merely transformations of individual consciousness.
(1) For objects might be objective to our consciousness without being extended.

me here is the logical jump, as I see it, to the conclusion that objects themselves are merely transformations of individual consciousness. That would mean that, in Berkeleyan terms, the whole being of an object of perception consisted in its being perceived by the mind. Now that clearly does not follow from the self-contradictory character of literal extension: for even if objects cannot be logically conceived as extended in this way, they might nevertheless exist quite apart from our awareness of them by possessing an objective and determinate character of a wholly different sort—like the monads of Leibniz's system, for example, which are relatively independent centers of mental energy or spiritual force, objective to each other in a way analogous to the sense in which finite minds, though unextended, may be conceived as objective to each other. Furthermore, unless perceived objects have some such status independent of our awareness of them (like the Idealist, I am talking here at the level of ordinary consciousness), I cannot understand how they can be perceived as distinct from each other at all, since being perceived by the mind is a property common to all such objects and therefore can provide no basis whatever for distinguishing them. For such reasons as this, I fail to see how the act of perceiving could, as such, constitute its own object of perception, since in that case there would be literally nothing that was being perceived. That some of the perceived qualities of objects are forms of our awareness of them (glasses, as it were, through which we see them, possibly for practical reasons) rather than literal properties of the objects themselves seems unquestionable to me; but that the ultimate objects of our awareness should have no objective, literal properties at all—that seems unthinkable!

(2) Act of perceiving could not, as such, constitute its own object of perception.

(3) Objects must have some literal properties in their own right.

For much of the rest of Mahayana philosophy, whether Voidist or Idealist, my reservations are far more serious and extensive. Both of these Mahayana schools share, as I have explained, the phenomenal illusionism and absolute monism of classical Taoism, for

b. Critical shortcomings of the Mahayana.
1. Incoherence of phenomenal illusionism.

which, at the level of ultimate truth, the world of distinguishable things and processes is an illusory, easily misunderstood appearance of an indeterminate, absolute Reality which is totally devoid of distinct qualities that could define its nature from the standpoint of the principles of conceptual reason. And as with classical Taoism, so here: there is, for such an outlook, no way to explain how such an illusory realm could arise, either as an objective order apprehended by finite, conscious minds, or as a series of successive transformations within those minds. Individual minds are, by hypothesis, themselves aspects of the illusion and can therefore provide no basis for explaining it. Nor is the suggestion reasonable that, through a series of intermediary levels (the "storehouse consciousness" or the "womb of the Tathagata," in Buddhist parlance, for example) between the absolute One and the phenomenal world, somehow the illusion could have its ground in absolute reality itself. For one thing, these levels themselves are just as difficult to explain as the illusory world order (in fact, they must ultimately be regarded, like conscious minds, as aspects of that order itself); and for another thing, there is no conceivable way in which anything which is determinate, even in an illusory sense, could find its determining ground in an Absolute that is presupposed to be wholly indeterminate.

a. No way to explain the basis of the illusion,

(1) either in individual minds,
(2) or in the Absolute itself.

But the Mahayana thinkers go beyond the main thrust of classical Taoism by attempting an intricate and detailed dialectic through which, using the ultimate principles of conceptual reason (especially the principle of self-contradiction), they purport to show that the realm of differences apprehended through such principles violates its own standard of meaningfulness by being riddled with the very sort of contradictions which reason refuses to accept. In all of this, however, the Buddhist is not trying to demonstrate anything, since he himself ultimately rejects the absolute validity of the principles through which he argues in constructing his dialectic; what he is trying to do is to persuade the rest

b. Yet the dialectical arguments attempt a basis for this view.

(1) Though the Buddhist is not trying to demonstrate anything,

(2) he is trying to persuade us to go beyond the intellectual standpoint.

of us to leave behind the principles of reason and the realm of difference, in order to ascend with him, as it were, to the highest level of undifferentiated oneness with the blessed *Dharmakaya*. And it is even admitted and urged that if we mistakenly view the Buddhist contention as itself an intellectual viewpoint, it will display as much incoherence as any other viewpoint of discursive reason.

2. Reaction to the dialectical arguments.
a. Difficulty of providing a relevant critique;

Now I readily acknowledge that it is, in principle, quite impossible to develop any sort of critical assessment of a stance which begins by admitting that it fails cognitively by the test embodied in the only objectively reasonable standards of critical evaluation at our disposal. Since there is really nothing to discuss, in the final analysis, a man either surrenders to the dialectical motivation provided by Buddhist philosophy, or he tries to find some way to avoid the disastrous consequences which seem to follow for his own discursive principles.

author's decision to opt for discursive intellect.

So at best I can only give some indication here as to why I feel uneasy about making any such surrender, and why therefore I feel constrained to reorganize the forces of discursive intellect and go on with the struggle, however agonizing it may seem.

b. State of enlightenment supposed to transcend all differences, while itself standing in obvious qualitative contrast to the state of ignorance and bondage.

At the very least, an enlightened person might reasonably be expected to believe, perhaps even claim, that he has realized an intuitive, conscious Oneness with the *Dharmakaya*—a stance of undifferentiated awareness for which all differences are dissolved. Yet the very fact that he proceeds to reach out to the rest of us with a self-giving love that is intent on bringing us to release shows that in practice at least, if not in theory, he views this new state of awareness (and all that goes with it ethically) as itself quite distinct from his own previous state of ignorance and bondage which he now sees as embodied in the rest of us. But the recognition of this difference would seem to me to imply that in some sense these two radically different states are distinct, objectively considered, only because they both possess determinate qualities which distinguish them for conceptual reason.

One is a state of bondage, ignorance, frustration, alienation, and despair; the other is a state of freedom, wisdom, peace, joy, insight, and love. Surely all this talk is more than mere words: it expresses a real difference; indeed, a part of the new state is precisely a wisdom fulfilled by the sensitivity to this difference, and a love made perfect by its sheer contrast with the selfish craving that has fallen away. It would seem, then, that the discernment of the difference between these two states is itself an essential quality of the new state of release.

Now then, consider, in the next place, the very nature of consciousness itself (enlightenment is admittedly a state of consciousness). Is there any basis for rendering intelligible, much less any reason for believing, that consciousness is capable of transcending all the distinctions of conceptual reason and discursive intellect? It would appear that the very notion of consciousness implies at least a difference between the activity of awareness and the object of awareness: is it not reasonable to maintain that no act of awareness can, as such, constitute its own object of awareness; that consciousness entails awareness of something other than its own act? It may even be reasonable to argue that there is a further difference between the subject that is aware and its own act of awareness. In fact, one of the Buddhist Idealist's own arguments implies this inference, since he himself argues that every conscious discernment takes place within a still more inclusive field (or subject) of awareness which therefore, as pure subject, transcends the distinctions that it discerns. If, then, the very *essence* of consciousness implies such differences, is it conceivable that consciousness, without ceasing to involve any awareness, could achieve a state of awareness from which all differences were excluded?

Continuing on the Idealist track just mentioned, I am puzzled by the conclusion which the Buddhist philosopher draws here from the concept of a pure subjectivity which itself transcends, in the activity of awareness,

c. Consciousness itself intrinsically incapable of transcending all distinctions. (1) For it is defined by the difference between act and object,

(2) and perhaps even between subject and act of awareness, a difference implied by the Buddhist's own basis for belief in Pure Consciousness.

d. The thesis that the pure subject of conscious awareness must be the

Absolute seems
unreasonable.

(1) Rather, the
individual
subject or ego
that is thus
disclosed.
(2) Any
objector must
be aware of his
own
subjectivity in
the act of
apprehending
his own
objection.

(3) No genuine
practical
problem of
individual self-
identity,
(a) partly
because of the
continuity of
experience,

(b) but
primarily
because of the
sheer activity
of awareness,
of just being a
pure subject.

every difference that it recognizes. In the tradition of
Kant, Husserl, and others of their kind, I call this pure
subjectivity the transcendental ego. Now the Buddhist
Idealist, along with Husserl, argues that this pure ego
cannot be any individual, personal subject, since it has,
as such, no quality that could distinguish it from any
other such pure subject; it must therefore be the Pure
Consciousness of the Absolute. I must confess that I
cannot go along with this reasoning: it seems to me quite
clear that it is precisely my own inviolable, individual
subjectivity that I discern through this process. And if
anyone argues that there are no qualities that individu-
ate this pure subjectivity, I am prompted to answer
along three lines: first, in saying this, such an individual
must clearly recognize his own pure subjectivity as apprehending this very "truth" (or anything else for that
matter)—and is not that inevitable subjective correlate
of every insight a sufficient mark of individuation in
this case? Again, I think it reasonable to argue that,
however baffling theoretically, no one has any practical
problem with the identity of himself as a pure subject in
contrast to other such individual subjects. In part, of
course, we solve this problem through the correlation of
our pure subjectivity with the relative stability and continuity of various sequences in the content of conscious
experience; but I am confident that such a correlation is
not the whole solution to this problem. Is the insistence
that individuation can be discerned here only by the recognition of distinct qualities that distinguish one pure
subject from another itself a reasonable insistence? I
think not. How do I achieve self-awareness? Certainly
not by noticing objectively that I am distinct from some
other self; for in that case the subject that noticed this
would transcend that very act of noticing. No, I achieve
self-awareness as an individual pure subject just by the
enduring and sustained activity of awareness itself; I
know myself *as* a subject, in the final analysis, just by
being myself that very subject! Logically and
philosophically, everything starts with that pure self-

awareness; and again, logically and philosophically, any insight which purports to deprive one of that pure, individual subjectivity must inevitably be a delusion and befuddlement. Quite unlike Mark Twain, then, no one ever needs to wonder, should he have been born a twin and should one of the two have died in infancy, whether the one that expired was himself or his brother.

But the ultimate agony confronts us in the intricacy of Buddhist dialectic. Since these critical arguments claim to argue from the basic concepts and principles of discursive reason, it follows that if I am to go on believing in the ultimacy of those concepts and principles on a satisfying objective basis I have to show that the destructive dialectic of the Buddhist is, in the main, groundless, and that its impression of reasonableness is based on a variable combination of factors like misinterpretation, ambiguity in the meaning of terms, and invalid inference. Of course, the no longer surprising truth is that the Buddhist himself regards his arguments as groundless and invalid too, not however, as in my case, because he believes the riddles can be solved, but rather because he believes that the whole methodology of conceptual reason must be set aside and transcended. His arguments, in other words, are merely tools of persuasion which he is motivated to use for spiritual ends.

e. The thrust of the dialectical arguments is itself characterized by misinterpretation and inconsistency.

(1) The Buddhist's admission of this point.

Now since the dialectician himself bases his use of rational arguments solely on ethical grounds in the way indicated, we may reasonably ask whether there are any morally justifiable limits to the range of persuasive devices which can be consistently used by a person whose motive is ethical love. The principle of love, I have previously urged, implies the intrinsic worth and inviolable dignity of the persons who are its objects. But I wonder if that principle and that worth do not provide the sort of limit I have referred to: if a persuasive device is fundamentally deceptive by appealing to premises and principles all of which are ultimately rejected by the person using this device, does it not seem that the use of such a method violates the worth of the person to whom

(2) The admittedly deceptive character of the dialectic seems to violate the Buddhist's own principle of ethical love.

the argument is directed and therefore also contravenes the principle of love? We often do argue from premises that we do not share in order to show another person an inconsistency in his structure of beliefs. But we can reasonably do so in love only because there is a belief that we do share with that person, namely, the belief that views and propositions cannot be true if they are logically and conceptually inconsistent or contradictory. Basically, in such a procedure, we are assuming that a person who believes inconsistent views is unwittingly presenting an affront to his own intrinsic worth as a person. But the Buddhist dialectician is on quite different ground here: he shares no principle with those whom he attempts to persuade, since he ultimately rejects as inadequate the principle of contradiction itself and therefore could not reasonably maintain, at the absolute level which he himself claims to occupy, that an inconsistent view could not be true. For this reason, the persuasive tool that he uses here is not merely provisional and tentative; it is rather, though admittedly, deceptive to the core. And I cannot regard it as consistent with the universal ethical love that motivates the Buddhist philosopher.

(3) The intrinsic incoherence of denying or rejecting the ultimacy of the principle of contradiction.

Since the dialectician claims a stance that transcends all viewpoints, I will not pause to ask, as I am inclined to do, how anyone can reject the ultimacy of the principle of contradiction without defining his rejection as conceptually distinct from the acceptance of that principle, since in that case he would be appealing to the principle of contradiction itself as a necessary ground for the intelligibility of his alleged rejection of it. Instead I will proceed, at least illustratively, to consider the logical structure of the dialectical arguments themselves.

(4) The dialectical arguments all rest on the questionable presupposition that no concept

Now my sincere opinion here is that all these arguments presuppose a principle that seems to me to be basically unreasonable in any of the various forms in which that principle can be stated. When the Buddhist argues, for example, that the concepts of substance and attribute are ultimately unintelligible because neither can be defined without the other or understood except through the other, he is presupposing that no concept can be fully and actually coherent or intelligible unless its meaning can be wholly understood in and through itself alone without any essential relation or reference to any other concept. But it is precisely this presupposition that I regard as thoroughly misleading and unsound. As I see it, no concept has a completely self-contained intelligibility in the sense required by this presupposition. Concepts become intelligible in a context of reciprocal relationships: each has a distinct meaning, but only in such a framework of interdependent connections. I happen, not quite by chance, to be one of those philosophers who believe that there are self-evident, logical starting points or necessary presuppositions of all intelligible thought. But even those categories, as I call them, become explicitly intelligible and clear only through their reciprocal relations to each other in a complex structure of reason, and they normally come to our conscious attention (when they do) through a complex of explicit examples and instances which provide the content of our overall experience. Just as we do not acquire any skill or competence except in conjunction with the development of other such abilities, so we do not, and in principle cannot, understand or define any concept except in conjunction with the whole conceptually structured fabric of thought and experience.

What applies to knowledge, I think, applies also to reality. When the Buddhist argues, for example, that no cause can be real at all if it in turn must be viewed as an effect of still further causes, he is presupposing that the very notion of contingent or dependent existence is absurd. But I cannot accept that thesis either: it may be reasonable to suppose that the more dependent a thing is on factors external to it, the less is its degree of being or reality. But I see no basis at all, on that ground, for supposing that such a dependent thing is ultimately unreal: it is only that its reality, though genuine, is con-

is fully intelligible unless it can be understood through itself alone.

(a) But this notion of self-contained intelligibility is actually spurious;

(b) even ultimate principles of reason are understood through their conceptual relations to each other.

(c) Nor is this presupposition any more plausible in metaphysics.

(1) A thing is not unreal merely because it is dependent or contingent in its existence.

(2) Even the concept of a self-existent Cause becomes clear to us through its relations to other concepts.

tingent. On the other hand, I have already agreed that no causal explanation is ultimately complete except through its relation to a self-existent and self-explanatory Cause; yet even the meager understanding of that Cause which we may come to possess becomes clear in our minds through our complex understanding in turn of its contingent products. Nor is there any reason to suppose, on the ground that reason seems to lead thought to an absolutely necessary being (the *Dharmakaya,* Absolute Suchness, etc.), that therefore nothing can be real at all unless it is itself absolutely necessary in the same sense.

Now it seems to me that the whole structure of the Buddhist dialectic rests upon the presupposition that I have thus illustrated and called into question. Of course substance and attribute, cause and effect, and indeed all concepts without exception can only be understood reciprocally: but that is no basis for rejecting either the ultimacy of conceptual reason or the complex of reality to which it applies; it is rather an attempt at clarifying the very nature of rational intelligibility. To identify something and explain it for what it is is unquestionably important; but it is no reason at all for casting it aside on the supposition that it is not some other thing, especially when it never really claimed to be anything but itself. And with that I conclude my account of the uneasiness I would feel about merely capitulating to the still persuasive appeal of the Buddhist dialectic; at the same time, I have provided the only sort of justification I know for going on with my conviction that nothing lies beyond the reach of rational intelligibility, except that which lies outside the scope of real being.

(d) No basis therefore for rejecting either conceptual reason or the contingent reality of the empirical world.

3. Unreasonable to regard love, wisdom, and firm resolve as truly manifesting the *Dharmakaya* unless they are essential qualities of it.

To the transformed *bodhisattva,* the qualities of love, wisdom, and firm resolve which are actualized in his new moral quality of being are clues to the nature of the blessed *Dharmakaya.* In his more speculative moments, he sees that somehow, in its absoluteness, the ultimate Reality is beyond all such determinate qualities for reasons we have already considered at length. But can such an enlightened individual reasonably cling to that awkward and cramping speculative posture? Can the unassailable authenticity of these moral qualities really manifest the *Dharmakaya* unless these qualities, in fully actualized form, constitute, in part, the intrinsic and essential nature of that absolute Reality? And can these qualities themselves be understood adequately unless they are viewed as possible only for a Being that is itself completely actualized personal being? The *bodhisattva* has realized his own true personhood through these qualities: can he reasonably continue to regard their ultimate ground as anything less? To follow the lead of such questions is no doubt to extend the boundaries of a Mahayana vision of reality; but it is not to forsake the moral core of that vision. Indeed, such an extension may in the end provide the most reasonable explanation for that inner spring of love that flowed from the heart of Gautama and itself expanded into a flood capable of engulfing the world.[1]

a. Since these qualities themselves are fully intelligible only as properties of personal being, the Absolute itself is best construed in this way.

b. Such a view extends the Mahayana perspective, but preserves its moral core.

1. For a discussion and critical evaluation of the doctrine of reincarnation—shared by Buddhism, Hinduism, and Jainism—see Appendix C.

Suggested Readings

General Background

Conze, Edward. *Buddhist Thought in India.* Pp. 17–118 (part 1).

Dasgupta, Surendranath. *A History of Indian Philosophy.* I, 78–168 (chap. 5).

Smart, Ninian. *Doctrine and Argument in Indian Philosophy.* Pp. 33–61 (chap. 2).

Theravada (or Hinayana) Buddhism

Conze, Edward. *Buddhist Thought.* Pp. 119–94 (part 2).

Jayatilleke, K. N. *Early Buddhist Theory of Knowledge.*

Radhakrishnan, S., and Moore, Charles A. *A Source Book in Indian Philosophy.* Pp. 272–328 (part of chap. 9).

Sharma, Chandradhar. *Indian Philosophy: A Critical Survey.* Pp. 57–71 (chap. 5).

Mahayana Buddhism

Chan, Wing-tsit. *A Source Book in Chinese Philosophy.* Pp. 336–95 (chaps. 20–23).

Conze, Edward. *Buddhist Thought.* Pp. 195–274 (part 3).

Fung Yu Lan. *A History of Chinese Philosophy.* II, 237–359 (chaps. 7, 8).

_____. *A Short History of Chinese Philosophy.* Pp. 241–54 (chap. 21).

Murti, T. R. V. *The Central Philosophy of Buddhism.*

Radhakrishnan, S., and Moore, Charles A. *Source Book.* Pp. 328–46 (part of chap. 9).

Rhys David, T. W. *The Questions of King Milinda.* 2 vols.

Sharma, Chandradhar. *Indian Philosophy.* Pp. 72–136 (chaps. 6–8).

Suzuki, D. T. *On Indian Mahayana Buddhism.*

_____. *Outlines of Mahayana Buddhism.*

Zen Buddhism

Chan, Wing-tsit. *Source Book.* Pp. 425–49 (chap. 26).

Fung Yu Lan. *History.* II, 360–406 (chap. 9).

_____. *Short History.* Pp. 255–65 (chap. 22).

Suzuki, D. T. *Essays in Zen Buddhism* (various series).

4 / Hinduism:
A Philosophy of
Release

The Formation of the Classical Orthodox Viewpoints

Buddhism sprang from the enlightened heart of Gautama as at least in part a reconstructive reaction to a cluster of basic concepts enshrined in the scriptures of Hinduism and providing the historical context from which emerged the classical traditions of both Buddhist and Hindu philosophy. As far as we know, Hinduism did not stem from the dynamic spiritual impetus of any single historical individual, but rather from the developing intuitive vision of a succession of seers whose personal identities have in most cases been obscured by the content and spiritual power of the insights they shared and ultimately reduced to definitive form in the last and greatest of the traditional scriptures, the Upanishads. These philosophical postscripts to the earlier segments of scripture embodied, as we explained previously, the veritable fountainhead of Indian philosophy. During the period extending from about 500 B.C. to about 500 A.D. (though these dates are intended to be no more than rough approximations) the classical traditions of both Hinduism and Buddhism achieved something approaching well-developed, systematic expression, while Buddhism, rejecting as it did the ultimate spiritual authority of the Hindu scriptures, accumulated at the same time a widely accepted canon of authoritative writings of its own. Of course, both of these great traditions were influenced as much by each other as by the division of either into distinguishable viewpoints within itself; and this continuous historical interaction not only began with concepts that both Buddhism and Hinduism shared from the beginning (*karma, samsara,* and the like), but it proceeded to extend this area of overlapping insight to the point where most of the distinctive features of Buddhist philosophy were absorbed by Hinduism in one or another of its widely diverse forms. Gautama himself came to be viewed, in Hindu religion, as one of the incarnations of Brahman or Vishnu (or whatever other name was assigned to the ultimate reality); and Sankara, perhaps the greatest of the Hindu philosophers in terms of the impact of his ideas, developed a philosophy so similar to that of some of the Mahayana Buddhist schools (especially Voidism) that his critics attempted to offset his influence by the charge that he was

really a Buddhist in disguise. In the end, the thrust of Buddhism was so well imbibed by the tolerant openness of Hindu thought that the former, after a brilliant history filling upwards of a millennium and a half, virtually died out in the land of its origin, though the core of its teaching continued to thrive in transplanted form in its native soil.

What made a philosophy orthodox, we may remind ourselves, was that it purported to accept the ultimate spiritual authority of the Hindu scriptures, however much its teachings might diverge from what seemed to be the obvious meaning of those scriptures. Some of the orthodox schools expended much labor in trying to show that their distinctive doctrines were implicitly contained in scripture; but all at least claimed that what they taught was not inconsistent with scriptural writings correctly understood. In the period to which we have referred, each of the orthodox schools gradually developed an oral tradition of teaching and exposition which finally achieved a relatively fixed and definitive form in a written treatise or *sutra* which became the official platform of that school. For the most part, these *sutras* were composed of highly condensed, aphoristic sentences which served more to remind an adherent of the teaching than to provide, as such, a clear explanation of them. And for this reason, the *sutras* were almost unintelligible except in conjunction with some sort of commentary provided as an exposition of their meaning. As a result of this fact, nearly all the great classical philosophical treatises were written either as commentaries on these *sutras* or as commentaries on the earlier commentaries of other thinkers in the same school.

2. Commentarial tradition.

By about the end of the millennium or more in which the *sutras* were achieving definitive form, six orthodox viewpoints had clearly emerged, each with its official treatise. Some, like the Sankhya school, claimed a comparatively ancient origin of their distinctive ideas, while others clearly seem to have defined their tenets rather late in this long period. Nor were these schools thought of as embodying philosophical claims that excluded necessarily those of the other viewpoints; in fact, a tendency ultimately prevailed for certain of these viewpoints to merge by reason of common tenets and mutual supplementation, until finally four basic systematic perspectives emerged. The Sankhya and Yoga schools merged historically and together formed a viewpoint which emphasized the eternal distinction between individual souls (*purushas*) and nature (*prakriti* or *pradhana*), and the development of techniques of mental and physical control for achieving the insight that would lead to spiritual liberation. The Vaishesika and Nyaya viewpoints combined in similar fashion to form an outlook which, though it too accepted a plurality of individual souls, understood nature as composed of ultimate, indestructible atoms and as fully meaningful only through a series of independently real categories, the most crucial of which was that of particularity (*vishesa*) or individuality; for its part the Nyaya provided a system of formal logic which functioned as methodology for explaining and arguing these Vaishesika views. The perspective called Purva Mimamsa (literally "former inquiry") started out, at least, as a method of scriptural

3. Emergence of the six viewpoints.
a. Supplementary relation to each other.

b. Four basic philosophies.
1. Sankhya-Yoga: dualistic distinctionism.

2. Vaishesika-Nyaya: atomistic pluralism.

3. Purva-Mimamsa: the Exegete school.

interpretation which defended the belief that those scriptures, in some transcendental form, were eternal and authorless, though they emerged in history through the vision of the seers; and they further interpreted the scriptures not as providing information about ultimate reality, but as containing a series of injunctions or prescriptions through conformity to which one might ultimately expect to achieve release. Eventually, however, partly because of its views about the Veda (the scriptures), this school became preoccupied first with the philosophy of language and finally with the whole field of epistemology or the theory of knowledge.

4. Vedanta: ultimate monism.

The last of the four main positions, and the only one still urged as a genuinely live option by contemporary Indian thinkers, is the so-called Vedanta (literally the "end of the Veda"—perhaps then its culminating and true meaning or explanation), which itself proliferated into three well-defined schools of its own. All the forms of the Vedanta stand in contrast to what I will call the *metaphysical pluralism* of the other schools, for all of which there is a plurality of eternal, individual souls, existing in their own right and confronting an equally independent order of nature. For the Vedanta philosophies, though strikingly different from each other in emphasis and in numerous details, share the view (which I call *monistic*) that there is a single, self-existing, independent Reality, namely Brahman, on which whatever else is real (if anything else *is*) in some sense depends.

c. Common elements of the views.

1. Yoga and Nyaya provided a universal methodology.

2. The goal of release and its realization

Of course, it would be a typical Western mistake to think of these positions as tightly compartmentalized: at varying levels and in varying degrees they all borrowed from and influenced each other; the techniques of Yoga self-discipline were utilized by all, and the rigor of Nyaya logic in its formal aspect was regarded as universally accessible. Underlying all the viewpoints, furthermore, was a universal aim and a common presupposition: the aim was the achievement of release from the cycle of births and from the enslaving consequences of *karma;* the presupposition was that the most effective and satisfying path to that release was through a knowledge of truth that dispelled the darkness of ignorance and the bondage of passion. Taken collectively, the philosophies of the four classical orthodox viewpoints (and variants of them) composed the so-called *jnana-marga,* or way of knowledge.

through right knowledge; the *jnana-marga.*

Yet on the whole the philosophers were not so steeped in their obsession with philosophy that they failed to realize its limits as a way of salvation. The average person needs release as much as the philosophical savant, but he possesses, as a rule, neither the ability nor the opportunity to take the way of philosophy with ultimate seriousness, much less to pursue it as a path to release. So for these others there are alternative ways which, though not as direct and effective as knowledge, may nevertheless move toward final release, if they do not ultimately achieve it. There is, for example, as recognized by the philosophers themselves, the *karma-marga,* or way of works, which instructs the individual in performing those actions and developing those habits, both ritualistic and ethical, that will, by right action, tend to cancel out the effects of wrong action in this or previous lives. And more significantly for our purposes, there is also the *bhakti-marga,* or way of devotion, which construes the ultimate reality as a personal Lord and therefore also as an appropriate object of individual worship.

4. Alternative ways of salvation.

a. *Karma-marga:* the way of works.

b. *Bhakti-marga,* the way of devotion.

For most of the philosophers, the ultimate grounds which explain existence either fall short of the notion of a personal God or go beyond that idea to an Absolute Reality that transcends all such determinate qualities. But for many in spiritual need, an ideal grounded in abstract principles or impersonal ultimates can not support the sustained self-discipline and commitment required for realizing the spiritual ideal. For them the example and object of spiritual reality must be a personal Lord who, at the least, changelessly embodies the liberated perfection that all are summoned to achieve, and at the most, is conceived as the personal God or Absolute,

1. Generally impersonal view of the Ultimate in the philosophical schools.
2. Need for a personalistic view.

on whom all creation is dependent for its reality in some sense or other. Through a transforming relation with the Lord, thus understood, the individual is to be engulfed in divine love and lifted up into an intimate moral union with God and other selves—a union which fulfills the true selfhood of each, but retains its individuality over against the Divine Reality. Such a way

3. The Gita.

of devotion is embodied in the most widely revered Hindu classic, *The Bhagavad Gita* or *Song of the Lord,* in which the personal God Krishna is depicted as transcending the impersonal Brahman of the Upanishads.

4. Influence of personalism on the philosophical schools.

So powerful was the appeal and impact of the personal concept of the Ultimate, that in various ways this theistic notion (as it is called) invaded the realm of the philosophers itself quite effectively. Pluralistic views, which in their original form were non-theistic, tended to develop a theistic form in which the notion of a personal Lord, though usually divested of creative functions, was put forth as an object and example of spiritual contemplation and perfection. The Vedanta philosopher Sankara aimed to keep the best of both worlds by holding that the absolute Brahman was qualityless, but that the highest concept of the qualified Brahman was that of a modified version of personal theism. And the other principal schools of the Vedanta, founded by Ramanuja and Madhva respectively, placed the personal view of God at the very top of the metaphysical ladder; for them there was no higher or more ultimate Reality than that of the personal Lord Himself.

c. Synthesis of the ways.

In actual practice, of course, even the most speculative of the philosophers tended to combine all the ways of salvation into a single, complex path to spiritual liberation. But for the many who could not reach this level of sophistication, there was always some practical way that they could correctly follow, some series of realistically possible steps that they might reasonably be expected to take in the direction of release. For such an outlook as this there emerges an inclusive outreach which offers deliverance to the most simple among us, while at the same time it provokes and challenges the keenest capacities of our most brilliant minds.

The Pluralistic Views: Release through Isolation

The pluralistic views of Sankhya-Yoga, Vaishesika-Nyaya, and Mimamsa, though clearly different views in many respects, share a broad base of common doctrinal outlook which makes it convenient to discuss them together as variations on a single theme quite in contrast to the rather different strain that runs through all the forms of the Vedanta. And to make the whole analysis less complex in its terminology, I will, somewhat arbitrarily, refer to the Sankhya-Yoga viewpoint as *dualistic distinctionism,* since it emphasizes very strongly the absolute difference between individual souls and nature; again, I will call the Vaishesika-Nyaya tradition *atomistic pluralism,* since it regards the basic constituents of nature as a plurality of indestructible atoms or ultimate particulars which combine in innumerable ways to form the various compounds of the order of nature; the Mimamsa philosophy, finally, I will speak of as the school of *Exegesis* because of its obvious preoccupation with scriptural interpretation.

1. The common outlook of the pluralistic views.

a. Terminology.

All three of these perspectives share a more or less common general metaphysical outlook. They accept an ultimate and ineradicable plurality of separate, individual souls, all of whom stand in contrast to the order of nature (*soul pluralism*); they take the position that the changes in nature are real transformations and not merely appearances of some changeless, underlying something or other, and that the material order of nature itself has a reality status that is quite independent of our awareness of it (*cosmological* and *perceptual realism*); and, except for Mimamsa, they further share with nearly all Indian philosophy the doctrine that the natural order passes through a beginningless series of cycles, in each of which nature passes from a state of

b. General metaphysical outlook.

1. Soul pluralism.

2. Cosmological and perceptual realism.

3. Cyclical recurrence.

4. Release as a state of isolation; discriminationism.

a. Bondage based on ignorance.

b. Release based on true and experiential knowledge of difference.

c. Interpretation of the distinction between soul and nature.
(1) A typical Western outlook.

(2) Contrast with Indian outlook.

dissolution or equilibrium of its constituent parts through a series of disruptive changes leading to a state of maximum development and differentiation, then back again to the original equilibrium (*cyclical recurrence*). Furthermore, these positions take a generally unitary view of release, according to which true deliverance involves the clear recognition of the absolute separateness of the soul as such from natural processes of whatever sort, so that the state of release is a state of individual isolation from all else; what this means in effect is that being in bondage to the cycle of births rests on a kind of mistaken identification, by the individual, of his soul with certain natural processes from which, in its essence, the soul is absolutely distinct. And just as bondage involves ignorance, so release involves knowledge, though it is hardly the knowledge of mere theory: the belief that the soul is distinct from nature is a start, to be sure; but it is little more than that, since the soul achieves release only as it incarnates existentially the ultimate difference which theory acknowledges. It is, for example, not enough to believe that the pain of a headache is not intrinsic to one's true self; I must achieve that level of insight for which the pain is as objective to me as any other state of the natural order (*discriminationism*).

Now it is of the utmost importance to see that the line between the soul and nature is drawn quite differently, for these views, from the way in which a similar distinction might be erected in a typical Western outlook. If we accept any sort of dualism here between soul or self and nature, we are likely to sweep all mental processes and conscious states into the soul, and then proceed to consign everything physical or material to the realm of nature; for such a view, my soul is mine indeed, with all that mental activity embraces, but my body, though also mine in a less intimate sense, really belongs to the order of nature. Indian thought, however, though in the pluralistic views it is no less confident about the difference, refuses to make the distinction in this way. Instead, for these thinkers the soul is essentially a passive and in itself inert witness, or, in Western terms, a permanent principle of pure subjectivity whose sole, intrinsic function is the awareness of conscious states which, though intimately correlated with the pure subject, really belong to nature and thus are objective to the true self in the sense of not belonging to its true nature. It is true that distinctionism takes a more rigorous view of this disjunction than does atomism: for the philosophers of the first school the soul, as such, even in a state of bondage, is intrinsically devoid of intellectual and conscious states, which belong exclusively to nature; the atomist thinkers, on the other hand, take the position that such states really do inhere in the soul, though only in conjunction with the soul's relation to the processes of phenomenal awareness which belong to nature and which are conjoined with the soul, once again, only in the state of bondage to the cycle of births. But it all comes to the same thing in the end, since for both views, when the soul achieves the liberating knowledge of its absolute separateness from nature the self will no longer be conjoined with conscious states of any sort.

In contrast, then, to the soul's role as a passive witness (however that notion may be clarified by the positions we have just compared), the active functions of intellect (*buddhi*—the capacity and process of conceptualizing and engaging in discursive thought) and sense-mind (*manas*—the capacity and process of sensory or perceptual awareness) belong, in unique correlation with each self, to the order of nature. And since the conjunction between each self and its corresponding intellectual and sensory function is both intricate and immediate, it is clear how easily the pure self slips into the groove of wrongly identifying itself with those natural processes. And difficult as it may be for the Western mind to grasp, the view that discriminates soul and nature in this way can be made to sound quite reasonable to at least some Western ears. We easily distinguish between the act of awareness and the object of aware-

Marginal notes:

(a) Soul as spectator or passive witness: pure subject of awareness.
(b) Mental processes as belonging to nature, though differently explained by distinctionism and atomism.

(3) Relative ease of mistaken identification.

(4) Plausibility of the Indian outlook on the soul/nature distinction.

(a) Some recognizable differences.

ness in a given case; for example, between being aware of a pain and the pain of which we are aware. Most of us would readily acknowledge, furthermore, that such an act, merely as an act of awareness, is not as such literally painful (in no direct, non-figurative sense is it painful just to think). But of course we can, in turn, make our acts of awareness themselves objects of awareness quite distinct from the pure, individual subjectivity which recognizes them as objects; and one can

(b) Particular acts of awareness not essential to the self.

now argue that such particular acts of awareness are not themselves essential to the self, since any other succession of acts could be substituted for them without violence to the true nature of the self. Still the pure subject, in its essential activity or subjectivity, cannot itself become, as such, an object of awareness in the same way, since the real subject always transcends any such objective discernment. Now if all this has at least a ring of plausibility, then it may seem equally reasonable to conclude that whatever can become truly objective to the self (including intellectual and sensory acts and

(c) Only pure subjectivity intrinsically essential to the self.

states) is not ultimately essential to the self, so that only pure subjectivity itself is inseparably essential and intrinsic to the self in its ultimate nature. And that is precisely the view of these philosophies on this difficult question.

(5) The soul as all-pervasive since not limited by a particular place.
(a) Meaning and basis of this position.

Space, too, in the next place, belongs to the natural order and cannot therefore function as any sort of limit to the self in its essence: for this reason, distinctionists and atomists spoke of the soul as, in itself, all-pervasive, not in the sense that it could act indiscriminately at any point in space (the soul *acts,* after all, only in conjunction with the phenomenal processes of mind and body which belong to nature), but rather in the sense that the soul as such and in itself is not limited to any particular space or locus. On the other hand, since the soul must act through its intellectual, sensory, and bodily correlates in nature, it is practically and functionally limited by the spatial restrictions which *are* intrinsic to those correlates. Yet the concept of all-pervasiveness did help to explain an otherwise awkward problem: if the soul were essentially restricted by space, it would be difficult to understand how it could be directly aware of bodily sensations in any given inner part or surface area of that body; on the other hand, as all-pervasive the soul can be directly present as pure subject wherever its sensory correlate functions.

(b) Problem of sensory awareness throughout the body.

If, finally, for these views, the relation of the soul to nature is understood in this over-all way, it follows that in the state of release finally achieved and culminated through authentic self-knowledge, the soul will have, in its true state of isolated pure subjectivity, no intellectual or conscious activities to perform, much less any sensory or other bodily rooted functions. And since bliss, joy, and other such positive qualities of awareness belong as such to the conscious functions that have thus ceased, it is clearly the case that such a state of release is construed here in a largely negative way: there is freedom from all pain and sorrow, but there can be no transition to the positive joy of salvation, since that too is ultimately consigned to its appropriate place in the order of nature from which the soul in its true essence is absolutely distinct. A high price to pay, perhaps: yet it may be that the ecstasy of that final moment in which the soul, though still conjoined with nature, feels its enslaving chains falling away as it rises at last toward the isolation of pure selfhood will more than compensate for the loss of an endless eternity of positive bliss.

d. Condition of the soul in the state of release.

(1) Its largely negative character.

(2) Compensation for this inactive and isolated destiny.

But the conceptual cords that bind the pluralistic views together do not quite compose an impenetrably solid front: for there are pervasive differences that disrupt this broad stretch of tranquil calm. Aside from some peripheral differences between distinctionism and atomism concerning the nature of the soul, the main contrasts among the pluralistic views appear in extensive disagreement about the ultimate constituents of nature—a difference that leads to an equally sharp contrast concerning the concept of causality. For the most part, the Exegete philosophers accept the metaphysic of

2. Significant differences among the pluralistic views.

a. Contrasting views of nature.

nature that is systematically developed by the atomists, while the distinctionists disagree with both: in the atomistic system, the ultimate particles whose varied combinations explain the differentiations that emerge in the process of natural evolution are qualitatively distinct, unextended atoms which, though inert in themselves, are put into motion by an unseen force (*adrishta*), which without conscious purpose correlates the state of nature with the proportion of merit and demerit which characterizes the soul in any given phase of its spiritual pilgrimage; quite otherwise, distinctionism, though it employs the concept of the atom, interprets the atoms as themselves composite derivatives of still more ultimate constituent principles (called *gunas*—qualities, attributes, or strands) which, in balanced equilibrium, constitute the primordial, unevolved state of nature.

Nature has then, for distinctionism, three such basic qualities or aspects: brightness (*sattva*), force or active energy (*rajas*), and mass or passive receptivity (*tamas*). The evolution of the world of nature takes place through the disruption of the original equilibrium of these aspects and their resultant interaction and differentiation. The rationale of this position is that the

unity of nature as we experience it requires a unitary cause which is infinite in the sense that there is no active principle external to it that could limit it (souls, of course, are merely passive witnesses). Nature itself, in its primordial state, is this unitary cause; still, the qualitative differences that emerge from nature—especially the differences between mental processes and physical processes, and those between the active and passive aspects of the latter—are so sharp that this unitary nature itself must have qualitatively distinct and relatively independent constituent qualities to explain those striking differences. Neither consciousness by itself nor material atoms by themselves would be adequate to explain the world; but the concept of a unitary nature which itself has qualitatively different components does meet this requirement.

The detailed explanation of this evolutionary process is intricate indeed, and a very general explanation is sufficient for our purposes. When the equilibrium of the qualities is disrupted, the quality of brightness becomes predominant and passes into a process of differentiation which finally results in the production of separate principles of intellect and sense-mind, together with the various sensory and active faculties; these are in turn correlated with the bound souls through the emergence of the individuating factor or self-consciousness. All this occasions a parallel process of differentiation in the other two qualities of nature, so that, through the interaction of active energy and passive inertness, eventually material counterparts of the various sensory and active faculties of the individual minds are produced— objects toward which these faculties may be directed. And this realm of objects is itself composed of qualitatively distinct atoms which, though derivative composites or by-products themselves, become, through various combinations, the basic elements of all actually observable things like trees and stones. And when nature has reached the maximum state of differentiation and determinateness, the whole thing starts, as it were, to fall apart again until the primordial state of equilibrium is again restored, only to be followed once more by the great cosmological rerun.

Atomism cannot accept all this: for what the philosophy of distinctionism takes as derivative here, the Atomists take as ultimate and underivable, since the atoms are regarded as the qualitatively distinct and indivisible particles which, having no magnitude or spatial extension, are instrinsically devoid of component parts and therefore unanalyzable into any more basic constituent elements or principles. The atoms are, as indicated, of different qualitative types, namely, earth, air, water, and fire; and they are combined into objects of larger magnitude through the power of the unseen force

(2) General order of the evolutionary process.
(a) Disruption of equilibrium.
(b) Differentiation of the qualities.

(c) Restoration of the primordial state: cyclical recurrence.
b. Reaction of atomism.

(1) Atoms viewed as unextended, indivisible, and underived.

(2) Process of atomic combination.

(*adrishta*) of merit and demerit, in the medium of space or ether which was non-atomic just because it was unsubstantial. Not only were so-called physical objects composed of combinations of atoms, but the sensory capacities and mind of the phenomenal individual were also regarded as material entities built from atoms, though the mind was itself a single atom for each individual.

3. Special features of atomism. *a.* The problem of magnitude: unextended particles and extended composites.

Atomism faced a special problem in trying to explain how atoms or particles which were themselves unextended could produce composite objects or aggregates that were actually (and not merely apparently) extended. To account for this the atomists contended that when two atoms combined a dyad was produced which contained the new quality of minute extension, so that the dyad was a minute quantum; and they went on to hold that when three dyads combined they formed a molecule which had gross extension, so that from such molecules larger extended objects could be formed. Without boggling over the details, I will simply point out that this explanation assumes that combinations can have new qualities that have no traceable continuity with the qualities of the elements of which those combinations are composed—a presupposition which becomes strategic for the atomist view of causality. Water, for example, though composed of hydrogen and oxygen, has qualities shared by neither of its constituent elements.

b. Ultimacy of the unique particular: the doctrine of categories. *1.* Uniqueness of ultimate substances.

The atomists also held that individual atoms, though of various generic types, as we have seen, have their own intrinsic and therefore indefinable individualities or particularities, a sort of unique "kinkiness," as it were. In fact, so strongly did they emphasize this notion of ultimate particulars that they developed, as a supplement to their atomism, a doctrine of logically ultimate metaphysical categories to explain that notion. The most

2. Analysis of the categories. *a.* Substance.

b. Quality.

c. Activity.

basic category was of course that of *substance:* but it can be clearly understood only as the substratum in which *quality* (embracing the permanent features of substance) and *activity* or *action* (including the transient features of substance and involving various kinds of motion) inhere. The ultimate spiritual substances are of course the eternal souls, while the ultimate physical or material substances are the atoms. While these first three categories have a real and objective existence which can be directly intuited, the rest of the categories, though no less real and objective, are products of intellectual discrimination in the sense that they must be logically inferred, rather than directly perceived. The category of *generality* or *universality,* for example, embraces the realm of class-concepts and is inferred from the conjunction of common characteristics belonging to individuals which are correctly viewed as belonging to the same class. But this does not imply that universals are merely subjective concepts in our minds: the doctrine is realistic, so that the universal is regarded as an objective, eternal, and changeless reality, in which the individuals of a given class participate. And thus we confront here a realm of transcendently real essences not unlike that of rationalistic Neo-Confucianism or even western Platonism.

d. Generality: real universals or essences.

The category of particularity (*vishesa*—after which the atomistic school is named in Sanskrit) becomes, as it were, the touchstone of this whole metaphysical scheme for which each soul and each atom, however similar to other entities of the same sort, has a unique individuality or particularity of its own which is apprehended not through conceptually definable differences (as in the case of compound objects like trees and stones), but by the direct intuition of this indefinable distinctness in the case of each ultimate particular.

e. Particularity.

Inherence is the inseparable eternal relation that subsists between objects that are logically inconceivable except through conjunction with each other (such as part and whole, substance and quality, particular and universal), and is quite distinct from mere separable and transient conjunctions of various sorts. And later atomists added, finally, the category of *non-being* on the ground that such a principle of negation was re-

f. Inherence.

g. Non-being.

quired to render intelligible the non-existence of an originated thing both before it comes into being and after it ceases to exist, as well as the determinateness of its characteristics which excludes from it those qualities which would make it some other thing which it is not. There is, from this point of view, no such thing as absolute negation or non-existence; and the three genuine phases of negation impart to this last category a relativity that contrasts with the absolute status of the other categories.

c. The problem of causality.

1. The identity theory: distinctionism.

a. Relation to concept of nature.

b. The meaning of identity.

c. Rationale of the view.

From the contrast of metaphysical outlook thus clarified, a further and far-reaching difference between distinctionism and atomism appears. Since, for the first perspective, the evolution of nature is a process in which what is *implicit* in the three aspects of nature, and *potential* in their relations to each other, simply becomes explicit and actualized through a process of differentiation, the distinctionist philosophers defended what was called the *identity* theory of causality (*satkaryavada*). According to this position, every effect pre-exists in its cause and is simply a different state of its being, hence (in that sense) identical with it in essence, but not in degree of explicitness or manifestation. At the same time this difference of state is no mere illusory appearance (as in the Vedanta philosophy of Sankara) but a real modification of the condition of the continuously identical cause. The main justification for this identity theory of causality was, of course, its being implied in the whole notion of nature with its three constituent aspects. But the distinctionists also argued the theory on grounds not so directly related to their own general metaphysical premises. Unless an effect does pre-exist in its cause, they contended, it would be a non-entity and could never be produced. Furthermore, on any other supposition, any effect at all could conceivably be produced by any cause at all; but experience shows that only certain restricted types of effect are produced by particular kinds of causes. We do not expect cottage cheese to be produced out of mere water, or kittens to

be born from fig trees; and these restrictions are best explained on the assumption that effects are limited to certain causes precisely for the reason that they are implicit
in them, rather than in other, different causes. If,
finally, the effect were absolutely distinct from its
cause, then the very moment that effect appeared it
would either lack the causal ground that it requires by
being thus utterly separate from its alleged cause, or
else, in the very independence of its distinctness, it
would, contrary to the original assumption, not be an
effect at all. Would butter, for example, be an effect of
milk if it were totally distinct from it? Basically, what is
at stake in all this is the dependable continuity and
rational intelligibility of the natural order itself.

Still the atomists disagreed and defended, on the contrary, the so-called non-identity theory (*asatkaryavada*).
According to this position, effects are not essentially
one with or implicit in their causes, but are quite distinct
from them. The main justification here was derived
from the metaphysical theory of atomism. Since all
compound things are aggregates of atoms (the ultimate
causes), and since the relations in which atoms stand to
each other in these aggregates are wholly external to the
intrinsic qualities of the atoms themselves, and since the
compounds frequently have entirely new characteristics
which are not in any discernible continuity with the
qualities of atoms (aggregates are extended, for example, but atoms are not), it follows that effects
(namely, aggregates and their qualities) are not implicit
in, or identical with, their causes. But again, like the
distinctionist defenders of the identity theory, atomists
tried to argue the non-identity theory on grounds not
wholly dependent on their peculiar presuppositions. If
effects were identical with their causes, there would be
no real causation at all, no genuine production of an effect, but merely the continued existence of the cause in
some further phase of its being, so that in that case it
would not really be a cause at all. And even if we view
an effect as a different phase of some cause with which

2. The non-identity theory.

a. Meaning of non-identity.

b. Rationale of the view.
(1) Basis in atomism.

(2) Independent arguments.

it is identical in essence, still the phases are wholly distinct (since we recognize them), and their difference can hardly be explained by a presupposed, though presumably deeper, identity of essence. Furthermore, we do find that effects often have qualities which are radically different from their alleged causes in nature; water, for example, has properties that could never be deduced from any independent investigation of the nature of hydrogen or oxygen. And that suggests another point: that if effects are implicit in their causes, it should be possible to arrive at some knowledge of the existence and nature of those effects from a consideration of the causes alone; but in fact we are able to correlate effects with their causes only by observing their more or less enduring conjunction in our empirical experience.

In principle, then, any effect could (logically) come about as the product of any cause; nor does the fact that there are reasonably predictable conjunctions of effects with certain kinds of causes contravene this point. We merely discover these conjunctions in experience, and we find it necessary to accept these conjunctions as more or less brute contingencies for which no further explanation is either practically important or theoretically possible. Chaos, then, is not the only alternative to the identity theory; and when we remember that the atoms themselves are directed, as it were, by the unseen force of merit and demerit through the principle of *karma,* a world of numerically distinct causes and effects seems quite capable of providing us with all the continuity that practical exigency requires.

3. A basic problem for pluralism: the relation between soul and nature as independent reals.

a. Plausibility of soul-pluralism.

But both distinctionism and atomism face difficult problems in explaining the intimate correlation between distinct and individual souls, on the one hand, and the independent order of nature which nevertheless provides the context of their moral self-realization, on the other. The thesis (common to the two views) that there is a plurality of really distinct and separate individual souls seems plausible enough: if there were, at some depth of metaphysical profundity, actually only one soul-principle of which particular finite individuals were so many mere appearances, there would be no way of accounting for either the direct awareness of individual self-consciousness or the separate lines of experience correlated with these selves, nor would there be any explanation for the fact that some souls are in a state of bondage to the cycle of births while others are liberated. But the crucial questions concern the relation of such individual souls, each of which is independent and ultimate in its being, to an order of nature which, on this view of things, is equally ultimate and independent. Distinctionism flatly holds that the moral well-being of souls functions as a kind of purposive end or goal for the processes of nature; and it even takes the position that it is the soul that disturbs the equilibrium of nature in its primordial end-state and thus initiates the whole cycle of natural development. Atomism views this overall relationship in a similar way: the equilibrium of the atoms in a state of general dissolution is disturbed by the so-called *adrishta* or unseen force—which is itself explained as the collective effect, through *karma,* of the moral condition of merit and demerit that characterizes individual souls.

b. But how relate independent ultimates?
1. Soul and nature as purposively and causally interacting.

All this, together with the fact that the soul, at least in a state of bondage, seems dependent on the mental aspect of nature for the processes of phenomenal awareness correlated with each such soul, would seem to compromise the supposed independence of the soul and nature in both directions. Nature seems dependent on the state of souls for the very initiation of the process of evolutionary development, and even for the restoration of those processes to equilibrium again at the end of any such cycle. And the soul, in turn, seems just as dependent on nature as a context of activity and as a total environment which matches the moral condition of the soul. And since the soul is supposed to be a merely passive witness of nature, it is difficult to see how such a spectator role could be intrinsic to the soul without an

2. Apparent compromise of independence.

3. Approach to this problem in later versions of these theories.

interdependent relation to nature as the object of this witnessing. And when, finally, we think of the purposive adaptation of the soul to nature, and vice versa, we are naturally led to wonder if this relation itself is not grounded in some deeper, unitary Ground of Being, whose world-purpose is actualized in the whole reciprocal connection of souls with each other and with the natural order. For reasons like these, it is not difficult to see why both atomism and distinctionism appeared in later forms that were decidedly theistic in outlook; in fact, in its conjunction with the school of Logic (*Nyaya*), atomism eventually produced the most impressive structure of arguments for the existence of God that can be found anywhere in the traditions of Indian philosophy.

4. Distinctive emphases of the Exegete school.

a. The Veda as eternal and authorless.

1. Resultant resistance to any theistic version,

2. and to doctrine of cycles.

3. Philosophical by-products.

The school of Exegesis, we may remind ourselves, largely identified itself with the metaphysical views of atomism, though it rejected any tendency to produce a theistic version and even rejected the doctrine of cyclical recurrence. Both of these disjoiners can be understood through the basic emphasis of Exegetes on the absoluteness of the scriptures, which were regarded as eternal and therefore authorless: the resistance to any concept of God can thus be seen as in part an attempt to preserve the ultimacy of the scriptures, which were regarded as without any authorship whatever, whether human or divine; and the rejection of cyclical recurrence can be viewed as an attempt to avoid any suggestion that in each cycle the scriptures would have to be originated. Although this obsession with scriptural authority may seem rather unpromising philosophically, nevertheless the attempt to defend the eternity of the Veda led to a preoccupation with the nature of language, the meaning of religious discourse, and, more generally, the whole field of epistemology.

b. Philosophy of language. *1.* Linguistic eternalism.

If the Veda is eternal, then since the Veda consists of words, it follows that language, in some transcendental sense, must also be eternal. Nor were the Exegete philosophers at all hesitant to adopt such a thesis: words

and their meanings are all eternal, though they have to
be distinguished from the sounds and symbols which are
their vehicles of manifestation in various conventional
human languages, like Chinese and German. And of
course, if language is in this sense eternal and necessary,
then the objects to which it ultimately refers must be
equally eternal and necessary: those objects cannot be
particular things that come into existence and pass
away; they must rather be a realm of eternal and
unchanging universals or essences—so that here again
we confront the realistic doctrine of such essences. At
first reading, this view appears to prove too much, if indeed it proves anything at all; for if we support the eternity of the Veda with the eternity of language, then it
will seem to follow that the daily newspaper is as eternal
as the Veda. But no: the words (not the conventional
symbols) in the daily newspaper are eternal indeed, but
the order of the words is the product of human authorship; the Veda, on the other hand, is not only composed, in its transcendental form, of eternal words and
their eternal meanings, but the *order* of its words is also
eternal and therefore self-determined and intrinsically
valid, quite independently of any authorship, human or
divine. We may, of course, regard the whole notion of
eternal words as a determined effort of theological dog-
matism to safeguard its favorite doctrine; but we might
temper this possibly premature judgment by recalling
that very recent Western thinkers have argued rather
persuasively that the origination of meaningful language by beings (human, I suppose) who did not already
possess a linguistic facility in understanding the significance of signs and symbols is simply preposterous as an
explanation. It appears that every attempt to explain the
origin of language as such presupposes the use of some
sort of language by the beings who were supposed to be
originating language itself. Hence, we might at least
reserve judgment about the whole question.

The problem of the meaning of religious discourse
has a still more contemporary ring. For the Exegete

a. Meaning of
this view.
(1) Relation of
language to
symbols.

(2) Real
essences as the
objects of
eternal
language.

(3) Special case
of the Veda.

b. Plausibility
of this view of
langauge.

2. Injunctivism
as a theory of

philosophers, the whole question emerges in this way: premising as always the absolute authority of the scriptures, they confronted the perplexing fact that the scriptures were full of talk about the gods, and in the later scriptures especially about the one true God (Brahman, Atman, or another), while Exegesis is wholly nontheistic in its view. But no such conundrum was to be allowed to daunt a courage as resolute as that of these bold thinkers. They adopted what I sincerely regard as the absolutely brilliant thesis that religious statements, especially scriptural ones, are not to be interpreted as providing information about reality—that would be to assign to religious discourse a cognitive role that it could not be expected to fill. Instead, scriptural statements were to be interpreted injunctively or prescriptively as a series of imperatives, instructions, or commands directing individuals to act in certain ways, morally and ritualistically, so as to express and implement their settled intent to achieve release from the cycle of births. Apparently informative statements were to be understood as elucidating this primarily injunctive thrust of scripture, or as expressing such prescriptions in a disguised way, or even as motivating submission to revealed commands or directives. It would be, these philosophers reasoned, to pervert the proper role and function of religious language to understand it in any way that did not entail the translation of the whole realm of religious discourse into this imperative mode. That this sophisticated hermeneutical system was, in Hinduism, affiliated with what may fairly be described as a fundamentalist mentality, may at least serve to remind certain Western interpreters of religious discourse that this kind of approach to religious language is a veritable nose of interpretive wax which can be twisted in more than one direction and which therefore witnesses to its need for cognitive guidance from *somewhere* if it is to subserve any useful purpose at all.

The involvement of Exegete philosophy in the whole field of epistemology, or theory of knowledge, entails the universal controversy in Indian thought about the number, nature. and relation of the so-called *pramanas* or criteria (ultimate grounds or first principles) of knowledge. While an adequate analysis of this question is possible only after a discussion of Vedanta (the last main school of Hindu orthodoxy), I will mention here that there were four generally recognized ultimate criteria of this sort: *perception* (which included not only empirical or sensory awareness, but the awareness of rational universals or essences), *inference* (which included the principles of inductive and deductive logic), *comparison* (reasoning by analogy of one sort or another), and *verbal testimony* (which meant, in general, the basing of a knowledge-claim on some recognized authority, and, more specifically, the authority of scripture). There was wide agreement about the ultimacy of perception and inference as logically basic criteria for ordinary knowledge claims; but there was equally extensive controversy about whether comparison and verbal testimony were ultimate standards, or whether instead they were logically reducible to perception and inference in some sense. The Exegetes, of course, regarded verbal testimony, at least in its scriptural form, as logically independent of the other standards. But whatever view one takes about these criteria, one still faces the problem of distinguishing, with some confidence, between valid and invalid knowledge-claims supposedly grounded in these ultimate standards; and that in turn involves the whole question of the nature of error and its relation to truth. But that problem will best be raised from a vantage point that has already been conditioned by the intricacies of the Vedanta tradition—by far the most impressive of the classical orthodox systems.

Indian thought.
1. The accepted means of right knowledge.

2. Agreement and controversy about these standards.

3. The validity of knowledge and the problem of error.

The Monistic Views: The Vedanta Concept of Release through Identification

The three principal Vedanta systems all take their point of departure first from the scriptures (especially the Upanishads), and then from the official treatise of their

1. Historical emergence of Vedanta.

school, the so-called *Brahma-sutra* or *Vedanta-sutra,*
attributed traditionally to a sage of approximately the
fourth century A.D. by the name of Badarayana.
Although the *Bhagavad Gita* (*Song of the Lord*) was
also an important source for this school, the three
greatest Vedanta thinkers, each the decisive exponent of
a different line of interpretation, produced individually
a significant commentary on the Vedanta-sutra; and
those commentaries by Sankara (788–820 A.D.),
Ramanuja (1017–1137 A.D.), and Madhva (1197–1276
A.D.) became the classic expressions of these divergent
forms of Vedanta thought. Much of the later literature
of these versions then consisted of commentaries on
these commentaries, or even commentaries on earlier
commentaries on those three original commentaries.

However different the three branches of Vedanta
were, there was much that bound them together as
variations on a common theme. Even though Madhva's
school was called *Dvaita* (duality) Vedanta—because he
emphasized the ultimate and ineradicable distinctions
between God, the individual self, and the world, it is
nevertheless illuminating to see the whole of Vedanta as
monistic in contrast to the metaphysical pluralism of
the other orthodox views. For while Sankara, Ramanuja, and Madhva differed radically on the *relation* between God and all else, they all maintained that God
alone was self-existent and self-dependent in His Reality; whatever else existed and however it existed, it all
depended for its existence and distinctive functioning on
that one sole and ultimate Reality. And there was a further common thread that ran through these distinguishable fabrics of Vedanta: while the pluralistic views
thought of release in terms of the distinction and
ultimately the isolation of the individual self from
nature, the Vedanta thinkers interpreted release as a
union of the individual both with his own true selfhood
and with God. It is true that for Sankara this union was
understood as the recognition of an absolute self-
identity with the Self of Brahman, so that all separate

individuality was left behind, while for Ramanuja and Madhva that union was thought of as a relation of moral oneness and devotional contemplation in which the selfhood of the individual was fulfilled in union but preserved in its personal integrity. Yet for all three traditions the state of release was a state in which the individual, in one sense or another, achieved an identifying union with his true place in the scheme of things through a fulfilling oneness with God. Finally, these perspectives together shared a seriousness about the ultimate authority of the scriptures that regarded them as the principal source of metaphysical knowledge, and that led each of the views to argue at great length that its system of interpretation conformed more perfectly with scriptural teaching than any alternative position could reasonably claim.

c. Seriousness about scriptural authority.

Sankara was presumably not the founder of *Advaita* Vedanta (or non-dualism, as we shall call it), but it is agreed on all hands that he was its most brilliant, remarkable, and energetic representative, and perhaps even the greatest of all the Indian philosophers of the commentarial period which extended from about 500 A.D. to modern times. What is virtually indisputable is that his philosophy became the fulcrum on which most of the subsequent development of classical Indian philosophy turned. The term *advaita* (non-duality) supplies the key to Sankara's whole outlook: for he holds that all differences and distinctions are ultimately superficial and, at the highest level of being and truth, unreal, and that therefore (though the logic probably moves, for Sankara, in the other direction—not from unreal difference to absolute identity, but rather from that identity to unreal difference) Reality is a single, all-inclusive, yet absolutely non-differenced Being, of which all else is the misinterpreted appearance, and with which all else is essentially and indistinguishably one.

3. Sankara's non-dualism.

a. Basic thesis: ultimate unreality of the realm of difference, but ultimate reality of absolutely non-differenced Being.

This massive thesis is grounded, from the standpoint of methodology, on a pervasive principle of interpretation which I will call the two-level principle or merely

b. Interpretive ground of the thesis: the two-level principle.

the concept of levels. This principle, like a musical theme, can be expressed only in some determinate context and form, but it is a single principle that runs through all these various manifestations. It means, basically, that we have to distinguish between ordinary truth (which is rational, discursive, and conceptual) and absolute truth (which transcends all conceptual distinctions and is both intuitive and immediate); between empirical reality (the realm of things, processes, and events) and absolute reality (the realm of absolutely non-differenced Being); and then in turn between the qualified (*saguna*) Brahman (the personal Lord and creator of all else—the material, efficient, formal, and final cause of all things, who calls all men to personal devotion and unqualified moral commitment) and the unqualified (*nirguna*) Brahman (the qualityless Absolute with which all else is undifferentiably one, and especially with which the self of each [apparent] individual is, in its deepest reality, absolutely identical).

The two-level principle stands, as Sankara sees it, squarely rooted in scripture and especially in the so-called identity-text of the Upanishads: "That art thou!" ("Tattvamasi"). He took this statement as affirming the absolute identity of the true self (*atman*) of the individual with the unqualified Brahman whose reality could only be designated ("That") and never described in terms of intellectually definable qualities. Then, guided by the frequent assertions of scripture that all things are one with or included in Brahman, while Brahman is itself completely devoid of difference, Sankara went on to conclude that the identity of the self with the absolute Brahman was a kind of exemplary paradigm of the essential identity of all things with Brahman at that highest level. But of course that meant that this identity was beyond all distinctions and differences, so that the realm of separate things and events was, as it were, a lower level appearance or manifestation, or in Sankara's words, *maya* or illusion. Those scriptures, in turn, which assigned conceptually definable qualities to

1. Ordinary truth and absolute truth.

2. Empirical reality and absolute reality.

3. Qualified Brahman and unqualified Brahman: the latter the true self of each individual.

c. The scriptural basis and its implications.
1. The identity-text: identity of the self with the unqualified Brahman.

2. Identity of all things with unqualified Brahman.

3. Realm of difference as *maya* or illusion.

Brahman, and which spoke of a qualified relation of difference between Brahman and the world, were accordingly also assigned, in this interpretive method, to the lower level of reality and truth.

4. Difference-texts assigned to lower level.

Yet Sankara does not discount, but rather emphasizes strongly, the practical reality of the lower level. From the standpoint of the higher or absolute level, the ordinary realm is, of course, *maya* or illusion, the manifestation through differences and limitations of the undifferentiable oneness of absolute reality; and, in epistemological terms, this lower level is a kind of cosmic or universal ignorance (*avidya*). Both the illusion and the ignorance are transcended *objectively* in the intuitive identity with Brahman that is achieved by the released soul. But the reality of the empirical order at the level of practical experience and activity is indisputable: even for the person who, like Sankara, is in a state of living release (so that he goes on living in the world even though no longer bound by the cycle of births), the distinguishable objects of that lower order of things do not absolutely vanish, but they are understood for what they *are,* namely, illusory appearances of the unqualified Absolute. Analogously, when a person discovers that what he sees in the road ahead is not wet pavement but a mirage, the road still looks wet to him, but he recognizes that wetness as an illusory appearance of something else. And when a man mistakenly identifies a rope as a snake, he does not cease to see what he saw before, but simply understands it in its true nature. If anything, the practical facility of a man in the affairs of ordinary life would be heightened rather than diminished by the recognition that differences which he previously regarded as ultimate were actually mere appearances. In fact, Sankara's empirical realism was so strong that he totally rejected the theory of Buddhist Idealism to the effect that the objects of ordinary experience were merely transformations of individual consciousness.

d. The status of the lower level.
1. The ordinary realm as illusion and ignorance.

2. The ordinary realm as a practical reality.

a. Qualified reality even for the released self.

b. Illustrations of the relation.

c. Sankara's perceptual realism as affirming this reality.

(1) Supporting arguments.

His arguments for perceptual realism are so impressive, in my opinion, that they are worth further discussion. He anticipates the theory of the intentional nature of consciousness by arguing (1) that perceptual consciousness always involves a duality between the *act* of perceiving and the *object* that is perceived, so that perception cannot constitute its own object; (2) that this distinction is clear both from the fact that when we perceive we are conscious not of perceptions, but of the things perceived through them, and from the fact that consciousness remains the same, in the active sense, while its objects vary; and finally (3) that, since an object perceived and later remembered is the same object, the object itself cannot be either the perception or the memory, which are clearly different (unless there is no such thing as memory at all). Such arguments as these

(2) Importance in Sankara's over-all view.

are significant in their own right; but it is important to see them, in the broad context of Sankara's thought, as indicating how seriously he took the empirical reality of the world at the ordinary level. This is phenomenal illusionism, without any question, but it is an illusionism that is tempered with a sober-minded, if qualified, realism which at least turns the edge of many standard objections to the illusionist view.

e. The relation of the two realms: response to objections.

Sankara thought it important to illustrate the relation between the unqualified Brahman (the sole reality underlying appearances) and the world of differences (the appearances *of* that sole reality). In response to the obvious objection that a pluralistic appearance of an absolutely unqualified Reality seemed inconceivable, Sankara answered in two ways. First, he admitted the objec-

1. Inexpressible in conceptual terms,

tion and, in Hegel-like fashion, assimilated it as a part of his theory—that the relation cannot be clarified in a fully satisfactory way by conceptual means, but can only be grasped by intuitive insight, is a part of what non-dualism is trying to say; and hence, the relation is,

2. But illuminated through conceptual models.

in this sense, referred to as inexpressible (*ānir-vacaniya*). Yet this does not mean that no progress can be made toward providing illuminating conceptual models of this relation; and these illustrations in turn were themselves of two main types. One type focussed on the notion of *reflection:* the sun or the moon, for example, can be reflected in many different images on many different sorts of reflecting surfaces; and even though these images have different properties conditioned by the nature and state of the medium in which they appear (a pool, a mirror, etc.), yet they are no less real as images, and the sun or moon is in no sense either differentiated by the plurality of those images or itself characterized by the properties that distinguish one image from another. The other type of illustration focussed on the idea of *limitation,* which itself subdivides into various lines of explanation: the universal essence of humanity, for example, can be exemplified in many distinct human beings without that essence itself being in any sense divided, or limited by the qualities that distinguish those human beings from each other; and the clay, which as such is the same matter in different clay vessels, is not in itself limited by the determinate objects into which it is moulded, or, again, by the features that distinguish those objects from each other. The implications of these two different sorts of illustrations seemed, to many of Sankara's later followers, to lead in rather different directions; so much so that they divided into two different schools of Nondualism, reflectionism and limitationism, each of which took its own line of illustration as basic for further interpretation. But Sankara himself was probably not aware of this disjunction, however important it may have become in later theory; and he would have been the first to acknowledge, as indeed he often did, that all these examples were susceptible of misinterpretation, and that at best they merely relieved, but did not eliminate, the intellectual strain which the illustrations were designed to ease. What must be discerned through all this is that it is a mark and expression of ignorance to ascribe to the absolute Brahman the properties that define and distinguish its many appearances in the em-

a. The analogy of reflection.

b. The analogy of limitation.

c. Resultant division of Sankara's followers into two main schools.

d. Limited relevance of the models: the concept of superimposition.

pirical world order; such a move, in fact, is a mistaken superimposition (*adhyasa*) upon Brahman of determine qualities that are wholly transcended in the Absolute.

f. The two levels of Brahman.

If, in all this, it seems that Sankara aims at preserving, as it were, the best of both worlds, without compromising the appropriately construed reality of either, that impression will gather greater strength when we turn to the two levels in their religious context. The

1. The qualified Brahman as personal Lord and causal ground of the world.
a. Aspects of the doctrine.

qualified Brahman is the personal Lord (*Ishvara*) who, from cycle to cycle (from one general dissolution to the next), creates the world as an extension of Himself, so that He is its cause in every sense: the matter of which it is composed, the efficient cause of its emergence, the ultimate locus of the essences that are exemplified in it, and the providential director of the whole process toward morally significant ends in accordance with the principle of *karma,* which is merely another name for the objective moral order that is grounded in the un-

b. Personal theism as the highest conceptual model of God.
c. Implied religious requirement.

changing moral character of the Lord. This view of Brahman is, for Sankara, the highest conceptual understanding of God that is achievable by the discursive intellect; and what the Lord requires of men at this level is unqualified moral commitment and uncompromising moral devotion in which the individual self both recognizes his union with the Lord, whose creative expression he is, and achieves a transforming rapport of reciprocal love which transcends in its worth any alternative that we may conceive as competing with it.

2. The unqualified Brahman as absolutely non-differenced Being.
a. As devoid of all qualities, Brahman can be known only through and in absolute, intuitive Oneness.

And all this is the truth, the highest truth attainable in conceptual terms: but it is itself, in the last analysis, also an aspect of the *maya,* the cosmic-illusion. The unqualified Brahman, though truly appearing as the personal Lord and at that level truly creating the world, is beyond all determinate qualities (even those connected with personality and causation) and therefore wholly devoid of all difference; as such Brahman cannot be apprehended by conceptual reason, but only by an indiscerptible, intuitive, and absolute Oneness in which the self achieves the realized awareness of absolute

Identity. In the bracing and exhilarating air of this unimaginable height that we have visited before, there is not a trace of subject-object duality; not even the objective discernment of an individual self that enjoys its undifferentiable Oneness with Brahman—even that is consigned to the lower level. Yes, there is Being (Sat)—unqualified and absolute; there is Pure Consciousness (Chit) from which every distinction is excluded; and there is Absolute Bliss (Ananda)—unsullied self-enjoyment. But even these designations are inapplicable if they are interpreted in ways that imply intellectual discrimination: for all that has been left behind.

b. Transcendence of all subject-object duality.

Yet there is, so to speak, a point of tangency between these (seemingly) distinct levels: for if one goes down to the depth of his own inner selfhood introspectively he will finally discover his true identity as that Pure Self of Brahman, not by discerning it as an object of his therefore still dualistic awareness, but by simply being that Pure Self from which all distinctions have fallen away. And there is much that an individual can do to prepare himself for this realization: moral rigor, mental and physical self-discipline, devotion to the personal Lord—all have their place. Yet the issue cannot be forced, there is no mechanical guarantee; and when the final truth dawns, it will just be that I discover myself, from Sankara's point of view, to be what I always was, namely, absolutely non-differenced Being, since in the end that is all there is. Just as I rouse myself from a dream and face the real world of waking consciousness, so I lift my inner eye to absolute truth and awaken in the reality of *Sacchidananda*—the Pure Being, Consciousness, and Bliss of the unqualified Brahman.

c. Tangency between the two levels.
(1) Introspective identity.

(2) Individual preparation.

(3) Awakening to final truth.

Later disciples of Sankara developed a structure of dialectical arguments to urge the plausibility of the *advaita* thesis that from an ultimate and absolute standpoint, the ordinary realm is an illusory appearance of absolutely non-differenced Being. And they even paralleled the arguments of Buddhist Voidism to the effect that the categories of substance, causation, and dif-

g. The relation of Sankara's philosophy:

1. to Buddhist Voidism;

ference violate their own basic criterion of intelligibility by being intrinsically self-contradictory. Without making any attempt to decide whether there was borrowing between the two traditions (although their continuous interaction makes the supposition of such reciprocal borrowing extremely plausible), I will merely observe that this parallelism of dialectical arguments greatly strengthened the impression that non-dualistic Vedanta was a disguised version of Buddhist Voidism. The very similarity between Sankara's over-all view and that of the Voidists had created this criticism in Sankara's own day. And when we add the surprising fact that Sankara, in his commentary, gives an extensive, even tedious, critique of Buddhist Idealism, while brushing aside Voidism in a single paragraph which criticizes only a perverse misinterpretation of that view, the hypothesis that Sankara's silence meant some kind of assent seems nearly inescapable. Historically, Sankara was also accused of being a disguised Buddhist Idealist, and some interpreters regard his long effort to distinguish his view from that of Idealism as a symptom of his concern to avoid this criticism.

2. to other versions of Vedanta.

In any case, we need not be jolted when we learn that other strains of Vedanta directed toward Sankara the accusation that he was indeed a crypto-Buddhist, with his absolute monism and his phenomenal illusionism. And it is important therefore to understand the so-called dualism (*dvaita*) of Madhva, as well as the qualified non-dualism (*visistadvaita*) of Ramanuja, as reactions to what these versions of Vedanta regarded as the unscriptural extremes of Sankara's non-dualism.[1]

4. Madhva's dualism. a. The ultimacy of difference.

Madhva's philosophy, in fact, is virtually the antithesis of Sankara's, since for his dualistic outlook it is not identity but difference which is ultimate. So intent was he on emphasizing this notion of difference that he seems to have pushed it to its logical outcome in literally every area of his thought. He accepts, for example, over against phenomenal illusionism, a rigorous cosmologi-

1. Selves and material

1. For a discussion of views similar to those of Sankara, see pp. 57 ff., 63 ff.

cal realism which holds not merely that individual selves and the material substances of the empirical realm are genuinely real and objective in their own right, but that these components of the real world of nature are not even the products of divine creativity, much less extensions of the divine Being, from which in fact they are all absolutely distinct. Not only so, but every individual self (or life-monad, as Madhva calls them) is indescribably unique, as is every material substance; there are, in fact, no real essences or universal natures common to similar entities which we, for our convenience, regard as belonging to the same class and therefore call by the same name (such as man, horse, or dog). Not even the notion of similarity has a real essence as its object, since, for Madhva, the similarity of any unique particular to any other unique particular is itself unique and therefore indescribably different from every other similarity. Madhva is therefore an unflinching nominalist: difference must be defended at all costs, even if it involves the sacrifice of real essences, although there is, so far as I know, no evidence for supposing that Madhva regarded such a sacrifice as any sort of strategic loss.

Yet there is a complex sense in which individual selves and material substances, though not created by the Lord, are nevertheless dependent upon Him, while the Lord alone is self-dependent in His Being. For the Lord causes the unique and distinct material substances to evolve from the primordial state of nature, so that nature is subject to divine control and providential direction. Individual selves, on the other hand, are intrinsically changeless; each such life-monad has unique qualities that determine the whole course of its existence and its ultimate destiny. Still the selves are also dependent on God, since he controls the details of their natural environment and life-circumstances; in a sense, he even controls their destinies by causing each self to realize what is inherent in its individual uniqueness. Yet the ignorance that implicates selves in the cycle of births and even the state of release that characterizes liberated

substances as separate and uncreated in their ultimate uniqueness: the doctrine of indescribable individuality.

2. Nominalism — the denial of real essences.

b. The unique self-dependence of God.

1. His providential control of nature.

2. Individual selves as both intrinsically predetermined and yet subject to external and internal divine control.

a. Uniqueness of selves.
b. Their ultimate destiny.

souls is unique and peculiar to each individual; and Madhva even holds the view, unprecedented in Indian thought, that some souls, by their unique individuality, are destined never to achieve release at all.

It is difficult to explain why Madhva was motivated to push the category of difference so far, qualifying it only by viewing all else as dependent in its activity on the direction and control of the personal Lord who alone was self-dependent. But from the context of his thought there is a rationale that emerges. On the one

hand, he felt that the absoluteness and transcendence of the personal Lord (personality was here, for Madhva, no mere appearance, but rather ultimate truth) could be fully safeguarded only if every monistic and pantheistic tendency was discarded and God was viewed as utterly distinct from all else. Even the notion of divine creation seemed to him a compromise, since he could construe the creation of selves and material substances only by viewing them as extensions of the Being and Substance of God. On the other hand, Madhva accepted the genu-

inely objective reality of the realm of distinct selves and material things; and he felt that any qualification of the ultimate distinction of every such reality from every other would be a first logical step, through all the intervening stages, to Sankara's cosmic illusionism. He alone is safe from such a world-denying intoxication who refuses to take, not the first drink, but the first sip of its bewitching dialectical potion. This rigorous cosmologi-

cal realism, Madhva seriously believed, was unquestionably rooted in the scriptures, which repeatedly emphasized the reality of the world of difference and its distinction from the transcendent personal Lord; and

for him the ultimate spiritual state of living release involved a loving devotion to the Lord in a moral rapport in which the individual achieves god-like qualities through contemplation of the Lord as the sole object of spiritual meditation. And it was in this light that

Madhva interpreted the identity-text: what this scripture teaches is nothing like the absolute identity of the individual soul with the Lord; it rather refers to a similarity of moral qualities which outline a character that is really possible for all those destined to achieve release. Yet, while every such liberated soul reflects the divine moral character in this way, each does so in his own unique way and thus enters into a salvation reserved for himself alone.

Ramanuja's qualified non-dualism, though historically earlier than Madhva's antithesis to Sankara, provides an appealing and plausible synthesis of these extremes. Historical order is, in any event, not really decisive here, since each of the classical versions of Vedanta represented the flowering of seeds planted and germinated in much earlier times. Nevertheless, Ramanuja had the advantage of a mature historical perspective in constructing a critical assessment of Sankara's non-dualism. Not only that, but his reaction was less extreme than that of Madhva; for he did not reject non-dualism, but merely qualified it. The scriptures, he thought, were too clear in their repeated assertion that Brahman was the only reality and that all things were included in that reality to admit of any such perspective as that of Madhva. There is an inclusive Identity here, but it is an Identity which, far from excluding difference, takes up all real differences into the organic, interdependent unity of an all-inclusive whole which is precisely Brahman. Like Madhva, therefore, Ramanuja is a cosmological realist: for him, however, the real world of individual selves and material nature is the body of God, His immanent self-expression; while the transcendent selfhood of God is related to that body of the world in a way analogous to that in which each individual self is related to his own body. It is clear that self and body are inseparably associated in that it is essential to each to be related to the other (the notions of selfless body and of disembodied self were regarded as unintelligible): a body, for example, is not a body (though it may be a lifeless mass) unless it is the body of a self; and a self is not a self unless it is the inner, con-

c. The transcendent Self of God as inner controlling principle of the world as His body.
d. Preservation of difference in the inclusive totality of God.
b. Clarification of the relation between God and the world.
1. God as the creator.

2. Soul-pluralism: oneness with distinction between individual self and the Self of God.

a. Real essence of selfhood.

b. The Lord as inner controller: problem of determinism.

trolling principle of a body which is both its instrument and self-expression. And it is equally clear that the transcendent selfhood of God, though distinct from the world which is His body and therefore His inseparable self-extension, is the inner controlling principle of the world as well. There is thus a distinction between individual selves and the selfhood of God, as well as a distinction between both and the material world; but it is a distinction which, though objectively real, falls within the inclusive totality of God in his wholeness.

In detail, this means that God is both transcendent personal Lord and also the creator of both selves and the natural order out of his own creative substance. The relation, of course, is eternal: and God's creative activity with respect to the material world is that He directs and controls the evolutionary process from one world cycle to another. Selves too are a part of God's body, but the relation here is somewhat differently described. As for Madhva, so too for Ramanuja, there is a plurality of finite individual selves, so that the view of Sankara that the true self of each individual is ultimately the Self of Brahman is decisively rejected: the oneness of the selves with Brahman leaves intact the distinction between the individual self (part of the body of Brahman) and the Self of Brahman, which is transcendent in relation to that body. On the other hand, unlike Madhva, Ramanuja was no nominalist and so held that in essence and intrinsic nature each self, though individually distinct from other selves, was generically the same. The Lord is regarded as the inner controller of these selves, although it is not clear whether or not this role involved a rigorous divine determinism of the destiny of selves. Ramanuja's followers were themselves divided on this issue; but the very ambiguity of their teacher on this subject makes it at least possible for an adherent to believe that the Lord's inner control of the working out of each individual's destiny followed a direction which was itself grounded in the person's basic decision whether or not to exercise believing faith and become a recipient of the Lord's grace.

What is clear is that the ultimate personal Lord calls men to just such devotion and faith, in response to which the Lord bestows a grace which initiates a spiritual transformation that progressively actualizes the true self of the individual as essentially characterized by god-like properties. Ramanuja rejects the concept of living release, since he holds that this spiritual revolution is never complete while the individual lives; but in that state of release which follows the death of those who express genuine faith and devotion the self enters fully into the bliss and well-being that characterize a completely adequate moral oneness and communion with the Lord. But since, for Ramanuja, the relation between self and body is inseparable, the self continues to have a body even in that state of release, though it is a body thoroughly subservient to spiritual fulfillment and thoroughly expressive of the self's fully actualized bliss in the Lord. Both Madhva and Ramanuja, though they believed that the soul was not in any sense a spatial or material entity, rejected the notion that it was all-pervasive, as the pluralistic systems held. Instead, they regarded it as atomic, but explained its capacity for sensation and activity throughout the body by positing an intervening or intermediary principle of attributive intelligence or consciousness which pervades the body like a sort of illuminating light. In Ramanuja's case this seemingly awkward thesis was intended to reaffirm in this context the interdependent relation which he regarded as subsisting between soul and body.

A system like Ramanuja's faces some difficult critical questions as to how a God who includes all differences within Himself (not merely as illusory appearances, but as genuinely real aspects) can be regarded as changeless and essentially good, since the world that He creatively evolves from Himself is both pervaded by change and infected, so to speak, by both the natural evil of suffering and the moral evil of sin. A reasonable solution to the problem of Divine changelessness is clearly available here: in His transcendent selfhood the Lord is change-

c. The moral requirement of God and the state of ultimate release.

1. Rejection of living release.

2. Final release as moral oneness with God, but still in an embodied condition.

3. The soul as atomic: its relation to attributive intelligence.

d. The problem of the changelessness and essential goodness of God.
1. Hints for solution in Ramanuja.
a. God as changeless as a whole and in His transcendent selfhood.

less as Pure Subject or Self in relation to changing contents of His awareness, and in relation to the real changes going on in the world which is His body; furthermore, as embracing all reality, God in his inclusiveness is of course changeless as a whole. The problem of evil is, in a sense, more difficult: basically, in this outlook, natural evil is subordinated to moral evil through the principle of *karma;* for moral beings, at least, subjection to pain and suffering is the consequence of the morally defective condition of the soul in a state of bondage. The problem of moral evil, here as in most Indian systems, is skirted by the supposition that the soul's state of bondage, and therefore of moral defection, is without beginning, though it need not be without end, as through divine grace and release it is not.

A contemporary reinterpretation of Ramanuja's over-all interpretation is perhaps more successful in grappling with these issues. Aurobindo Ghose, like others before him, also rejects Sankara's illusionism and holds that the identity of the soul with God in the state of release is a spiritual oneness in which individual selfhood is fulfilled and transformed rather than obliterated or dissolved in the absolute selfhood of Brahman. The problem of evil, both natural and moral, is most acute, he maintains, for the sort of theistic view which regards the world as the free creation of an extra-cosmic Deity who, as ultimate personal Mind, produces a world distinct from His own Being and Essence. But if God is, so to speak, one existence without a second, so that the world is an aspect of God Himself in the form of evolutionary self-expression, then the most awkward part of the problem disappears. For it is no longer God exposing His creatures to sufferings of which He Himself, as distinct from the world, is incapable; instead, it is God, as the sole existence, exposing Himself to suffering in His creatures. And the only problem that remains is that of why God's ultimate goodness and bliss should admit into itself its apparent opposite.

Basically, Aurobindo proposes a twofold solution to this question. From one point of view, the production within Himself of such a world is the correlate of a Divine self-delight in Being which buries itself in its apparent opposite in order to recover itself, as it were, in a process through which the inner spiritual truth or reality becomes increasingly explicit and manifest. All this is the *Lila*—the sport, joy, and play—of pure Self-Delight. But this general thesis implies a further explanation with respect to the problem of evil. For if the world is, at every level of its emergence, the self-development of God, then it is a mistake to take some limited phase of this self-development as providing decisive categories for the evaluation of the whole. The ethical level, then, is a transitional stage of this evolutionary process: and it is from the limited vantage point provided by the categories of this limited level that the problem of evil seems crucial. Surely the ethical is a significant phase in the urge of God toward self-expression, and it represents a stage in the struggle toward a higher and more universal harmony of Being; but the opposition between good and evil must ultimately itself be transcended in a supra-ethical stage for which the so-called problem of evil ceases to be a perplexity. From the standpoint of the Infinite Self-Delight of God, and at the supra-ethical level, these ethical oppositions will be viewed as merging in a current of higher unity. Just as a man can attain in moments of hypnosis, high excitement, or even sheer aesthetic contemplation a kind of temporary aloofness from the normal keenness of his sensitivity to pain and pleasure in ordinary waking consciousness, so he can aim, through the rigors of self-discipline, to approximate such a liberated and transcendent selfhood as a more or less permanent possession. And if he does this, he is in the very vanguard which moves toward the fuller actualization of Divine Self-Delight. In the realization of this higher unity in God, the problem of evil, whether natural or moral, simply disappears because it has been transcended.

(3) Evil susceptible of a double explanation: (a) through the concept of Divine self-delight in projecting an opposite,

(b) Through regarding the ethical level as itself a transitional stage,

the good/evil opposition ultimately transcended.

e. Ramanuja's
critique of
non-dualism.

1. Absolutely
non-
differenced
Being
insusceptible
of support by
any means of
right
knowledge.

a. Perception.
(1) As
immediate
conscious
awareness.
(a) Essentially
characterized
by difference:
(1) between
subject, act,
and object,

(2) between
subject and
predicate of
the act's
judgment
form.

(b) Conscious-
ness of non-
differenced
Being must be
qualitatively
distinct from
ordinary
consciousness
of particular
objects.

But no account of Ramanuja's qualified non-dualism is complete without a consideration of the searching criticisms that he directs toward Sankara's absolute and unqualified monism. At the outset, Ramanuja argues that the notion of absolutely non-differenced Being, which is crucial for non-dualism in its pure form, is insusceptible of proof, or even relevant evidence, by any of the commonly recognized *pramanas* or means of right knowledge, even when those ultimate criteria are interpreted to include the very sort of intuitive and direct awareness to which Sankara and his followers appeal. If by *perception,* for example, we mean immediate conscious awareness, then it is clear on any plausible view of consciousness that it is essentially characterized by difference and therefore cannot be a means of apprehending what is totally devoid of difference. In the first place, consciousness intrinsically involves a distinction between the subject or agent of consciousness, its act of consciousness, and the object of that act; the distinction between subject and act is not only clear from the form in which knowledge-claims are typically expressed (that "I know" anything implies a distinction between the "I" and the act of knowing), but it follows also from the fact that the self that knows remains the same as pure subject, while its particular acts change by succeeding one another. But even if we confine our attention to the act of consciousness itself as apprehending an object, the judgment form of every such conscious state involves a difference between the subject of the judgment and the predicate through which something is understood about that subject (which in turn is itself an object of thought to the pure subject or self that is thinking about it). Even if there were a state of consciousness in which non-differenced Being seemed to be apprehended, that state and its object would have to have characteristics other than mere being to distinguish them from the determinate objects of ordinary consciousness and the states through which they were apprehended; and in that case, there would be a set of differences which would characterize the very object which was supposedly devoid of all such differences. And at the level of theory, finally, even the non-dualists try to render their view reasonable by distinguishing it from other views which they regard as opposing it: but how could there be any such distinction from other views if the very core of the non-dualist view is absolutely non-differenced Being and its method is that of an intuitive oneness that has transcended all distinctions?

(c) Non-dualists distinguish their view from other views.

On the other hand, if by perception we mean ordinary empirical awareness, then it is clear at once that any such perception involves a distinguishable content (over against other objects of perception) that can be apprehended only by a determinate state of awareness that is itself distinct from the states through which other perceived objects are apprehended. And this clearly means that being as such could not possibly be the object of such a perceptual act without possessing limits analogous to those of any other such object of perception. Of course, the non-dualist realizes this and does not even try to argue that the Absolute Reality can be apprehended by ordinary empirical awareness; but Ramanuja is merely trying to make his case complete. And it follows that if this analysis of perception is essentially correct, then on no reasonable interpretation whatever can absolutely non-differenced Being be the object of perception.

(2) As ordinary empirical awareness.
(a) Involves distinct content and determinate state of awareness.
(b) Hence, impossible to apprehend Being as such through any determinate act; admitted by non-dualists.

The criterion of *verbal testimony* means, in general, speech or language, and then, in particular, the witness of scripture. As for speech in general, it is scarcely debatable that the intelligibility of a word in its linguistic context depends on its symbolizing meanings that are conceptually distinguishable from each other, however vaguely and imperfectly that distinction may be recognized by a person using language as a tool of communication. And if such determinate meaning is a necessary condition of the intelligibility of words, then it must be logically impossible to express in speech that which is, by hypothesis, wholly devoid of all such determinations.

b. Verbal testimony.

(1) Intelligibility of speech depends on its symbolizing determinate conceptual meanings.

(2) Hence, the scriptures, as composed of words, cannot meaningfully express the totally indeterminate.

Now then, since the scriptures are composed of linguistic units which, if they are intelligible at all (and Ramanuja shared with Sankara the conviction that they were intelligible and indeed one of the ultimate means of right knowledge), cannot meaningfully express that which is supposed to be totally indeterminate (namely, the unqualified Brahman as understood by non-dualism), then it follows logically that no proposition of scripture can possibly teach the notion of absolutely non-differenced Being—to expect otherwise would be like expecting, after much labored searching and trial, to construct a geometrical figure that was both square and circular in the same sense and in the same respect. Yet Sankara based a significant part of his case on the so-called identity-texts of scripture; and if Ramanuja's thesis about language is correct here, then whatever else the identity-texts teach, they logically cannot teach being devoid of all difference. The scriptural statement "That art thou!" would in fact be unintelligible if we did not regard the subject-predicate distinction that characterizes this statement as expressing a unity that subsists in a twofold form; and if we were to interpret the text as teaching unqualified identity, then there would be no way of accounting for the many texts that teach a difference between the individual finite self and the transcendent self of God. The kind of difference that *is* denied by scripture, according to Ramanuja, is the sort of difference that would oppose the inclusive unity of all reality, with all the differences entailed by it, within the being of Brahman. And for Ramanuja, this inclusive unity is sufficiently established by the supposition that the world of nature and of finite selves is the body of Brahman, the inseparable correlate of His ultimate personal selfhood. For all these reasons, then, the scriptures do not, and indeed logically cannot, teach the doctrine of non-dualism.

(3) As for identity-text:
(a) cannot logically teach non-dualism,
(1) because of the nature of language,
(2) because of the subject-predicate distinction in the judgment.
(3) No way to account for the difference-texts.
(b) The difference that scripture does deny is that between Brahman as a whole and any reality believed external to Brahman.
(c) The self-body analogy as a reasonable explanation of the identity-text.

c. Inference:

If absolutely non-differenced Being can be known neither by perception nor by verbal testimony, however construed, then it is clear that it cannot be known by *in-*

ference either. For inference can take place only on
the basis of premises that are themselves ultimately
grounded in the use of the other means of right knowledge; and it depends, for the propriety of its conclusion
from those premises, on the valid relation of determinate conceptual elements in those premises, since
from premises devoid of determinate meaning no conclusion follows at all.

Any attempt to base the knowledge of the non-dual
Absolute on *comparison* or *analogy* is of course bound
to be inadequate, both because the very notion of comparison is unintelligible apart from the supposition of a
distinction between the things compared, and because
all that might be compared with the Absolute is, by the
very nature of the case, essentially characterized by difference, since only the unqualified Brahman is devoid of
all differences. For these reasons, Sankara himself admitted that the relation between the absolute Brahman
and the empirical world could not be clarified without
inconsistency and was therefore inexpressible. The examples and analogies which Sankara used were thus, as
indicated previously, imperfect models designed more
to provoke an insight than to establish a case.

But if no generally recognized means of right knowledge can provide any basis for the non-dualist concept
of non-differenced Being, Ramanuja asks, is there any
way at all of rendering that notion reasonable or intelligible to thought? The doctrine of phenomenal illusionism, it is argued, is clearly self-contradictory, since
there is no substrate for the ignorance that apprehends
it, no way of explaining how the illusion of a realm of
difference could conceivably have arisen. This pervasive
mistake cannot be traced to the individual, finite self,
since that self, as individual and finite, is merely one aspect of the error to be explained. But it cannot be traced
to Brahman either, since the qualified Brahman, the
personal Lord, is again, like the finite self, an aspect of
the illusion itself, while the unqualified Brahman is supposed to be wholly devoid of all such difference and

(1) must derive
its premises
from other
means of right
knowledge;
(2) depends on
determinate
conceptual
relations in the
premises and
conclusion.
d. Compari-
son.
(1) Implies
distinction
between things
compared.

(2) Every
analogy to the
Absolute is
admittedly
characterized
by difference.
(3) Sankara's
acknowledge-
ment of this
point.

2. Phenomenal
illusionism
clearly self-
contradictory:
no identifiable
ground from
which the
illusion could
arise.

could therefore provide no explanation for the illusory recognition of difference.

3. Intuitive knowledge of Brahman not a reasonable basis for setting aside the alleged wrong knowledge of the world.
a. Notion of such knowledge cannot be clarified.

If, finally, the non-dualists argue that the intuitive knowledge of the absolute Brahman is a sufficient basis for sublating or setting aside the wrong knowledge of the world, then Ramanuja has a plausible answer to that thesis also. For it has already been argued that there is no consistent way of clarifying the notion of such an intuitive knowledge of the non-dual Absolute. And even if, which is impossible, that clarification could be provided, then it could be a basis of setting aside wrong knowledge only if it contradicted what was regarded as wrong. However, an awareness of the wholly indeterminate can clearly not contradict anything at all: only a determinate thesis can logically contradict a determinate thesis. Hence, even if one could know the non-dual Absolute by immediate intuition, that knowledge could provide no logical grounds for consigning the world of differences to illusion and unreality.

b. The indeterminate cannot logically contradict anything.

4. The personal Lord as the absolute reality.

With such a dialectical criticism, as it were, behind him, Ramanuja now embraces not only the real world of things and individual selves as the body of God, but he also acknowledges the qualified Brahman, the personal Lord, as the ultimate Reality. If, as Sankara had himself insisted, the concept of such a personal Lord was the highest knowledge of God available to the discursive intellect, then the Lord in whose presence we find ourselves is no periphery or final limit of illusion, but rather the one true God Himself, beside whom there is no other, and beyond whom there is no higher.

a. Personal view of God not part of any world illusion.

b. The epistemological issue between Sankara and Ramanuja.
(1) Truth/ error distinction as part of the cosmic ignorance.

Much is at stake in this controversy between Sankara and Ramanuja. But at the level of epistemology the crucial issue is between an outlook which regards the whole notion of a distinction between truth and error as itself a contrast that is part of a larger error, namely, the cosmic illusion or ignorance, which must itself ultimately be transcended in spiritual intuition (Sankara); and, on the other hand, an outlook which takes the distinction between truth and error with an ultimate seriousness which cannot logically be set aside, although all error, for this view, is a kind of partial truth, an imperfect and incomplete knowledge which consists in failing to apprehend the difference between a fragment of the truth and the whole. At the level of ordinary knowledge, however, both Sankara and Ramanuja accepted the rationalistic thesis that all knowledge-claims are grounded in intrinsically valid or self-evident principles which provide the structure and framework of all intelligible thought at the conceptual level; and they therefore opposed those views which, like Nyaya-Vaishesika and some schools of Buddhism, held that there were no such intrinsically valid principles and that the propriety of all knowledge-claims had to be inferred from grounds external to the principles themselves and involving correspondence together with fruitful activity. Any such thesis, they clearly saw, would involve an infinite regress, since every premise would in turn have to be grounded in previous premises and so on without assignable limit, and that would mean that no conclusion could ever be established as sound. It is perhaps therefore to the joint credit of both Ramanuja and Sankara that they recognized so clearly the self-contradictory character of any theory that sets out to justify every knowledge-claim on independent logical grounds, even if those grounds lie in the context of successful practical activity. In the end, then, what differentiates Sankara from Ramanuja is not primarily ordinary epistemology; it is rather the question whether that ordinary epistemology must itself be finally set aside, so that what God reveals to the world, in manifesting himself as the personal Lord, is at last to be viewed as a mask, rather than, as Ramanuja believed, the true face of the Absolute.

(2) Truth/error distinction as ultimate, though error itself viewed as incomplete knowledge. (3) Both views accept the notion of self-evident first principles as starting points for ordinary knowledge; self-contradictory character of any alternative view.

c. The final difference between Sankara and Ramanuja.

Critical Problems of Hindu Philosophy: A Personal Response

Woven through all the perspectives of orthodox Hinduism is a thread of truth which our critical concern with previous views, both Chinese and Indian, has already

1. Positive value of orthodox perspectives.

a. Aspects argued in earlier contexts, and common to all the perspectives.

recognized as sound. That man is essentially a moral being capable of conscious participation in the principles of the objective moral order of reality in which he finds himself; that spiritual fulfillment involves the recognition, acceptance, and progressive realization of man's true nature as a self in the whole framework of reality rightly understood; that man has a destiny which transcends in its implications the merely biological and natural environment in which he views himself in the present scheme of things; and that true deliverance means a transformation from ignorance to knowledge, as well as from bondage to genuine spiritual freedom—all these convictions run through the otherwise distinct traditions of Hindu thought like a recurring musical theme in the successive movements of a great symphony. And since I have already expressed at some length my own conviction that these insights are reasonable, there is no need here either to rehearse these themes again or to trace the directions of thought which seem to me to emerge from them.

b. Soundness of the concept of ultimate criteria of right knowledge.

1. This includes:
a. givenness of empirical content;
b. necessity of rational categories.
2. Role of empirical perception and its basic practical reliability.

Nor is it necessary, in view of my previous defense of a qualified rationalistic apriorism, to register more than my agreement with the widely held thesis that there are ultimate standards or criteria of right knowledge, necessary first principles or starting points, as I would call them, for all intelligible thought and understanding. I further agree that among these ultimate criteria are, on the one hand, the givenness of basic empirical content as discerned in correctly interpreted ordinary perception, and the rational necessity of interpretive categories and inferential principles of formal logic. And while I believe that empirical perception provides for us more practical guidance in manipulating the objects of ordinary experience than it does pictorial representation in understanding the true nature of those objects in themselves, it nevertheless seems reasonable to me to argue that unless our basic empirical perceptions are counted on to be generally reliable in the role that they fill in

practical experience, there is no way to recognize perceptual errors, much less to correct them. Furthermore,
I also think it sound to argue, with much of the Hindu
tradition, that unless there are ultimate rational and
logical grounds for thought, no truth-claim can even be
supported as probable, since otherwise it would require
a literally infinite regression of premises to justify ac-
cepting any thesis as even plausible. In effect, I am saying that, in the end, a self-stultifying scepticism is the
only alternative (if it is an alternative at all) to the view
that the basic principles and grounds of knowledge, in
perception and reason, must be presupposed as intrinsically valid.

> 3. Essential role of ultimate rational principles.

On the other hand, and again in agreement with
some Hindu views against others, I cannot accept the
ultimacy of verbal testimony as a basic criterion of right
knowledge. That in practice we inevitably *do* rely on the
testimony of others (and especially on the established
authority of experts) for by far the greatest proportion
of what we claim to know, seems virtually indisputable.
But it seems equally clear that the ultimate grounds for
the reasonableness of any statement of testimony or authority cannot themselves be a matter of testimony or
authority. And this point can be seen in several ways:
first of all, a testimony or authoritative declaration is
itself an expression of some truth which is quite distinct
from the fact that someone testifies to it—whatever is
true, is true whether or not anyone states it, testifies to
it, or believes it; and hence truth itself cannot ultimately
be dependent upon testimony, since the grounds of
truth—however construed—are logically independent
of its being the object of testimony. Furthermore, testi-
monies and even authorities sometimes oppose one
another; and the fact that where it is important to resolve such conflicts we inevitably search for independent grounds of truth to settle these oppositions clearly
shows that testimony or authority is not an ultimate
criterion of right knowledge. There can, of course, be

> c. Critique of the ultimacy of verbal testimony.
> *1.* Verbal authority, though useful, cannot be an ultimate basis of knowledge:

> *a.* because of the distinction between testimony and truth;

> *b.* because of conflicts between authorities and the methods used to resolve them.

disagreement about those independent grounds too; disagreement, for example, about what is disclosed by perception and inference; but while it would be reasonable to take certain basic perceptual data and certain rational principles as ultimate starting points (since there is no conceivable ground of truth that is logically prior to them), it does not appear that verbal testimony can be regarded as ultimate in the same way (since by the very nature of the case such testimony always refers to a supposed truth that is logically distinct from it). More briefly, perception and inference seem to be self-correcting and self-vindicating in a way that verbal testimony does not. Of course Sankara and Ramanuja were concerned to recognize the ultimacy of verbal authority because they were committed to the view that the scriptures were the ultimate and decisive source for metaphysical truth; in this conviction they went so far as to deny that there were, in the end, any valid grounds of ultimate metaphysical truth that were independent of scriptural presuppositions—the oneness of all things with Brahman could never be known by other means of knowledge (much less established thereby) if that truth were not authoritatively grounded in, and revealed in, scripture. But there are of course other scriptures, and even those who accepted the absolute authority of the Hindu scriptures could not agree as to what they taught. Here too, then, there is a conflict of testimony which, however remote from solution in actual practice, is in principle capable of solution only on grounds that are logically independent of scriptural statements and interpretations. To put the matter bluntly, I agree with Buddha here: scriptures are authoritative only to the extent that their claims can be directly or indirectly vindicated on grounds of reason and experience which are logically independent of those claims.

But I must turn to an assessment of the relative claims of pluralism and monism in the context of orthodox philosophy. And on this issue Sankara himself has pro-

2. Not even scriptural authority can be ultimate:

a. because of other scriptures;

b. because of conflicts in interpretation;

c. because of the limitation of scriptural authority to its reasonableness on other grounds.

2. The relative claims of pluralism and monism.

duced an extensive critique of the various pluralistic views—a searching evaluation which, for the most part, I recognize as sound. In various contexts he argues that there logically cannot be a plurality of independent reals, since in that case the fact that each provided a limit to the independence of the others would be quite unintelligible. Distinctionism claims to accept a plurality of independent souls over against an equally independent order of nature: but it turns out that the status of the soul as a passive spectator is unthinkable without nature as its object, and that the subservience of the order of nature to the purposive ends of the soul implies a dependent relationship. Indeed, without the dependence of nature on the soul, there is no way at all of explaining that disruption of equilibrium, among the three qualities of nature, with which the process of natural evolution begins. Furthermore, the independent qualities of nature, as understood in distinctionism, require a further causal ground for their reciprocal relation to each other in the order of nature itself. In all these ways, the presumed plurality of independent metaphysical reals appears to fade.

Precisely similar problems, according to Sankara, confront the perspective of atomism, except that the concept of an ultimate atom, itself devoid of spatial magnitude and yet possessing qualitative differences, brings with it a whole host of further insoluble problems. The thesis of a quantum jump in which two atoms, themselves devoid of magnitude, compose a minute quantum which has magnitude seems both unintelligible and arbitrary—a device concocted, perhaps, to avoid the self-contradictory notion of the infinite divisibility of extended parts. Furthermore, if the atoms themselves are unextended and have no parts, the very supposition that they could be physically joined together becomes unthinkable: they cannot touch each other, since they have no surfaces to make such contact possible; and if they joined together as wholes they would then be indistinguishable and therefore identical.

And how can it possibly be held reasonable that atoms possess qualitative differences of type (earth, air, fire, and water): the conditions necessary for such differences involve parts that are extended—how could an unextended particle have the quality of earth? In all of this, and correctly in my opinion, Sankara sides with the so-called identity theory of causality and holds that causes must at least have those qualities required to explain the distinctive characteristics of their effects, since otherwise the causal relations would be unintelligible.

(3) Unextended atoms cannot be qualitatively different in substance.

And this last point about causality entails another criticism that Sankara directs at both distinctionism and atomism. Not only does he argue that behind every pluralism of real entities there must be a single ultimate reality. But he goes on to hold that, on the presuppositions of these pluralistic views, the evolution of the world would be grounded in a non-intelligent cause, namely, nature. But the purposive order of the world of nature, and its apparent subservience to spiritual ends, cannot be adequately explained as originating from a non-intelligent cause: only the intelligent will of the qualified, personal Brahman provides the required sort of explanation.

2. Inadequate causal explanation of evolutionary process: purposive order of nature inexplicable as product of a non-intelligent cause.

Sankara also believed, finally, that at least atomism had muddied its own metaphysical waters by introducing the notion of a realm of independently real categories, the status of which further limited the supposed ultimacy of both nature and souls. The logical order of essences implied by the doctrine of categories seemed itself to be a sort of ground for the being of these other supposedly independent real entities. And this fact further strengthens Sankara's contention that whatever the ultimate Reality is, it is unique in its independent self-existence and therefore One without a second.

3. Atomistic doctrine of real categories increases the incoherence of that perspective.

If we find, as I do, that Sankara is essentially right in his criticism of the pluralistic views (he also argues at length against the injunctivist theory of scriptural interpretation accepted by the Exegete philosophers), then we are left finally with the issues that divide the various

b. Issues that divide the Vedanta views.

Vedanta perspectives. And here both Sankara and Ramanuja provide a telling critique which, though obviously directed toward earlier versions of the view systematically elaborated by Madhva, is nevertheless a provocative and, in my opinion, effective assessment of Madhva's so-called dualistic view. As I explained previously, dualism here is quite distinct from the metaphysical pluralisms of the distinctionists and the atomists, since Madhva is basically monistic in contending that although selves and material entities are distinct from God, they are nevertheless dependent upon Him, while He alone is self-dependent. It is not difficult to see why critics could insist, against such a view and its denial that nature and souls were created by God, that the notion of dependence on God is unintelligible, in this ultimate metaphysical context, unless it involves derivation of being from God. Otherwise, this so-called dependence would be no different from the reciprocal causal relation between two or more finite things; and that analogy would suggest that God is not independent and self-existent at all. If what God does in the world of nature is merely to supervise the course of the evolutionary process, it is difficult to see how this involves a true and ultimate dependence upon God. And the case with selves is even more awkward, since what God does as inner controller here is merely to bring out the destiny already determined by the intrinsic character of each unique self. And more significant still is the contention of Ramanuja that God's self-existence and independence are compromised if, as follows from a view like Madhva's, He faces, in material entities and finite selves, limits of being and operation which in the end are neither self-imposed nor self-involved: God's transcendence and perfection are clearly threatened unless all real being is in some way not merely subject to the divine causality, but also the product of it. Ramanuja of course agreed with Madhva in rejecting Sankara's cosmic illusionism; but his own qualified non-dualism is supposed to be reasonable evidence that one need not go

1. Effective critique of dualistic outlook.

a. Independence of God compromised if souls and nature are not derived from His being.

b. No real dependence of souls and nature on God in this scheme,

and they therefore limit the transcendence and perfection of God.

to the extremes of Madhva in defending the genuine reality of the world of difference.

c. Nominalistic doctrine of universals intrinsically sceptical.

And it will be further clear, for reasons long since elaborated, that I agree with Madhva's critics in regarding the nominalistic theory of universals as self-contradictory: unless there are real essences, however construed, there is no way of adequately explaining those similarities that make the division of things into real, natural classes or types possible. On the other hand, I am both fascinated and convinced by Madhva's thesis that individual entities, whether souls or material things, are, as he puts it, ineluctably or indescribably unique. I have already argued the intrinsic individuality of each personal self as a transcendental ego; and I cannot believe that the difference between even the most similar material entities is merely numerical distinction. I rather think that every distinct reality is a unique and unparalleled focus of divine creativity which reflects the whole of being in itself, as it were, but does so in a way that is utterly unique to each such individual. However, I see no reason why, at least in the case of selves, this individual uniqueness must involve a determinateness of being that excludes all genuine freedom, as Madhva apparently held with a rigor that matches, if it does not out-distance, the rigidity of double predestinarianism in Western theology. For my part, I reject this kind of determinism in all its forms: if divine creativity can produce unique individual souls, there is no reason in principle why that uniqueness itself should not involve a capacity for creative originality in the possession of genuine moral freedom. On the whole, therefore, I agree with Sankara and Ramanuja that the sort of perspective represented by Madhva is both an unwarranted and basically unscriptural version of Vedanta, but I have tried to explain why this judgment does not, I hope, blind me to rays of genuine insight that radiate forth even here.

d. But the concept of individual uniqueness seems reasonable. (1) Illustration of the transcendental ego.

(2) This need not involve the unreality of true freedom.

e. Summary estimate of Madhva's view.

2. Soundness of Ramanuja's critique of

As for the clear disjunction between Sankara and Ramanuja themselves, all that I have accumulated by way of personal critical response places me on Ramanuja's side of the fence. There is no reason to reiterate again my objections to cosmic illusionism, or my grounds for rejecting the notion of absolutely non-differenced Being, or my cavils about a presumed state of awareness in which every principle of conceptual reason or of discursive intellect has been left behind, or even, finally, my basis for agreeing with Ramanuja in taking the concept of God, as transcendent personal mind, with absolute and ultimate seriousness. Nor can I accept Sankara's attempt, as it were, to preserve the best of both worlds by conjoining a qualified Brahman, who is personal and creative, with an unqualified Brahman that, in the final analysis, is neither. In any such interpretive juggling, for me at least, the mask of personalism would simply have to go, with the shocking discovery that underneath that mask there had never been any real face at all. And I will not even stop to quibble with Sankara about how he can defend particular views about the empirical world against other views which he rejects (perceptual realism, for example, against the qualified subjectivism of the Buddhist Idealists), when as a matter of fact he finally dismisses all such views as unreal and illusory: can there be any objectively right way of thinking about a world which, in the end, has no genuine reality, especially when there is by hypothesis no true state of determinate things of which this pervasive illusion is a perversion?

I find, then, in a perspective like Ramanuja's, the closest approximation in all oriental philosophy to a perspective that my deepest convictions and restless critical sensitivity would allow me to recognize as adequate. And I even agree with those scholars, both oriental and occidental, who view Ramanuja's system as exhibiting a greater and more serious fidelity to the Hindu scriptures than any alternative among the orthodox Hindu viewpoints. Yet here again my generally favorable attitude is scarcely unqualified. In expressing my dissatisfaction with Ramanuja's view of scriptural

Sankara and non-dualism. *a.* Previous basis for this judgment.

b. In Sankara's scheme, the doctrine of qualified Brahman could not be taken with final seriousness.

c. Implausibility of defending particular views of the determinate realm.

3. Ramanuja's view, though more adequate than any other, nevertheless involves some critical shortcomings.

a. Previous criticisms.

authority, and in opting for Madhva's view of individual uniqueness (which Ramanuja would not have accepted, since he held that liberated souls in a state of final release are distinct from one another only in the numerical sense), I have already begun to develop some of my qualifications about Ramanuja's type of view.

b. Divine transcendence and perfection compromised by Ramanuja's pantheistic stance.

But there are still deeper issues that disturb me: for one thing, I see no satisfactory way in which a monistic pantheism of this sort, for which all reality is included within the being of God, can defend itself against the charge that the divine transendence and perfection are compromised if we include in God all the processes and changes of the world, as well as all the natural and moral evil that characterizes the world. I have already

(1) Process and change inconsistent with nature of absolute reality.

explained in a much earlier context, when critically assessing Confucianism, why I think process and change are logically inconsistent with the nature of absolute reality. And I cannot regard the objective moral order and ultimate perfection or goodness, which for Ramanuja are grounded in God, as unsullied if all the

(2) Inadequacy of Ramanuja's solution to problem of evil.

natural and moral evils of the world are part of God's body, which is as essential to God as His transcendent selfhood. Ramanuja, of course, is clearly sensitive to these problems, and tries to ward them off by the twofold thesis that all these limits are aspects of the world as God's body, rather than intrinsic qualities of His transcendent selfhood, and that, in any case, all the limits, as internal to God, provide no external restriction to the divine self-completeness and perfection. But if, as this

(a) Change and evil would be as essential to God as transcendent selfhood.
(b) These limits not transcended merely by being included in God.

view holds, the Self and Body of God are essentially and inseparably related, then it would follow that change and evil are as essential to God as transcendent selfhood, and the problem remains. And I cannot resist observing that the attempt to solve these problems by making all these limits internal to God is rather like an American's dismissing the problem of the national debt by the simple suggestion that after all we owe the money to ourselves—an observation which leaves that debt right where it was before.

In all fairness, I should say that Ramanuja also suggests that the problem of evil can be alleviated for his view by the thesis that the distinction between good and evil is itself an aspect of a limited, partial, fragmentary, and transitional view of things, a sort of provisional phase whose place in the whole scheme of things more or less sublimates the inappropriate and awkward consequences of this thesis taken in isolation. But of course it is Aurobindo who, among others, works out this suggestion in detail. Now I shall have to say frankly that I feel extremely uncomfortable about this whole suggestion. What it amounts to in the end is the idea that the difference between good and evil is, from the standpoint of the whole truth, cancelled out in its consequences; and that is the same as saying that this distinction is finally illusory. Not only, in my opinion, is such an implication an unwarranted concession to Sankara and his clan; but it seriously threatens, if it does not destroy, the concept of an objective moral order of reality and the correlated notions of individual moral obligation and responsibility. I can understand a God who, as an expression of his absolute goodness, sets out to conquer the evils made possible in the world by conditions intended for better use in the service of that same ideal goodness. But I cannot understand a God who finally obliterates those very principles of moral order which, as grounded in Himself, He places on finite moral beings like ourselves as an objective framework of moral obligation and responsibility. To put it more directly to Aurobindo, for me the ethical level of reality is no mere phase of evolutionary process, finally to be made irrelevant by some higher stage; instead, that ethical level is the rediscovery of an ultimate structure of objective moral order which is as ultimate as God Himself, not, however, because it is any sort of alter ego for God, but rather because it is the very essence of the divine moral character. In the end, then, only a God whose essence excludes all process and evil while at the same time it incarnates absolute changelessness and ulti-

(3) Problems with Aurobindo's solution to the question of evil.

(a) Makes the distinction between good and evil finally illusory.

(1) Unwarranted concession to Sankara.
(2) Threatens the concepts of objective moral order, obligation, and responsibility.

(b) Unreasonableness of view that God finally obliterates the very principles that are grounded in Himself and determine human destiny.

(c) The ethical order ultimate as the essence of divine moral character.

c. View of God that emerges from these criticisms.

mate goodness can be the personal Lord before whom I can reasonably and without cavil bow in an adoration and worship through which I both recognize and fulfil my own highest selfhood.

Suggested Readings

General Background

Dasgupta, Surendranath. *A History of Indian Philosophy.* I, 1–77 (chaps. 1–4); II, 437–552 (chap. 14)—"The Philosophy of the Bhagavad Gita."

Radhakrishnan, S., and Moore, Charles A. *A Source Book in Indian Philosophy.* Pp. 3–223 (chaps. 1–6); 349–55.

Sharma, Chandradhar. *Indian Philosophy: A Critical Survey.* Pp. 1–27 (chaps. 1, 2).

Smart, Ninian. *Doctrine and Argument in Indian Philosophy.* Pp. 23–32 (chap. 1); 149–208 (chaps. 11–15).

The Orthodox Viewpoints

Distinctionism-Yoga (Sankhya-Yoga).

Dasgupta, Surendranath. *History.* I, 208–273 (chap. 7).

Radhakrishnan, S., and Moore, Charles A. *Source Book.* Pp. 424–85 (chaps. 12, 13).

Sharma, Chandradhar. *Indian Philosophy.* Pp. 137–62 (chaps. 9, 10).

Smart, Ninian. *Doctrine and Argument.* Pp. 76–88 (chap. 5).

Logic-Atomism (Nyaya-Vaishesika).

Dasgupta, Surendranath. *History.* I, 274–366 (chap. 8).

Radhakrishnan, S., and Moore, Charles A. *Source Book.* Pp. 356– 423 (chaps. 10, 11).

Sharma, Chandradhar. *Indian Philosophy.* Pp. 163–98 (chaps. 11, 12).

Smart, Ninian. *Doctrine and Argument.* Pp. 89–96 (chap. 6).

Exegesis (Purva-Mimamsa).

Dasgupta, Surendranath. *History.* I, 367–405 (chap. 9).

Radhakrishnan, S., and Moore, Charles A. *Source Book.* Pp. 486–505 (chap. 14).

Sharma, Chandradhar. *Indian Philosophy.* Pp. 199–226 (chap. 13).

Smart, Ninian. *Doctrine and Argument.* Pp. 72–75 (part of chap. 4).

Vedanta.

Absolute non-dualism (Advaita Vedanta).

Dasgupta, Surendranath. *History.* I, 406–494 (chap. 10); II, 1–227 (chap. 11); IV, 204–319 (chaps. 29, 30)—"Controversy between the Monists and the Dualists."

Radhakrishnan, S , and Moore, Charles A. *Source Book.* Pp. 506–543 (part of chap. 15).

Sharma, Chandradhar. *Indian Philosophy.* Pp. 227–77 (chaps. 14, 15).

Smart, Ninian. *Doctrine and Argument.* Pp. 97–105 (chap. 7).

Thibaut, George. *The Vedanta Sutras of Badarayana: With the Commentary by Sankara.* 2 vols.

Qualified non-dualism (Visistadvaita Vedanta).

Dasgupta, Surendranath. *History.* III, 94–138 (chap. 18), 165–398 (chap. 20).

Radhakrishnan, S , and Moore, Charles A. *Source Book.* Pp. 543–55 (part of chap. 15).

Sharma, Chandradhar. *Indian Philosophy.* Pp. 323–59 (chap. 18).

Smart, Ninian. *Doctrine and Argument.* Pp. 106–114 (chap. 8).

Thibaut, George. *Vedanta Sutras.*

Dualism (Dvaita Vedanta).

Dasgupta, Surendranath. *History.* IV, 51–203 (chaps. 25–28), 204–319 (chaps. 29, 30)—"Controversy between the Dualists and the Monists."

Radhakrishnan, S., and Moore, Charles A. *Source Book.* Pp. 555–72 (part of chap. 15).

Sharma, Chandradhar. *Indian Philosophy.* Pp. 360–63 (part of chap. 19).

Smart, Ninian. *Doctrine and Argument.* Pp. 115–22 (part of chap. 9).

Epilogue

A Concluding Reflection

And so we come at last to the end of our philosophical journey through the East, though for some it may perhaps be only the beginning of an expanding vision and a deepening insight which promise much to those who approach this still greater journey with unwavering commitment and enlightened understanding. My most profound hope is that I may have provided some ray of light, some framework of insight, or some impelling motive to all who are ready to embark on this ultimately inescapable journey in the right frame of mind. Among other things, I have tried to give some account, in my critical responses, of the way that the pieces of the existential puzzle have been gradually fitting together in a unified outlook to the implications of which I can sincerely commit myself even in my most agonizing dialectical moments. Of course, the way cannot be easy for any sincere and earnest inquirer. Still, love demands that we take seriously the deepest convictions of our fellow human beings in every age of history and every focal point of culture; and in the end, it is from the ongoing struggle to see these convictions in their true light that each man will be able to forge that chain of beliefs which will bind him in fulfilling ethical love to the inclusive moral community of being to which he truly belongs.

Reference Matter

Appendix A / Jainism:
A Philosophy of Individualism
and Self-Denial

Historical Roots: The Relation of Jainism
to Other Indian Traditions

The historical origin of Jainism, as an alternative to Buddhist
and Hindu perspectives, is veiled in considerable obscurity.
While Vardhamana (known religiously as Mahavira or the
great hero) is commonly referred to by certain scholars as the
founder of the Jain religion, there is significant evidence that
actually he was the last prophet and systematizer of an ancient
religious tradition that extends back at least to the Vedic
period and perhaps even earlier. In any case, Jain tradition
and literature have it that Mahavira (599–527 B.C.) was the
last in a line of twenty-four *jinas* (victors), or founders of the
path, whose collective spiritual achievements are responsible
for the Jain religion.

Mahavira was then an older contemporary of the Buddha,
and the details of his spiritual pilgrimage are similar—born
in a noble (possibly even royal) household, he grew up in
luxury and married at a young age; but when he had turned
thirty, full of inner unrest, he set out to seek spiritual self-
realization through a vigorous program of self-denial which
ultimately included nakedness as an expression of his renunciation of all worldly goods. After twelve years of searching,
he finally achieved *kevala* (infinite and perfect knowledge),
while sitting meditatively in a field under the warm sunshine.
In this experience he destroyed the effect of *karma,* achieved
release from the cycle of births, and thus became the last
founder of the Jain path. As in the case of Gautama, Maha-

1. Possible
antiquity of
Jainism.
a. Mahavira as
the last of the
prophets.

b. Sketch of
Mahavira's
spiritual quest:
its similarity to
that of
Buddha, his
contemporary.

vira's experience was not a confrontation with Brahman or God, but rather an individual self-conquest, self-knowledge, and self-realization. Buoyed up by this fulfilling experience, he gave himself for the balance of his life to the energetic teaching of the truths he felt he had inherited and discerned, and to the founding of the actual ascetic order of the Jains.

2. Rejection of the ultimate authority of the Hindu Veda.
a. The gradual emergence of the Jain sacred writings.
1. Period of oral tradition.
2. Traditional view of the fixing of the Jain sacred canon.
b. The commentarial tradition: some chief writings.

As a heterodox system, Jainism from the first rejected the ultimate spiritual authority of the Veda (the sacred literature of Hinduism). But through the accumulation of traditional teaching, the Jains ultimately developed their own sacred literature—at first preserved through oral tradition for an indeterminate period of time, then gradually and partially written down until at last it achieved definitive literary form many centuries after Mahavira's death. One widely held scholarly opinion contends that the *Angas* and / or *Siddhantas* (precepts and treatises), as the sacred lore was called, achieved a fairly fixed oral and written determinateness about 300 B.C., but that the final redaction of this literature into something like an authoritative canon did not take place until about the fifth century A.D., or a millennium after the time of Mahavira. As in the case of Hinduism, an extensive commentarial tradition grew up around the sacred writings of Jainism over many centuries of time, and it is to the literature composing and surrounding this tradition that we must turn to find the great classical expositions of Jain philosophy. Among the most influential writings of this sort would be *An Examination in Thirty-two Stanzas of the Doctrines of Other Systems* by the Jain scholar Hemacandra (1088–1172 A.D.), and an extensive thirteenth-century A.D. commentary on this work by Malli-shena.

3. Relation of Jain philosophy to other Indian viewpoints.
a. Core of common beliefs: cycle of births, transmigration, *karma,* and release.
b. Distinctive comparative features.
1. Non-theistic outlook.

If now we try to characterize and situate the Jain philosophy conceptually in relation to other Indian perspectives, it is clear that Jainism shares the basic core of religious conceptions common to Hinduism and Buddhism—the belief in a cycle of births through which individuals in a state of bondage transmigrate in a succession of life circumstances determined by the principle of *karma* and the expectation of release from that bondage through a self-realization that destroys the effect of *karma* and introduces the individual into a state of perfect knowledge and enlightenment. Like Buddhism in its original (Hinayana) form, Jainism is non-theistic, if not atheistic, so that salvation is an individual achievement inspired by the "founders of the path." But unlike Buddhism, and in agreement with Hinduism, the Jain perspective believes in the permanent soul or self (called *jiva*) as enduring relatively unchanged through successive experiences and lives. More specifically, Jainism exhibits many similarities to the pluralistic realism of the Sankhya (distinctionism) and Vaishesika (atomism) philosophies of Hinduism: it holds with these views to the existence of eternal individual souls over against an eternally existing order of physical nature; and further agrees in rejecting the phenomenal illusionism of nondualistic Vedanta in Hinduism and the Mahayana perspectives in Buddhism. The further characterization of these distinctive emphases involves the systematic exposition of the Jain perspective—a task to which we now turn.

2. Permanent soul.

3. Pluralistic realism.
a. Plurality of individual souls.
b. Objective reality of the empirical world order (rejection of phenomenal illusionism).

The Jain Theory of Knowledge and Its Application to Metaphysics and Ethics

Jainism purports to base the truth-claim of its philosophical position not on any arbitrary appeal to religious authority, but on a reasoned interpretation of relevant human experience. It follows that the theory of knowledge is crucial for the whole perspective. There are, it is contended, five basic kinds of knowledge: the first two are regarded as mediate and indirect, since they result in knowledge only through a process of conceptual interpretation. Thus ordinary knowledge-claims are grounded in perception and inference, neither of which can constitute genuine knowledge by itself since the former lacks meaning and intelligible order, while the latter lacks content as a basis for inferring. Through the interaction of perception and inference, however, genuine cognition is possible and involves structured perceptual awareness, memory, recognition, empirical generalization, etc. The other sort of mediate knowledge involves the analysis of various linguistic signs and symbols, and the achievement of an understanding of the various ways in which words are both vehicles of meaning and at the same time refer to objects. This sort of insight involves the recognition that if any proposition or statement can be considered from many different aspects or standpoints, then no truth-claim can be absolute or unconditional—a recognition that leads, as we shall see, to the Jain doctrine of the relativity of knowledge.

1. Theory of knowledge.
a. Logical priority of a reasoned interpretation of experience.
b. Five basic kinds of knowledge.
1. Mediate.
a. Ordinary cognition involving perception and inference.

b. Knowledge based on linguistic signs and symbols combined in statements: the doctrine of multiple viewpoints, and the resultant relativity of knowledge.
2. Immediate.

The other three kinds of knowledge are considered by the Jains to be direct and immediate, since they apprehend their objects without intervening logical steps grounded in conceptual interpretation through perception and inference: such are

a. Clairvoyance.
b. Telepathy.
c. Omniscience.

clairvoyance (direct knowledge of things remote in space and time), telepathy (direct knowledge of the thoughts of other minds), and the all-comprehensive, perfect omniscience which characterizes only the liberated soul in a state of release from the cycle of births.

c. Contrast between perfect knowledge and the limited degrees of lesser knowledge grounded in the state of bondage.

According to Jain theory, every soul is intrinsically conscious and potentially characterized by the infinite knowledge which only the liberated soul possesses in fully actualized form. Lesser degrees of knowledge are the result of the obscuring effect of the embodied state of bondage through the operation of the principle of *karma.* And this thesis returns us again to the consideration of the Jain doctrine of the relativity of all ordinary truth claims.

1. Relativity of all ordinary truth claims.
a. Variety of standpoints as implying that no statement is unconditionally true,

so that statements from different standpoints may oppose one another.
b. Philosophical error largely due to wrongly universalizing a limited standpoint.
(1) Illustration of this error in other systems.

Since any object of thought about which a statement may be made can be considered from an unlimited variety of aspects or standpoints (*nayas*), it follows that the truth-claim of such a statement is relative to the limited context prescribed by that standpoint or framework of consideration. No statement, therefore, is absolutely or unconditionally true; and it is even possible for a given statement to be true from one standpoint and false from another. It is important to see, however, that this thesis does not mean that a statement can be both true and false from the same standpoint, as if contradictory statements could both be true. If, however, one mistakes a limited standpoint for the whole truth, one will be in error by regarding as absolutely true a statement that is true only from that limited standpoint. According to the Jain philosophers, that is exactly the mistake that proponents of other systems of philosophy have made. Absolute non-dualists, for example, emphasize the understanding of things from the point of view of the universal classes to which they belong, and end up by dissolving all particular differences in the abstract, indeterminate Being of the unqualified Brahman; while Buddhist theory, at the other extreme, regards things from the standpoint of their status as fleeting, momentary particulars constituted through a collection of individual qualities. Both standpoints are misinterpretations if they are regarded as absolute: the real truth is found in the synthesis of all the standpoints in an all-inclusive whole.

(2) Real truth as a synthesis of standpoints.

c. Resultant conditional status of ordinary truth claims:

Because this all-inclusive vision is accessible only to the liberated soul, all ordinary truth-claims must be conditionally stated with a "maybe" or a "perhaps"—or, in the original language, a "*syad.*" With this qualification, one can then proceed to sketch a framework for comprehensive understanding by discerning that from one point of view a thing is, from another it is not, from still another it is indescribable, etc. A thing can be a clay pot only by not being an indefinite variety of other things and therefore not possessing existence in the absolute or unlimited sense of all-inclusive being in general; and precisely because of the difference among these various standpoints, the thing may also be regarded as indescribable.

various ways in which an object may be considered.

This Jain doctrine of contextual relativisim (the relativity of any truth-claim to the limited context in which the claim is propounded) was perhaps sometimes regarded as itself an absolute or unconditional truth; but in the hands of wiser interpreters even the relativity doctrine was regarded as a limited mode of understanding, and it therefore provoked a corresponding humility in those who advocated Jain philosophy, so that in principle at least other systems of thought were also tolerantly regarded as partial truths.

2. Contextual relativism as motivating humility and tolerance.

All this theorizing had, of course, extensive implications for the Jain view of reality. From an epistemological standpoint, at the level of ordinary knowledge, the Jains are perceptual realists: that is, they hold that the soul's conscious empirical experience of objects as relatively enduring sets of qualities corresponds to the real and independent state of those objects as they exist independently of consciousness. And hence, metaphysically, this perceptual realism involves cosmological realism, the doctrine that the real world itself is not a phenomenal illusion but an order of reality actually characterized by distinct things and changes as those are disclosed to conscious experience. In a way, therefore, knowledge of the real world arises through sense perception; but since the soul itself is intrinsically conscious and characterized potentially by full and perfect knowledge, the role of sense perception consists more in occasioning and provoking the rise of knowledge than in providing the generative source of it—it is more a case of the veil of obscurity being removed than of the content of knowledge being externally supplied by the senses.

2. Metaphysics
a. The Jain view of reality and its relation to epistemology.
1. Perceptual realism as correlated with cosmological realism.
2. Rejection of phenomenal illusionism.
3. Real world apprehended through sense perception as occasion for the manifesting of the soul's intrinsic knowledge.

The general framework of Jain metaphysics is thus a counterpart of the pluralistic realism of certain orthodox Hindu views like distinctionism (*Sankhya*) and atomism (*Vaishesika*). A plurality of eternally existing individual souls (*jivas*), each intrinsically conscious and intelligent, over against an equally eternal and independently real order of

b. Pluralistic realism involving:
1. eternal individual souls (*jivas*);

2. real order of physical

existence
(*ajiva*)

3. Concept of souls at every level of life, all capable of progressing toward release: degrees of consciousness determined by degrees of material infiltration.

4. Atomic structure of matter.

3. Jain ethical theory.
a. Bondage as involving ignorance and enslavement by passion.
b. Meditation and moral austerity as the path to release.

1. Rigor of the moral requirement.

2. Release as an individual achievement.

physical existence (the *ajiva* or non-living): that is the Jain picture of reality. All living things, from the lowest to the highest, contain souls which are co-extensive in space with the bodies they occupy; and the different souls differ in degrees of consciousness according to their degree of involvement in matter through the principle of *karma,* so that it is the soul's infiltration by matter that obstructs its vision and understanding. As the Jains see it, all souls, from those of plants at one extreme to those of human beings at the other, are capable of rising above their obstructive material bonds through a succession of lives, and eventually achieving final release from the cycle of births.

The material world itself (*ajiva*) is basically atomic in its structure, and it is important to distinguish between matter as thus structured and possessing form, on the one hand, and those aspects of the external nature that are non-substantial and therefore without form such as motion, rest, time, and space. It is, of course, the involvement of the soul in this non-conscious world, its infiltration by matter according to the principle of *karma,* that accounts for, and constitutes, the soul's state of bondage.

The final aspect of Jain teaching therefore concerns its ethical theory and its concept of release through knowledge and right conduct. Basically, the bondage of the soul to the cycle of births exhibits itself in ignorance of the soul's true condition and a consequent enslavement by disruptive passions and emotions. These symptoms of bondage can be overcome through a process of disciplined meditation and moral austerity which, rightly followed out, will break the effects of *karma* and lead to that state of *kevala* or perfect knowledge in which involvement in the cycle of births is finally transcended and emotional enslavement decisively left behind. The moral demand is rigorous for those intent on full release: it requires a way of life which pledges non-injury to all living things (*ahimsa*); complete fidelity to truth in thought, word, and deed; an absolute ban on stealing of any sort; abstention from all forms of self-indulgence; and the sheer renunciation of all but the most minimal worldly goods. And it is an achievement that each individual must win for himself—inspired, no doubt, by the example of the founders of the path, but carried through by intense personal self-discipline. Yet the goal of release is well worth the effort, since it involves a state of infinite knowledge, infinite bliss, and infinite power—a glorious condition which we can but dimly glimpse in our present obstructed state of bondage.

3. Aspects of the state of final release.

Critical Problems of Jain Philosophy: A Personal Response

The Jain philosophical perspective bears so many affinities to positions I have previously analyzed and evaluated that it is hardly necessary, for the most part, to do more than summarily refer to those earlier results. On the positive side of the ledger, for example, I have already expressed my sympathy with the helpful corrective role that can be played by recognizing, within limits, the tentative and approximative status of all ordinary truth-claims, in view of the limited context and complex influencing factors within which such claims are propounded (see my critical response to Taoism). And I have, with the Hindu pluralistic realists as well as with the Vedanta perspectives of Ramanuja and Madhva, defended the real existence of the realm of empirical reality against all forms of phenomenal illusionism, such as occur in the philosophies of Sankara and the Mahayana Buddhists. It has likewise been made clear that I side with both Buddhism and Jainism in defending the logical priority of a reasoned interpretation of experience over all ultimate and therefore arbitrary appeals to religious authority as itself logically ultimate. Finally, I am committed, along with most oriental perspectives, to the concept of an objective moral order of being which poses a framework of unconditional moral requirement for all rational moral selves—a thesis which Jainism also shares.

1. Implications of previous criticism for the evaluation of Jain philosophy.
a. Summary of positive critical results.

On the negative side of the ledger, I have pointed out the potentially self-contradictory character of any universal doctrine of the relativity of ordinary knowledge, I have argued against all metaphysical pluralisms on the ground that a plurality of ultimate beings is unintelligible in the final analysis, so that, beyond and behind every plurality of beings or principles, it is reasonable to believe that there is a single, self-existent, self-explanatory ground of being to the causal operation of which all contingent beings might ultimately be attributed; and I have even suggested that an objective moral order of being is rendered fully intelligible only if we regard

b. Summary of negative critical results.

this framework of moral obligation as grounded in the moral character of an ultimate personal Mind.

2. Critique of some special Jain emphases.

It is therefore obvious that the cumulative effect of my previous critical responses bears heavily on my evaluative assessment of a perspective like Jainism. Yet the Jain position embodies certain distinctive emphases that merit further critical consideration. If, with this outlook, for example, we are to hold that all ordinary truth-claims are contextually relative in the sense explained, what is the logical status of this claim itself? Is this claim limited to some further context and so on without assignable limit? Or is there some discoverable ultimate framework of ultimate categories and interpretive principles which is itself the logically final basis of all contextually limited truth-claims as well as being the arbiter of all opposition among such contexts themselves? If we subscribe to an infinite regress of contexts, what keeps the whole position from undermining the reasonableness of any truth-claim whatever? And if we subscribe to a framework of ultimate categories and principles which function as necessary presuppositions of all possible thought, have we not, in principle at least, transcended the contextual relativism doctrine itself? Such questions, at the very least, provide an extended area for further investigation into the problem of the grounds of knowledge. Jainism itself envisions a totality of insight which combines the various limited and often conflicting contexts into an inclusive integrative understanding that weaves the fragments of truth into a sort of organic whole; but perhaps more needs to be said by this tradition to clarify the ultimate epistemological implications of that vision.

a. Possible self-stultifying character of contextual relativism.
1. Statement of the difficulty.

2. Jain concept of truth as organic totality.

b. Implausibility of the claim that finite souls, though liberated, are omniscient.

Of course, all partial viewpoints, by hypothesis, are left behind, according to Jain theory, in the infinitely perfect knowledge of the liberated soul. But I find it difficult to understand the claim that finite souls, even though released from the cycle of births, are omniscient. It would seem, on the one hand, that the defining limitations of a finite individual would preclude the sort of all-inclusive, exhaustive insight that such a claim entails, since a finite consciousness could not plausibly be regarded as capable, given its temporally successive and restricted character, of being at any time explicitly conscious of all the objects of knowledge and their complex relationships; and it appears reasonable, on the other hand, that perfect knowledge would be genuinely predicable only of an infinitely perfect reality that was both self-existent and self-explanatory in such a way that all contingent being depended upon it for existence, whereas Jainism has no room for such a religious and metaphysical Absolute.

Finally, even if one accepts a view of reality in which existence at every level involves the correlation of a material substratum with some sort of immaterial soul, it is baffling to contemplate the means by which the souls of plants, insects, and lower animals could transmigrate to higher levels and ultimately achieve release. At such levels, the soul principle lacks the operative conditions necessary to make the spiritual ascent conceivable: such ascent would seem to require the sort of clear self-conscious awareness that is capable of recognizing the soul's plight and spontaneously moving toward the spiritual goal through organized, purposive self-discipline. So far as we can discern, these qualifications begin to appear only at the human and personal level of life.

c. Possibility of spiritual progress difficult to conceive below the personal level.

Yet the Jain vision is nevertheless a stirring challenge that provokes in all of us a humility that becomes the hampering restrictions of our present state, while it summons the most courageous among us to the sort of rigorous self-discipline which at the very least points us in the direction of spiritual self-realization.

3. Summary statement of the Jain challenge.

Suggested Readings

Dasgupta, Surendranath. *A History of Indian Philosophy.* I, 169–207 (chap. 6).

Radhakrishnan, S., and Moore, Charles A. *A Source Book in Indian Philosophy.* Pp. 250–71 (chap. 8).

Sharma, Chandradhar. *Indian Philosophy: A Critical Survey.* Pp. 36–56 (chap. 4).

Smart, Ninian. *Doctrine and Argument in Indian Philosophy.* Pp. 62–69 (chap. 3).

Appendix B / Materialism
in Indian Philosophy

Historical Roots

Although the overwhelming impression created by the classical traditions of Indian philosophy is clearly religious and spiritualistic in viewing the soul as having a destiny distinct from that of the material world and the physical body—a destiny, further, that is ultimately understood and determined on religious grounds—it is nevertheless generally conceded that an opposing anti-religious and essentially materialistic tradition extends back to very early times, perhaps to the early Vedic period itself. However, since most of the original source materials of this tradition have been lost and we are indebted for our knowledge of materialism to negative polemical sections in the treatises of the other Indian philosophical schools, there seems to be very little reliable information about the historical origin and development of the school. It is usual to refer to the school with the term *Carvaka*, but it is not certain whether this is the name of the school's founder or is to be interpreted as a descriptive term based on the root of the word, which literally means *to eat;* and in the latter case, there is no agreement as to the significance of the term, whether, for example, it refers to the school's emphasis on bodily pleasures as the only plausible goal of human life, or perhaps refers to the sceptical trend of this perspective in voraciously gobbling up the theories of other philosophical systems by means of destructive criticism. Other designations include *Lokayata* (since it holds that only this present world order or *loka* exists) and *Svabhavavada* (literally, the doctrine of self-being, since it holds that the natural world requires no explanation beyond itself).

1. Antiquity of the materialist tradition.
a. Essentially spiritualistic tenor of Indian thought.
b. Anti-religious character of materialism.
c. Nature of historical source materials.
2. Terminology and definitions.
a. *Carvaka.*

b. *Lokayata* and *Svabhavavada.*

195

The acknowledged *sutra* or treatise of the school is traditionally ascribed to a sage named Brihaspati who is thought
to have lived about 600 B.C., but that treatise too has per-
ished in antiquity. While there are summaries of materialistic
doctrine in various other treatises, therefore, it appears that
the only surviving authentic text is a book of the seventh century A.D. entitled, as literally translated, *The Lion Assaulting
All Philosophical Principles,* by Jayarashi Bhatta.

A Summary of Carvaka *(Materialistic Doctrine)*

From an epistemological point of view, the sole *pramana,* or
means of right knowledge, that the materialists accepted was
that of perception, which they regarded as the only plausible
basis for grounding a truth-claim. Partly because of the anti-
religious stance of the school, verbal testimony, especially as
involving any appeal to religious authority, was rejected out of
hand as arbitrary and logically dependent upon perception itself as its final basis. But even logical inference was disowned
as an ultimate *pramana:* deductive inference, or formal logical demonstration of a conclusion from premises which, if
true, would necessarily entail the truth of the conclusion, was
rejected as indecisive on the ground that in such an argument
the truth of the major premise already presupposes as its basis
the truth of the conclusion, so that the reasoning is circular
and question-begging; inductive inference, or the establishment of a generalized thesis from the consideration of particular observed instances of the phenomenon in question,
was held to be limited to actually perceived cases, while the extension of a general truth to unperceived cases would depend
on an invariable association or causal relationship which was
regarded by the materialists as a sheer arbitrary assumption.
For example, when deductively one argues from (1) All men
are mortal, and (2) Socrates is a man, to the conclusion (3)
Therefore Socrates is mortal, it seems evident that the truth of
the first premise (1) is based on the assumed truth of the conclusion (3), since (1) could be true if, and only if, (3) were also
true. And when one argues inductively from cases of being
burned by fire to the conclusion that one will be burned by fire
in an as yet unperceived instance, one must assume an invariable causal connection or association between fire and
being burned; but that assumption is clearly arbitrary, since it

cannot, by hypothesis, be observed, and it cannot be established by inductive inference, since all such inference is based on that very assumption itself. The materialists, therefore, were intrinsically sceptical of all truth-claims that went beyond the realm of present perception or observation, although they acknowledged as probable inferences from what is actually perceived to conclusions about what is in principle perceptible, though not actually perceived. But they strongly rejected all inference from the perceptible to any conclusion about what is in principle imperceptible, such as an immaterial soul, or an ultimate spiritual Being (God, Brahman, or whatever).

The materialist doctrine of reality parallels its epistemological perspective: since matter is the only reality apprehended by sense perception, material substance was regarded as the only reality. In turn, it was held that matter itself was fundamentally composed of the four basic elements: earth, air, fire, and water. These eternal elements enter into various combinations to produce the succession of changing entities that make up the world in process. The soul is not therefore a qualitatively distinct substance, but is either identical with the physical body or some physical process within it, or else it is the capacity for consciousness generated by the unique combination of bodily elements in a certain proportion. Mental operations are therefore either identical with certain bodily processes or alternatively the functional by-product of those processes, and in either case, the cessation of bodily existence at death involves the destruction of mental operations for any given individual. Consequently, the soul does not survive physical death in any sense, and there can be no such thing as the transmigration of the soul through a succession of lives. In answer to the obvious objection that mental states appear introspectively to be so different in quality from physical states that the derivation of mental processes from physical causes (much less their identification with those causes themselves) seems totally implausible, the materialists answered that there are numerous cases in perceived experience to illustrate the emergence of effects from causes that are totally different in quality from the effects they produce. The stupor produced as an effect of drinking an alcoholic beverage, for example, has no observable qualities in common with the beverage that is regarded as producing that stupor; and analogously, it is not unreasonable to regard consciousness as an effect of causes that are as distinct in quality from mental states as wine is from stupor. More generally, the material universe as a whole is regarded as both eternal and self-explanatory, so that it requires no causal explanation by reference to an ultimate spiritual ground.

The ethical implications of the materialist outlook seem clearly compatible with its epistemological and metaphysical perspective: the notion of an objective moral order involving, through the operation of *karma,* a reciprocal relation between life circumstances and the individual's moral state was totally rejected. There are, then, no objective moral values; and moral beliefs are either a projection of individual desires, or a product of social convention, or a combination of the two in varying proportions. From such a relativistic point of view, the only expedient goal of life for the individual would be the pursuit of personal pleasure and the avoidance of personal pain, so far as wit and prudential self-interest could bring these about.

c. Ultimacy of the material universe.

3. Ethical implications.

a. Rejection of an objective moral order.
b. Moral beliefs grounded in desire and convention.
c. Pleasure as the expedient goal of life.

Some Critical Reflections: A Personal Response

It is hardly surprising that the main traditions of Indian philosophy, preoccupied as they were with the destiny of the soul and its bondage to the cycle of births through the operation of *karma,* were not only unattracted by the materialist alternative but virtually buried it in obscurity under a mountain of criticism. It was argued by representatives of those main traditions, for example, that perception alone could provide no basis for truth-claims without being conjoined with inference and interpretation, and that the materialist criticisms of inference were themselves grounded in the very sort of inferential processes that it was the point of that criticism to reject. Against the materialist doctrine of consciousness as a by-product of bodily processes, it was urged that the qualitative difference is too extensive to permit such a derivation; that mental states are known directly only in private introspection by each individual for himself while physical states are in principle publicly observable; that the materialist thesis could not explain the subjective unity that pervades conscious states and accounts for their continuity as phases of a single inner self; and that the mere correlation between mental

1. General opposition of Indian philosophy to materialism; summary of some negative critical arguments.
a. Epistemological.

b. Metaphysical.

states and bodily states does not establish the total dependence of the former on the latter. As for the ethical radicalism of *Carvaka,* it was universally argued that the materialist outlook would destroy any defensible notion of the meaningfulness or enduring significance of human life; and that the hedonistic defense of the pleasure-principle on grounds of pure individual expediency was not so much a moral ideal as it was the destruction of all morality without exception.

c. Ethical.

The whole orientation of my personal critical responses to the oriental perspectives I have discussed should make it clear that I am in full sympathy with the general criticism of materialism in the main traditions of Indian philosophy. In various contexts, for example, and especially in my discussion of Confucianism, I have defended at length the very sort of moral objectivism that the Indian materialists rejected; and in equally numerous contexts, I have argued the reasonableness of regarding the natural order of existence as dependent upon a transcendent realm of being. I therefore refer the reader to the cumulative effect of all that previous discussion on the critical evaluation of materialism. If there is any respect in which I have not expressed myself fully enough to provide a summarily adequate framework for reflecting critically on the materialist outlook, it would be in not providing a thorough discussion of the reasonableness of the thesis (widely shared by oriental perspectives) that man has an essential spiritual selfhood which cannot, as materialism supposes, be adequately explained as a sheer chance by-product of physical forces and bodily processes. It will hardly be contested, however, that this is not the place—in a brief appendix on a relatively insignificant aspect of Indian philosophy—to discuss the nature of the mind and its relation to the body: that would require another treatise greater in length than the present one. Suffice it to say in passing, first, that if mental processes and states are wholly the by-product of purely physical causes, then there is little reason to suppose that the functioning of these processes will lead to any defensible truth-claims unless we make the incredible and monumental assumption that physical causes are totally parallel to, and productive of, the logical grounds of reasonable belief—and that assumption, if accepted, would cast all other evidence of teleology or purpose in the universe (a result that materialism would hardly welcome) into the shade; and the implication of these develop-

2. Author's general acceptance of this negative criticism; a reference to previous critical results.

a. Acknowledged incompleteness of the criticism.

b. Two consequences of materialism. *1.* Undermining of the reasonableness of all truth-claims.

2. General
impertinence
of religious
philosophy.

ments would be that neither materialism nor any opposing thesis could consistently claim to be even an approximation of truth. And more generally, to regard the spiritual self of man as the accidental by-product of the churning of the physical universe with mindless motion would be to reduce the pertinence of any discussion of religious philosophy to very small proportions indeed, unless it would, more drastically, render the whole analysis totally irrelevant. Such a consideration does not of course settle the argument one way or the other; but it does recognize the enormous price that must be paid by the advocate of a rigorously materialist outlook.

Suggested Readings

Radhakrishnan, S., and Moore, Charles A. *A Source Book in Indian Philosophy.* Pp. 227–49 (chap. 7).

Sharma, Chandradhar. *Indian Philosophy: A Critical Survey.* Pp. 28–35 (chap. 3).

Smart, Ninian. *Doctrine and Argument in Indian Philosophy.* Pp. 70–72 (part of chap. 4).

A recurrent theme in practically all the Indian philosophies, and one with which I have yet to deal in a reflectively critical way, is the whole concept of reincarnation. It is not difficult to sketch the grounds which make this notion all but universally plausible among Indian thinkers: for one thing, the concept is woven into the very fabric of the cloth of primordial religious tradition from which the various Indian views, in one way or another, emerged. But more importantly this doctrine appears on the whole to provide a basis for reconciling the concept of moral order embodied in the principle of *karma* with the empirical facts about our human situation. The circumstances and native endowments of different human individuals, and even of entire cultures, are so strikingly various and, apparently at least, so uncorrelated with the moral state of these individuals in the present life that, if we confine our attention to this context, it seems extremely difficult to suppose that the distribution of privileges and powers is expressive of any sort of principle of reasonable and proportionate justice; indeed, at least in the short range, the very opposite seems to be the case. On the other hand, if these conditions of life are themselves the appropriate consequences of moral choices and responses made in previous lives, then that would at least make it reasonable to believe in an objective and ideal moral order of being. And when we add to this the whole body of testimony provided by those who claim that they remember their previous lives and even provide testable details to support those claims, at least in some well-documented cases, the case seems even stronger.

> 1. Supporting grounds for the concept.
>
> a. Tradition.
>
> b. Moral order and distributive justice.
>
> c. Memory claims.

2. Critical difficulties.
a. Relative absence of memory data; possibility of an alternative explanation.

b. No way to explain the origin of the cycle.

1. Implausible to regard the cycle as without beginning.
(a) Infinite series self-contradictory.
(b) Makes the cycle of births an inexplicable and brute fact.
(c) In an infinite time, the process of release should have been completed in the infinite past.
2. Sankara's illusionism equally unreasonable.
3. Plausibility of a symbolic reinterpretation of the concept.

Yet the concept of reincarnation is certainly beset with difficulties in the context of Indian philosophy. For one thing, most people, whether in the East or in the West, have no memory whatever of having lived previously, much less of any details of previous lives; and as for those who do claim such memories, it is at least possible to explain them as presumably sincere misinterpretations of mental contents acquired by some sort of clairvoyance or telepathic thought transference, although that subject is far beyond the scope of what I would attempt to deal with here. But more importantly from a philosophical point of view, it is difficult to understand how any such cycle of births could be initiated in the first place, if variation in life circumstances and capacities must always be the consequence of previous choices; and if there is any exception to this rule which would explain the circumstances of one's first incarnation, there is no reason in principle why that exception could not provide an explanation for this set of circumstances for the present life, in which case the hypothesis of reincarnation would become superfluous.

Indian views commonly solve these problems by supposing that the state of bondage to the cycle of births is without beginning. But I regard this view as unreasonable for several reasons: first, the concept of an actually infinite and successive series of lives is, I think, self-contradictory; second, the thesis that the cycle is without beginning leaves every view that accepts it with a kind of ultimate and inexplicable metaphysical surd which has to be accepted as a kind of brute fact about which nothing further can be said. My most serious objection, however, is that, since most Indian views believe that ultimately everyone will achieve release from the cycle of births, it is difficult for me to see why, in an infinite series of such chances, this release has not already been achieved by all. It is not surprising therefore that Sankara dismisses these problems with the supposition that the whole notion of rebirth is a part of the grand illusion; but that thesis, as we have seen, has difficulties of its own.

Frankly, then, I do not know how to resolve this whole muddle on philosophical grounds. But if the concept of reincarnation could be symbolically interpreted as a commitment to the view that in the end every rational, moral being will have to accept and deal with the consequences of his own responsible moral choices, then that position seems to me to be unquestionably sound. And if that is so, then two further things may also be the case: that many of the inequities of the human situation may themselves be the effect of irresponsible moral choices, and that each man may be viewed as bearing about in the quality of his own moral character the irreversible imprint of his own ethical choices. In the end, the worst consequence of wrong moral choice is that I become thereby a worse person; and the only truly valuable consequence of right moral choice is that I become thereby a better one, or that I reinforce the responsible determination of some other person to do the same.

adhyasa: lit. "super-imposition," in the Hindu school of non-dualistic Vedanta, a term for the mistaken identification of one thing (for example, a shell) with another (for example, silver) which it is not; applied by this school to the mistaken identification of the realm of ordinary experience with the absolute Brahman.

adrishta: In the atomist philosophy of Hinduism, the unseen force which, without conscious purpose, produces a correlation between states of nature and the merit or demerit of an individual soul in any given phase of its existence in the cycle of births.

Advaita Vedanta: the Vedanta school of absolute non-dualism in Hinduism, so called because it holds that, from the standpoint of absolute knowledge, only the unqualified and absolutely non-differenced being of Brahman exists. Propounded originally by Sankara, this view holds that the self of each individual is identical with the Self of Brahman.

ahimsa: in Jainism, the ethical doctrine of non-injury to all living things.

ajiva: in Jainism, *lit.* the "non-living," a name for the order of nature that is objective to the living self (*jiva*) of an individual.

anatman: in Buddhism, *lit.* "no soul"; (1) specifically, the doctrine that there is no permanent self as a pure subject of awareness that persists through the changing series of psychological states; (2) more generally, the doctrine that there is no such reality as a permanent substance of any sort.

angas: in Jainism, the precepts which comprise a part of the sacred literature of the Jains.

anirvacaniya: lit. "that which cannot be expressed"; in the Hindu school of non-dualistic Vedanta, a term for the inexpressible and logically inconceivable relationship between the realm of ordinary experience and the realm of absolutely non-differenced Being or unqualified Brahman.

asatkaryavada: the non-identity theory of causality in Indian thought, that is, the theory that every effect is numerically and totally distinct from its cause, though produced by it; contrasting with *satkaryavada* (q.v.); for example, this theory is defended by the Vaishesika school of Hindu philosophy.

atman: in Hinduism, the soul or self, whether that of the individual or that of the ultimate reality (or Brahman); the concept of such a permanent self is rejected, at least for the individual, in the main traditions of Buddhism.

atom: in Hinduism, a term for the ultimate and indivisible particles which function as the basic elements of observable things.

atomism: a descriptive title for the Vaishesika philosophy of Hinduism (q.v.).

avidya: lit. "ignorance"; in the Hindu school of non-dualistic Vedanta, a term for the cosmic ignorance which mistakenly apprehends the realm of ordinary experience as genuinely and finally real, whereas from the standpoint of absolute knowledge it is regarded as ultimately unreal; cf. phenomenal illusionism.

bhakti-marga: in Hinduism, *lit.* the "way of devotion," that is, the method of achieving salvation through devotion to the personal Lord; cf. *jnana-marga* and *karma-marga.*

bhutatathata: in Mahayana Buddhism, "absolute suchness," or the ultimate reality of the Buddha essence as above all conceptual distinctions and determinate qualities; equivalent to *dharmakaya* (q.v.).

bodhisattva: in Mahayana Buddhism, an individual whose true being consists in a pure enlightenment that is pervaded by universal love and grounded in firm resolve; in particular, one whose enlightenment finds its true expression in loving devotion to others; in contrast to a *pratyekabuddha* (q.v.).

Brahma(n): in Hinduism, the principal name for the ultimate reality as including all being within itself; cf. pantheism.

buddhi: in Indian philosophy, the intellect of an individual as involving the capacity for discursive, conceptual thought.

Carvaka: in Indian philosophy, the school of materialism which reduces all substantially real things to states and processes of matter and therefore denies the existence of the soul (as a distinct spiritual substance) and of the cycle of births.

chi: in rationalistic neo-Confucianism, *lit.* a perfection point—that is, another name for the *li* or essence of some class of real beings.

ch'i: in rationalistic neo-Confucianism, the principle of matter or potentiality, also regarded as the active cause of the existence of particular things; in contrast to *li* in the sense of essence or ideal pattern.

contextual relativism: in Jainism, the doctrine of *syadvada* (q.v.) that no truth-claim can be more than probable, since it is relative to the viewpoint from which it is propounded.

contradiction: that basic principle of thought which stipulates that one and the same subject of thought cannot both be and not be the same thing at the same time in the same sense; cf. rational coherence.

cosmological realism: the doctrine that the realm of distinct things, relations, and processes (the natural order of existence) is genuinely real essentially as it appears to ordinary conceptual understanding, irrespective of whether the natural order depends on a transcendent realm; in contrast to phenomenal illusionism (q.v.).

cyclical recurrence: the doctrine, common to many Indian schools of philosophy, that the world-whole passes through a repeating cycle of phases ranging from a state of dissolution into distinct things and back again to a state of dissolution; sometimes called the doctrine of the alternation of worlds.

Dhammapada: in Buddhism, "The Way of Virtue," a traditional collection of the sayings of Buddha, supplementing *The Teaching Basket;* cf. *Tripitaka.*

dharma: (1) in Indian thought, sacred doctrine, religion, moral duty, etc.; (2) in Buddhism, the name for the Buddha's body of pure being or absolute reality, as in the term *dharmakaya* or body of *dharma.*

Dharmakaya: In Mahayana Buddhism, *lit.* the "body of pure being" or "essence," that is, the universal Buddha essence as absolute reality with no determinate qualities or attributes; equivalent in spiritual experience to the state of final, unqualified *nirvana* (q.v.) and in the order of reality to absolute suchness or *bhutatathata* (q.v.).

dhyana: the methods and disciplines of spiritual meditation and concentration in certain schools of Mahayana Buddhism, especially Zen.

discriminationism: in the distinctionist philosophy of Hinduism, the doctrine that distinguishes sharply between the soul as a passive witness, on the one hand, and both psychological and physical processes as states of objective nature, on the other.

Distinctionism: a descriptive title for the Sankhya philosophy of Hinduism (q.v.).

Dvaita Vedanta: the Vedanta school of dualism in Hinduism, so called because it emphasizes the distinction between Brahman and the world, as well as between individual selves and physical nature. Propounded in definitive form by Madhva, this view holds that though Brahman is the only independent reality, the world and individual selves are co-eternal with Brahman and do not derive their being from him.

epistemology: that basic subdivision of philosophical study which investigates questions about the origin, nature, and limits of knowledge, the nature and tests of truth, and the relation between ideas and their objects.

ethics: that basic subdivision of philosophical study which investigates questions about moral goodness or rightness, such as (1) the meaning and logical status of ethical terms, judgments, and arguments (meta-ethics); (2) the nature of the ultimately good or right as clarified by a general theory (normative ethics); (3) the application of a general theory and its specific moral principles to actual moral policies and choices (applied ethics).

Exegesis: a descriptive title for the Mimamsa philosophy of Hinduism (q.v.).

experiential relevance: that basic principle of thought which stipulates that the truth or adequacy of any proposition is proportionate, in part, to its effectiveness in providing a satisfactory causal explanation of the facts (or data) of experience that the proposition was formulated to account for.

formal concept: in Chinese philosophy, the concept of that which is real but which cannot be regarded as an actually or possibly existing thing; examples are necessary logical laws, ideal essences, etc.; in contrast to a positive concept (q.v.).

Great Whole: in Confucianism, a name for the whole of reality, including both the natural order of things and whatever realms of being may be regarded as transcending that order.

guna: (1) in Hinduism, a quality or characteristic; (2) in the Sankhya philosophy, a descriptive title for any one of the three ultimate aspects of nature; cf. *prakriti.*

hedonism: the ethical doctrine that the ultimate, self-contained good for man consists in maximizing pleasures and minimizing pains.

Hinayana: one of the vehicles or traditional schools of Buddhism; another name for the Theravada or Elder School, though strictly the Theravada is a subdivision of Hinayana; the term *hinayana* actually means "lesser vehicle" and is usually regarded as a critical designation; in contrast to *Mahayana* (q.v.).

hsiao: in Confucianism, the principle and virtue of filial piety which requires that an individual show deference to those in authority over him in the social order, and condescending understanding to those over whom he is himself in authority.

Idealism (Buddhist): a name for the Vijnanavada or Yogacara school of Mahayana Buddhism (q.v.).

idealistic Neo-Confucianism: that branch of Neo-Confucianism which emphasizes the inclusion of all reality in a single, all-embracing universal mind.

Ishvara: in Hinduism, a name for Brahman as the personal Lord, whether regarded as provisionally (Sankara) or ultimately (Ramanuja, Madhva) real.

jen: in Confucianism, the basic virtue and principle of ethical love which recognizes persons as intrinsically valuable and aims at implementing that recognition in actual conduct.

jina: in Jainism, a title (*lit.* "a victor") for any one of the traditionally recognized founders of the Jain religion.

jiva: in Jainism (and some other Indian traditions), the individual soul as an enduring, active agent and subject of awareness; cf. *jivatman.*

jivatman: in Hinduism, the individual soul or self as an enduring entity; cf. *atman.*

jnana-marga: in Hinduism, *lit.* "the way of knowledge," that is, the method of achieving salvation through philosophical insight and understanding; cf. *karma-marga* and *bhakti-marga.*

karma: in Buddhism, Hinduism, and Jainism, the law of the deed and the effect, according to which the life circumstances of an individual in any given phase of the cycle of births are an effect of his deeds and character in previous lives; cf. *samsara.*

karma-marga: in Hinduism, *lit.* "the way of works," that is, the method of achieving salvation through rigorous adherence to moral and ritual prescriptions; cf. *jnana-marga* and *bhakti-marga.*

kevala: in Jainism, the infinite and perfect knowledge of a person who has achieved spiritual self-realization and release from the cycle of births.

koan: a puzzling or baffling question used by Zen Buddhist masters to provoke their disciples to renounce rational methods for achieving ultimate enlightenment.

li: (1) in Confucianism, that basic virtue and principle of propriety which aims at appropriate conduct and moral character so far as these have been embodied in established traditional moral practice; (2) in rationalistic Neo-Confucianism, the form, essence, or ideal pattern of any class of actual or possible things.

Li, School of: a name for rationalistic Neo-Confucianism (q.v.).

lila: in the Vedanta tradition of Hinduism (e.g., Aurobindo Ghose), the sport or play of the ultimate Brahman in its self-manifestation as the universe.

limitationism: a subdivision of the Hindu school of non-dualistic Vedanta which emphasizes the relation between a substance (for example, clay) and the objects into which it can be fashioned (for example, clay pots) as the most appropriate symbolism for understanding the relationship between the unqualified Brahman and the realm of ordinary experience.

Lokayata: in Indian philosophy, the doctrine of materialism that only the natural world order (or *loka*) exists (cf. *Carvaka*).

Madhyamika: lit. "the Middle Way," one of the schools of Mahayana Buddhism—Voidism or *Shunyavada* (q.v.); called the Middle Way because its theory is logically between the nihilism which holds that nothing is real and the cosmological realism which holds that everything is real substantially as it appears in the realm of ordinary experience.

Mahayana: lit. the "greater vehicle," one of the traditional schools of Buddhism; in contrast to *Hinayana* or *Theravada* (q.v.); Mahayana is commonly viewed as a substantial modification and reinterpretation of Buddha's original teachings, which are said to be preserved in Hinayana.

manas: in Indian philosophy, the sense-mind as the capacity for sensory awareness and discrimination of particular sense objects with their qualities; more briefly, the capacity of sense perception.

materialism: in Indian philosophy, the doctrine of the *Carvaka* school (q.v.).

maya: lit. "magic" or "illusion"; in the Hindu school of non-dualistic Vedanta, a term for the ultimately illusory and finally unreal status of the realm of ordinary experiences; cf. phenomenal illusionism.

metaphysics: that subdivision of philosophical study which investigates questions about the nature of reality, such as (1) What sorts of things are real? (2) How are those real things generally related to each other? (3) What sort of reality is man? (4) Is there an ultimate reality, the being and activity of which is the ground of all dependent real things?

Mimamsa (= *Purva Mimamsa*): in Hinduism, one of the six orthodox viewpoints, *lit.* "inquiry" or "former inquiry," so called because it is a system of exegetical interpretation applied to the sacred Hindu scriptures. For that reason, it is also called the school of Exegesis.

moksha: in Indian thought, salvation or deliverance in the religious sense, usually involving release from the cycle of births; cf. *samsara.*

mondo: a puzzling story or dialogue used by Zen Buddhist masters to induce their disciples to abandon conceptual reason and rational methods in the search for spiritual enlightenment.

monism: any philosophical theory that attempts explanation in terms of a single ultimate principle or reality; for example, classical Taoism, Mahayana Buddhism, non-dualistic Vedanta in Hinduism (or either of the other schools of Vedanta if properly qualified).

moral sphere: in Chinese philosophy, that context of ethical living in which the individual aims at implementing the well-being of the social order through moral principles that are binding on him, irrespective of his own feelings and opinions, but that also and at the same time implement his own true ethical well-being; cf. sphere (ethical).

mystical oneness: a descriptive phrase referring to the realized union of the individual with the ultimate reality in direct, intuitive religious experience (for example, in classical Taoism).

natural sphere: see sphere (ethical).

naturalistic symbolism: a descriptive characterization of the Neo-Taoist theory that the natural order of existence is the only realm of being and that references to the ultimate Tao in religious discourse are merely metaphorical symbols for expressing truths about that natural order.

naya: in Jainism, a relative standpoint or context from which a truth-claim is propounded and which therefore renders that claim relative to the context.

nirguna Brahman: in the non-dualist school of Vedanta, the unqualified Brahman, or Brahman as absolutely non-differenced Being totally devoid of attributes and apprehended only at the absolute level of knowledge; cf. *saguna Brahman.*

nirmanakaya: in Mahayana Buddhism, *lit.* "the body of transformation," that is, the manifestation of the universal Buddha essence in and as the realm of ordinary experience (the natural, empirically discernible realm of particular things and processes); equivalent to the realm of *samsara* or the cycle of births (q.v.)

nirvana: in Buddhism, *lit.* "cessation" or "extinction," the state of spiritual release and insight which characterizes those who have achieved genuine enlightenment, but differently interpreted by different branches of Buddhism. It at least involves the extinction of selfish craving and of spiritual ignorance.

nominalism: the theory that there are no universal essences or natures to which general words (for example, *man, triangle*) refer, but that such words are tags or names for groups of particular things (for example, individual men, individual triangles).

Nyaya: in Hinduism, one of the six orthodox viewpoints, *lit.* "argumentation," so called because it consists of a comprehensive system of logic and epistemology. While it generally merges with Vaishesika to form a single philosophical perspective, its logical forms and techniques are employed by all Hindu schools.

objectivism, ethical: the theory that there are moral principles whose validity and binding character for moral agents are logically independent of individually and culturally variable states of opinion, preference, feeling, or response.

pantheism: any philosophical outlook for which all that is real is, in some sense, essentially one in being with the sole ultimate and therefore self-existing reality.

pantheistic mysticism: a descriptive phrase for any religious philosophy which, like classical Taoism, includes all reality within the being of the absolute reality and aims at the individual's realization of this oneness in spiritual experience; also applicable to Mahayana Buddhism and the Hindu school of non-dualistic Vedanta.

perceptual realism: in several traditions of Indian philosophy, the doctrine that the individual's conscious perception of objects corresponds to the real and independent state of those objects as they exist independently of consciousness.

phenomenal: that which appears or is disclosed to ordinary empirical observation; the phenomenal realm, for example, would be the realm of the things and processes of ordinary experience; cf. shapes and features.

phenomenal illusionism: the doctrine (common to classical Taoism, Mahayana Buddhism, and non-dualistic Vedanta in Hinduism) that the realm of ordinary experience (things distinct from, and related to, each other) is a misleading, deceptive, and ultimately unreal appearance of a single ultimate reality which transcends all distinctions and qualities.

pluralism, metaphysical: any theory of reality which believes in a plurality of ultimate, underived, and irreducible entities which are viewed as the basic constituents of reality.

positive concept: in Chinese philosophy, the concept of a class of actually or possibly existing things, such as chairs, tables, trees, stones, etc.; in contrast to a formal concept (q.v.).

pradhana: another designation for nature or *prakriti* in the Sankhya school of Hinduism; cf. *prakriti, Sankhya.*

prajna: in Mahayana Buddhism, the ultimate wisdom or insight which consists in complete identity of being and knowledge with the absolute Buddha essence beyond all difference or distinction; hence, the epistemological aspect of *nirvana* as involving oneness with the blessed *dharmakaya* (q.v.).

prakriti: in the Sankhya school of Hinduism (and some other schools), a designation for nature regarded as irreducibly distinct from individual souls and as constituted by three basic aspects or *gunas*—brightness (*sattva*), force (*rajas*), and mass (*tamas*); cf. *Sankhya.*

pramana: in Indian thought, an ultimate standard, criterion, or means of right knowledge. Basically, four *pramanas* are distinguished in the various schools—perception, inference, analogy, and verbal testimony; but some schools do not accept all four as ultimate and irreducible.

pratyekabuddha: in Hinayana Buddhism, an individual or separate Buddha, that is, a person who achieves enlightenment and enters a state of living release or qualified *nirvana* alone or in isolation from other persons, in contrast to the Mahayana ideal of a *bodhisattva,* (q.v.) whose living release consists in loving devotion to other persons, especially to those still in a state of bondage to ignorance and selfish desire.

pudgala: in the personalistic school of Hinayana Buddhism, a relatively enduring principle of personal selfhood which persists through successive experiences but is not to be interpreted as a permanent, changeless substance.

purusha: in Hinduism (especially in Sankhya or Distinctionism), the individual soul as a pure subject of experience or passive witness; in contrast to *prakriti* or *pradhana* as the order of nature which functions as an environment for the *purusha.*

rajas: in the Sankhya philosophy of Hinduism, the force (active energy) aspect or *guna* of nature or *prakriti* (q.v.); cf. *guna.*

rational coherence: that basic principle of thought which requires that all the predicates ascribed to any given subject must be mutually compatible with each other and with the nature of the subject to which they are ascribed; basically, a generalized version of the principle of contradiction (q.v.).

rationalism: (1) the general thesis that there are ultimate principles of knowledge which reflect the nature of objective reason itself and which therefore do not depend for their status as ultimate on a voluntary commitment of will by the individual; (2) more specifically, the doctrine that the ultimate principles and categories of knowledge characterize the structure of the mind prior to and independently of experience.

rationalistic Neo-Confucianism: that branch of Neo-Confucianism which emphasizes the reality of a transcendent realm of essences, forms, or ideal patterns (*li*) which particular things in the ordinary realm embody and exemplify.

reflectionism: a subdivision of the Hindu school of non-dualistic Vedanta which emphasizes the relation between an object (for example, the moon) and its multiple reflections in a reflecting medium (for example, pools of water) as the most appropriate symbolism for understanding the relationship between the unqualified Brahman and the realm of ordinary experience.

relativism, ethical: the theory that all moral values and principles are relative, in their validity and binding character, to individually and culturally variable states of opinion, preference, feeling, or response; in contrast to objectivism, ethical (q.v.).

relativity of knowledge: (1) in Taoism, the doctrine that all ordinary knowledge-claims, based on conceptual reason and perceptual awareness, are relative to the circumstances and opinions of the individuals propounding them, so that such claims should be transcended in a higher knowledge beyond all distinctions; (2) in Jainism, a similar view regarding knowledge but without the notion of higher knowledge beyond distinctions.

Sacchidananda: a descriptive designation of Brahman in Hindu thought; *lit.* Being (*sat*), Consciousness (*chit*), and Bliss (*ananda*).

saguna Brahman: in the non-dualist school of Vedanta, the qualified Brahman, or Brahman as characterized by defining attributes. For this view, the qualified Brahman is understood only at the level of relative knowledge and is to be transcended at the absolute level of knowledge, for which Brahman is totally without attributes; cf. *nirguna Brahman.*

samadhi: in Buddhism, the state of fully unified concentration and oneness with truth which culminates the noble eightfold path to spiritual release and realization.

sambhogakaya: in Mahayana Buddhism, *lit.* "the body of pure delight," that is, the manifestation of the universal Buddha essence in symbolic forms for the self-enjoyment of Buddha and for the spiritual edification of the *bodhisattvas* (q.v.).

samsara: in Buddhism and Hinduism, the cycle of births through which successively the individual transmigrates in circumstances determined by the operation of *karma* (q.v.).

Sankhya: in Hinduism, one of the six orthodox viewpoints, *lit.* "right knowledge," commonly called Distinctionism because it emphasizes the ultimate and irreducible distinction between the soul (*purusha*) and nature (*prakriti* or *pradhana*).

satkaryavada: the identity theory of causality in Indian thought, that is, the theory that any effect is essentially identical with its cause, but in a distinguishable phase of its manifestation; contrasting with *asatkaryavada* (q.v.); for example, this theory is defended by the Sankhya school of Hindu philosophy.

satori: the state of fully realized oneness with the *Dharmakaya* or absolute Buddha essence, as that state is referred to in Zen Buddhism.

sattva: in the Sankhya philosophy of Hinduism, the brightness *guna* or aspect of nature or *prakriti* (q.v.); cf. *guna.*

scepticism: the negative philosophical thesis that genuine knowledge is impossible, either in general or in some limited field of thought. Religious scepticism, for example, would be the theory (or implication) that genuine knowledge of religious truth is impossible.

self-transcendence: the religious experience of rising above one's limited individual selfhood to achieve oneness with the ultimate reality (for example, in classical Taoism).

shapes and features: in Chinese philosophy, a name for the things and processes of ordinary experience—the natural, empirically discernible order of things, in contrast to whatever spheres of being are regarded as transcending that natural order (for example, the realm of *li* or ideal essences in rationalistic Neo-Confucianism).

shu: in Confucianism, that basic principle of moral reciprocity which requires that an individual treat other persons in the manner in which he himself would morally will to be treated if the roles of the involved parties were reversed.

Shunyavada: the school of Voidism in Mahayana Buddhism; *lit.* "the way of emptiness," so called because it holds that the objects of ordinary experience are empty in the sense of being ultimately unreal from the standpoint of absolute reality, while the absolute itself is regarded as empty because, though unconditionally real, it is beyond all qualities or attributes; cf. phenomenal illusionism.

Siddhantas: in Jainism, the treatises that comprise part of the sacred literature of the Jains.

situational realtivity: the theory that the application of moral principles to a specific moral problem varies with, and is dependent upon, all the relevant facts and circumstances about that problem; in distinction from ethical relativism (q.v.—relativism, ethical).

smriti: in Hinduism, *lit.* "that which is remembered," a descriptive name for the body of traditional writings which comment on sacred scriptures or *sruti* but are not regarded as ultimately binding in their authority; cf. *sruti.*

soul pluralism: (1) the doctrine (for example, in the Sankhya and Vaishesika philosophies of Hinduism) that there is an ultimate plurality of separate, individual souls which are eternal, irreducible, and underived; (2) more generally, any doctrine that accepts a plurality of individual souls, whether ultimate or not.

sphere (ethical): in Chinese philosophy (especially Confucianism), a context of individual and social relations pervaded and constituted by a determining motivation or prevailing attitude; the *natural* sphere, for example, would be the ethical context of a person who allows the bent of his life to be governed by the combined effect of instincts, impulses, emotions, and customary habits of response.

sruti: in Hinduism, *lit.* "that which is heard," the descriptive name for the whole body of authoritative sacred scripture; cf. *smriti.*

sutra: an oral or written treatise comprising more or less the official platform of some identifiable school of Indian philosophy; *lit.* "a discourse."

Svabhavavada: in Indian philosophy, another name for *Carvaka* (q.v.). The term literally means "self-being" and refers to the view that the natural world requires no explanation beyond itself.

syadvada: in Jainism, the doctrine that because all viewpoints are relative, any truth-claim must be characterized by probability, at best (*syad* = "maybe" or "perhaps").

tamas: in the Sankhya philosophy of Hinduism, the mass (inertness, lethargy) aspect or *guna* of nature or *prakriti* (q.v.); cf. *guna.*

Tao: lit. "way" or "path"; in Chinese philosophy, the term for the harmony or order of the universe as symbolizing an ideal pattern for human behavior (Confucianism); or the ultimate reality itself, of which the universe is an aspect or surface manifestation (Taoism).

Tao Axis: in classical Taoism, the stance occupied by one who has achieved realized oneness with the Tao as ultimate reality, and who therefore has transcended all the limited viewpoints about reality at the level of conceptual reason or discursive intellect.

tattvamasi: the so-called identity-text of the Hindu Upanishads, *lit.* "That art thou!" It is interpreted by non-dualistic Vedanta as teaching that the individual self is ultimately identical with the Self of Brahman.

Theravada: the Elder School of Buddhism; another name for *Hinayana* and with it standing in contrast to *Mahayana* (q.v.).

transcendent sphere: in Chinese philosophy (1) that context of ethical living in which the individual recognizes his place in the Great Whole of the universe and aims at embodying those principles of Tao or right order that pervade that Whole (cf. sphere [ethical]); (2) a name for whatever realms of being are regarded as independent of the realm of ordinary experience.

transmigration: in Indian philosophy, the doctrine that each individual soul passes through a succession of lives through being reborn in an innumerable sequence of life circumstances; hence, the cycle of births or *samsara* (q.v.).

trikaya: in Mahayana Buddhism, *lit.* "the triple body" of the Buddha, that is, the three different forms in which the universal Buddha essence subsists or manifests itself: (1) the *nirmanakaya,* (2) the *sambhogakaya,* and (3) the *dharmakaya* (q.v.).

Tripitaka: in Buddhism, *lit.* "The Three Baskets," that is, the three basic authoritative texts accepted by both vehicles (i.e., by Hinayana and Mahayana); called baskets because the palm leaves on which they were written, in one collection of manuscripts, were stored in cases of basketwork; the baskets are (1) *The Teaching Basket* (containing discourses ascribed to Buddha), (2) *The Discipline Basket* (containing rules for initiates in the Buddhist monastic order), and (3) *The Higher Doctrine Basket* (containing detailed exposition of psychological and metaphysical doctrines).

Universal Mind, School of: a name for idealistic Neo-Confucianism (q.v.).

Upanishads: in Hinduism, the final subdivision of authoritative sacred scripture, consisting of a series of philosophical postscripts to the Vedas (q.v.) and purporting to explain the true, inner meaning of the earlier scriptures.

upaya: in Mahayana Buddhism, the doctrine of "means," that is, the use of persuasion and condescension to convince those in a state of spiritual bondage and ignorance to begin on the journey to spiritual enlightenment and release, or to continue therein, excluding only those methods that would be essentially deceptive and therefore inconsistent with universal love.

utilitarian egoism: a descriptive name for the Yang Chu phase of Taoism, which recommends the implementation of individual self-interest and advantage.

utilitarian sphere: in Chinese philosophy, that context of ethical living in which the individual explicitly and consciously aims to realize his own self-seeking advantage or personal profit; cf. sphere (ethical).

Vaishesika: in Hinduism, one of the six orthodox viewpoints, *lit.* "particularity," so called because it emphasizes the reality of a plurality of ultimate particulars (either souls or atoms) which are irreducible and underived;

commonly called atomism because it views nature as composed of ultimate, eternal, and unextended physical particles; generally merging with Nyaya to form a single philosophical perspective.

Vedanta: in Hinduism, historically the most influential of the six orthodox viewpoints, *lit.* "the end of the Veda"; divided into various sub-schools, all of which emphasize the dependence of the rest of reality on Brahman (the sole independent, ultimate reality); cf. *Advaita Vedanta, Dvaita Vendanta,* and *Visistadvaita Vedanta.*

Vedas: in Hinduism, the first major subdivision of authoritative sacred scripture, consisting primarily of *mantras* (hymns to the gods) and *brahmanas* (priestly regulations); but sometimes the term *Veda* refers to the whole sacred canon of Hinduism, including the *Upanishads* (q.v.).

Vijnanavada: the Idealist school of Mahayana Buddhism; *lit.* "the way of consciousness," so called because it holds both that the objects of ordinary experience exist only provisionally as transformations or states of consciousness, and that the absolute reality is essentially pure, undifferentiated consciousness; cf. phenomenal illusionism.

vishesa: in the atomist (Vaishesika) school of Hinduism, the ultimate category of particularity; souls and atoms are examples of such ultimate and irreducible particulars.

Visistadvaita Vedanta: the Vedanta school of qualified non-dualism in Hinduism, so called because it holds that all reality is included within the being of Brahman, but that there is a real distinction between the self of Brahman and the world as the body of Brahman. Propounded in definitive form by Ramanuja, this view denies that individual selves are identical with the Self or Brahman, and holds that they are part of his body.

Voidism: another name for the Mahayana school of *Madhyamika* or *Shunyavada* (q.v.).

voluntarism: the doctrine that an ultimate and ungrounded commitment of will is the decisive basis for the status of those fundamental principles which are the logical grounds of all truth-claims.

Yang: in Chinese philosophy (especially Taoism), a name for the active, assertive, and aggressive forces in the universe; always coupled with *Yin* (q.v.).

yi: in Confucianism, that basic virtue of moral righteousness which, stated as a principle, recognizes an unconditionally authoritative and objective principle of moral duty or obligation; cf. objectivism (ethical).

Yin: in Chinese philosophy (especially Taoism), a name for the passive and receptive aspects of the universe; always coupled with *Yang* (q.v.).

Yoga: in Hinduism and Buddhism, *lit.* "union"; (1) a complex of techniques for achieving mental and physical control with a view to spiritual realization; (2) one of the six orthodox viewpoints of Hinduism, so called because it emphasizes those techniques, and commonly merging into a single philosophical perspective with Sankhya (q.v.).

Yogacara: another name for the Idealist or *Vijnanavada* shool of Mahayana Buddhism, so called because it emphasized the techniques of Yoga (methods of physical and mental control) for the realization of oneness with the ultimate Buddha essence as pure consciousness.

Selected Bibliography

General Works on Oriental Philosophy

Chan, Wing-tsit. *A Source Book in Chinese Philosophy*. Princeton, New Jersey: Princeton University Press, 1963.

Fung, Yu-lan. *A History of Chinese Philosophy*. 2 vols. Princeton, New Jersey: Princeton University Press, 1952–53.

————. *A Short History of Chinese Philosophy*. New York: Free Press (Macmillan), 1948.

————. *The Spirit of Chinese Philosophy*. Boston: Beacon Press, 1962 (first English ed., 1947).

Potter, Karl H. *Presuppositions of India's Philosophies*. Englewood Cliffs, New Jersey: Prentice-Hall, 1963.

Radhakrishnan, S., and Moore, Charles A. *A Source Book in Indian Philosophy*. Princeton, New Jersey: Princeton University Press, 1957.

Sharma, Chandradhar. *Indian Philosophy: A Critical Survey*. New York: Barnes and Noble, 1962.

Smart, Ninian. *Doctrine and Argument in Indian Philosophy*. London: George Allen and Unwin, 1964.

Confucianism

Chan, Wing-tsit, ed. and trans. *Instructions for Practical Living and Other Neo-Confucian Writings by Wang Yang-Ming*. New York: Columbia University Press, 1963.

Legge, James, ed. and trans. *The I Ching: The Book of Changes*. 2d ed. New York: Dover Publications, 1963.

————, ed. and trans. *The Works of Mencius*. New York: Dover, 1970.

Liu, Wu-Chi. *A Short History of Confucian Philosophy*. New York: Dell (Delta Book), 1955.

Waley, Arthur. *The Analects of Confucius.* London: George Allen and Unwin, 1938.

Taoism

Legge, James, ed. and trans. *The Texts of Taoism.* 2 vols. New York: Dover, 1962.

Buddhism

Burtt, Edwin A., ed. and trans. *The Teachings of the Compassionate Buddha.* New York: New American Library (Mentor Religious Classic), 1955.

Conze, Edward. *Buddhism: Its Essence and Development.* New York: Harper and Row (Torchbook), 1959.

_____. *Buddhist Thought in India.* Ann Arbor, Michigan: University of Michigan Press, 1967 (copr. 1962).

Jayatilleke, K. N. *Early Buddhist Theory of Knowledge.* London: George Allen and Unwin, 1963.

Kern, H., ed. and trans. *Saddharma-Pundarika: The Lotus of the True Law.* New York: Dover, 1963.

Murti, T. R. V. *The Central Philosophy of Buddhism.* London: George Allen and Unwin, 1960.

Rhys David, T. W., ed. and trans. *The Questions of King Milinda.* 2 vols. New York: Dover, 1963.

Stcherbatsky, Th. *Buddhist Logic.* 2 vols. (vol. II includes many primary sources). New York: Dover, 1962.

_____. *The Conception of Buddhist Nirvana* (with portions of Nagarjuna's Treatise on Relativity). Varanasi, India: Bharatiya Vidya Prakashan, n.d.

Suzuki, D. T. *Essays in Zen Buddhism* (various series: first series, 1949, 1961). New York: Grove Press.

_____. *On Indian Mahayana Buddhism.* Edited by Edward Conze. New York: Harper and Row, 1968.

_____. *Outlines of Mahayana Buddhism.* New York: Schocken Books, 1963.

Warren, Henry Clarke. *Buddhism in Translations.* New York: Atheneum, 1970.

Hinduism

Dasgupta, Surendranath. *A History of Indian Philosophy.* 5 vols. Cambridge, England: Cambridge University Press, 1955–57.

Deussen, Paul. *The Philosophy of the Upanishads.* New York: Dover, 1966.

Edgerton, Franklin, ed. and trans. *The Bhagavad Gita.* New York: Harper and Row (Torchbook), 1944.

Ghose, Aurobindo. *The Life Divine.* New York: Greystone Press (Sri Aurobindo Library), 1949.

Mahadevan, T. M. P. *The Philosophy of Advaita*. Madras, India: Ganesh and Company, 1938, 1969

Müller, F. Max, ed. and trans. *The Upanishads* (twelve of the principal Upanishads). New York: Dover, 1962.

Thibaut, George, ed. and trans. *The Vedanta Sutras of Badarayana: With the Commentary by Sankara*. 2 vols. New York: Dover, 1962.

_____, ed. and trans. *The Vedanta Sutras: With the Commentary by Ramanuja*. Delh, India: Motilal Banarsidass, 1962.

Jainism

Jacobi, Hermann, ed. and trans. *Jaina Sutras*. 2 vols. New York: Dover, 1968.

Index

Absolute, 110, 111; unqualified, 149; non-dual, 165. *See also* Being, non-differenced; Brahman, unqualified
Absolutism, monistic, 65. 89
Action: as volitional life-response, 12; atomist metaphysical category of, 136–37
Adhyasa, 152
Adrishta, 134, 135–36, 141
Advaita, 147. 153
Ahimsa, 190
Air: atomist view of, 135, 172; materialist view of, 197
Ajiva, 189, 190
All-pervasiveness: pluralistic Hindu concept of, 132–33
Analects, 21–22
Analogy. *See* Comparison
Ananda, 153
Anatman (nc-soul), 81
Ancestor worship, 24
Angas, 186
Ānirvacaniya (inexpressible), 150
Appearance, 58
Aquinas, Thomas, 34
Arguments, philosophical, 13. *See also* Dialectics
Aristotle, 47
Asanga, 92
Asatkaryavada, 139
Ashvaghosha, 87

Atman, 73, 144; Upanishadic emphasis on, 80; Buddha's reinterpretation of, 81; doctrine of impermanence negates, 107; and Upanishad identity text, 148
Atom: distinctionist concept of, 134; place of, in distinctionist evolution concept, 134, 135; atomist concept of, 134, 135–39; combinations of, 136, 139; particularlity of, 137; qualities of, 139; and *adrishta,* 141; Sankara criticizes concept of ultimate, 171
Atomism: concept of self, 131, 132, 133, 137, 140–42; concept of atom, 134, 135–36, 137, 139; natural evolution concept of, 135–36; magnitude theory of, 136; view of mind. 136; view of sensory capacities, 136; ultimate metaphysical categories doctrine of, 136–38, 139; rationalism of, 137; Sanskrit name for, 137; view of non-existence idea, 137–38; causality theory of, 139–40; and School of Exegesis, 142; and School of Logic, 142; Sankara criticizes concepts of, 171, 172; Madhva's dualism *vs.* pluralism of, 173; compared to Jainism, 186–87, 189
Attitudes: as emotional life-response, 12
Attribute: and quality, 94; and substance, 94; Buddhist view of, 119; reciprocal understanding of concept of, 120
Augustine, Saint, 34

Materialism, 195; anti-religious stance of, 196; scepticism of, 197; view of reality, 197–98; ethical implications of views of, 198; view of causality, 198; Indian criticism of, 198, 199; rejects moral objectivism, 199

Matter: Chang Tsai's concept of, 36; formed *vs.* pure, 38; relativity of concept of, 38; non-existence of pure, 38, 49; and principle of efficient causality, 49; Jain view of, 190; materialist view of, 197

Maya, realm of, 148, 149, 152

Means, principle of (*Upaya*), 91

Meditation: Mahayana's view of, 88; yogic, 92; Zen discouragement of, 102; Madhva's view of, 156; Jain belief in power of, 190

Memory: and idea of enduring self, 106; Sankara's view of, 150; Jain concept of, 187; claims, and reincarnation, 201–2

Mencius, 22, 29, 55

Mentalism, 97

Mental processes, 134

Merit and demerit, force of (*adrishta*), 135–36, 140, 141

Metaphysical categories: atomist doctrine of, 136–38

Metaphysics, 13

Middle Way, the (*Madhyamika*), 92

Milinda, King, 106

Mimamsa. *See* Purva Mimamsa

Mind: all-inclusive, 37; ultimate, 39, 48; Personal, 52; universal, 65; ultimate personal, 160, 191; /body relationship (criticism of materialist view), 199–200

Minute quantum, 136, 171

Moksha, 74

Molecule, 136

Monads, 112

Mondo, 102

Monism, 170; classical Taoist, 57; Mahayana Idealist absolute, 112–13; Voidist absolute, 112–13; of the Vedanta, 126; Sankara's absolute, 154; Ramanuja

criticizes Sankara's absolute, 162–66; Sankara criticizes atomist, 171–72; Madhva's, 173

Moore, George E., 15

Moral causality, 105

Moral character, 106

Moral ideal: Confucian view of, 26; Indian criticism of materialist, 199

Moral law, 25, 26, 33

Moral objectivism: Confucian, 26, 27, 41, 51; Western criticism of, 43; argument for soundness of, 43–45; and nature of objective moral worth, 45–46; criticism of materialist rejection of, 199

Moral obligation, 46

Moral order, objective, 191; Confucian idea of, 25, 27, 28; Oriental concept of man's participation in, 168; and problem of evil in Ramanuja's system, 176; and Aurobindo's solution to problem of evil, 177; materialist rejection of idea of, 198. *See also* Moral objectivism

Moral reciprocity, principle of (*shu*), 31

Moral responsibility: Hinayana personalist doctrine preserves, 87; idea of impermanence negates, 106; Aurobindo's solution to the problem of evil and, 177

Moral values: materialist rejection of, 198

Moral worth, objective, 46. *See also* Intrinsic personal worth

Motion: and atomist metaphysical category of activity, 137

Mysticism, 57

Nagarjuna (Verses on the Middle Way), 91

Naturalistic symbolism, 61

Natural order: Confucian view of, 25, 26, 27; problem of causal explanation for, 49; Neo-Taoist view of, 61; and transcendent realm of being, 63–64, 199; and the Tao, 64; cosmological realist view of, 65; problem in Neo-Taoist view of, 65; transcendental monistic absolutist view of, 65; Ramanuja believes God creates, 158

Rationalism, 6–7, 163

Real, the. *See* Reality, ultimate

Realism: Voidist qualified, 93; Sankara's empirical, 149, 150

—cosmological, 65; Hinayana, 90; of pluralistic Hinduism, 129; Madhva's, 154–55, 156; Ramanuja's, 157; Jain, 189

—perceptual: John Locke's, 97; of pluralistic Hinduism, 129; Sankara's, 150, 175; Jain, 189

—pluralistic, 189; Sankhya's, 186; Hindu, 191

Realism, cosmic. *See* Realism, cosmological

Reality, 8, 9, 13 Taoist distinguishes, from appearance, 58; as requiring causal explanation, 63; Mahayana Idealist concept of Pure Consciousness as true, 100; as contingent, 119–20; Vedanta views, as Brahman, 126; Divine, 128; Sankara's view of, 147, 148, 150–51; Ramanuja's idea of inclusive unity of, 164; ethical level of, 177; Jain view of, 189, 192–93; materialist doctrine of, 197–98

—Absolute: infinite reality of, 16; Indian gods as manifestations of single, 72; concept of Brahman as, 72–73; called *Atman* (Self), 73; Oriental view of, as non-personal, 73; Voidist idea of, 93; Mahayana Idealist idea of, 93, 109; as identical with empirical world, 96, 149; unlimited by pure Consciousness, 97; knowledge of, 111, 163; classical Taoist view of, 113; *Dharmakaya* as, 121; relation of personal Lord to, 127–28; process and change as inconsistent with, 176

—ultimate: and category of spiritual personality, 16; as personal, 17; Taoist idea of, 22–23; Confucian idea of, 23; human ignorance of, 108; *bodhisattva's* view of, as *Dharmakaya*, 120; Voidists view knowledge of, as oneness, 95; Buddha as incarnation of, 124; *bhakti-marga* views, as personal Lord, 127;

Vedanta idea of, 128, 146; Ramanuja's concept of, 166; Sankara's view of, 172

Realm of being, transcendent, 199

Realm of form. *See* Ideal form, realm of

Realm of ordinary experience, 93, 94, 97, 104. *See also* Realm of shapes and features

Realm of shapes and features: positive concept of a thing in, 35; Neo-Confucian idea of, 35, 38; sage acts in, 36; relation of realm of form to, 37; School of Universal Mind view of, 39; Confucian view of, 41, 48; rationalist sees differences in, 48; and ultimate cause, 50, 51; conceptual knowledge as relative to, 59; Neo-Taoist view of, 61

Reals, independent. *See* Selves, individual

Reason: nature of, 6; Confucian confidence in, 40–41, 51, 58; adequacy of, 41–42; eternal, 52; Hinyana confidence in, 90; Voidist view of, 94; Mahayana view of, 113; intrinsic validity of basic principles of, 169; scriptural claims vindicated on grounds of, 170

—conceptual, 114; Taoist view of, 58–59, 60, 113; *Dharmakaya* as unknowable by, 89; Mahayana replacement of, with intuition, 90; Mahayana use of principles of, 91, 113; Zen view of, 102; adequacy of, 110, 120; and enlightenment, 115; Buddhist view of, 117; Sankara's view of, 152, 175; Jain view of, 187

Reason, analytic. *See* Reason, conceptual

Recognition, 187

Reflection: Sankara's analogy of, 151

Reflectionism, 151

Reincarnation, 73; Buddha's view of, 82; requires concept of permanence, 106, 107; assures justice of principle of *karma*, 201; Indian acceptance of concept of, 201; and memory claims, 201–2; symbolic reinterpretation of, 202–3

Relativism: cultural, 15–16; ethical, 45; Jain doctrine of contextual, 189, 192

Relativity, situational, 26

Release, 87, 88; Mahayana view of, 90; recognizes difference between ignorance and enlightenment, 115; pluralistic Hindu unitary view of, 130, 133, 146; Vedanta concepts of, 146–47; Madhva's concept of living, 155–56; Ramanuja's rejection of concept of living, 159; Ramanuja's concept of, 159, 160, 176; Aurobindo's concept of, 160; Jain view of, 186, 187, 190, 193; inadequacy of Indian idea of, 202

Religion, 12; and philosophy, 12–13; traditional Oriental, 14; eastern view of object of, 16; western view of object of, 16; heritage of, in China, 22–24; popular, 23; Indian, 17, 201

Religious discourse, 142–44

"Revealing shining virtue," 40

Righteousness, principle of (*yi*), 29–30; *vs.* moral beliefs, 30; and utilitarian motive, 30; goal of, 30–31; unconditional obligation to, 30–31; and ethical love, 31; and standard of propriety, 32; Taoist view of Confucian virtue of, 59

Right order: Tao as meaning, 23; social extension of idea of, 24; in harmony of natural order, 25; principles of, pervade Great Whole, 28; and Confucian view of character formation process, 46; as impersonal, 52. *See also* Tao

Rites, Book of (Confucian classic), 21, 22

Rome, 72

Sacchidananda, 153

Sage, 29, 33, 36, 39

Saguna, 148

Salvation: Orthodox Hindu ways of, 127, 128; pluralistic Hindu concept of, 133; Madhva's idea of uniqueness of individual's, 157; Jain concept of, 186. *See also* Deliverance; Release

Samadhi (unified concentration), 85

Sambhogakaya, 90

Samsara, 73; as condition of bondage, 74; as identical with true *nirvana,* 88, 89, 96; body of transformation of Buddha

as, 89; Buddhism and Hinduism share idea of, 124. *See also* Cycle of births

Sankara: and Mahayana, 124; view of personal Lord concept, 128, 166; *vs.* atomist theories, 138, 172; commentary on Vedanta-sutra, 146; view of release, 146; concept of God, 146, 167; concept of reality, 147, 148, 150–51; non-dualism of, 147–49, 157; empirical realism of, 149; rejects Mahayana Idealist theory, 149, 154; perceptual realism of, 150; phenomenal illusionism of, 150, 160, 173, 177, 191; later followers of, 151; on value of analogy, 151, 152; dialectics of followers of, 153; thought of, compared to Mahayana Voidism, 153–54; Ramanuja's criticism of ideas of, 157, 162–67, 173, 174–75; identity theory of, 158, 172; appeals to intuitive awareness, 162; absolute monism of, 162–66; identity-texts of, 164; similarities between Ramanuja and, 164, 167; truth/error distinction of, 166; believes in ultimacy of verbal testimony, 170; criticizes pluralism, 170–71, 172; criticizes monism, 171–72; criticizes Exegete injunctivist theory, 172; criticizes Madhva's views, 173, 174; sees reincarnation as illusion, 202

Sankhya, 189

Sankhya school, 124

Sankhya-Yoga, 125, 129

Santayana, George, 15, 53

Sat, 153

Satkaryavada, 138

Satori, 103

Sattva, 134

Scepticism, 7, 48, 169

Scriptures, Hindu: Orthodox Hinduism accepts authority of, 124; Purva Mimamsa interpretation of role of, 126; and school of Exegesis, 142, 144, 145, 172; and Vedanta, 145, 147; Sankara's two level principle as rooted in, 148; Madhva's cosmological realism as rooted in, 156; Ramanuja's interpreta-

DESIGNED BY TED SMITH/GRAPHICS
COMPOSED BY FOX VALLEY TYPESETTING, MENASHA, WISCONSIN
MANUFACTURED BY BANTA DIVISION,
GEORGE BANTA COMPANY, INC., MENASHA, WISCONSIN
TEXT AND DISPLAY LINES ARE SET IN TIMES ROMAN

ⓌⒿ

Library of Congress Cataloging in Publication Data
Hackett, Stuart Cornelius.
Oriental philosophy.
Bibliography: pp. 219–221.
Includes index.
1. Philosophy, Oriental.
2. Philosophy, Comparative. I. Title.
B121.H3   181   78–65010
ISBN 0-299-07790-X
ISBN 0-299-07794-2 pbk.